KANT'S AESTHETIC THEORY

Kant's Aesthetic Theory

An Introduction

Salim Kemal

Second Edition

First edition 1992
Reprinted 1993
Second edition 1997

Published by
MACMILLAN PRESS LTD
Houndmills, Basingstoke, Hampshire RG21 6XS
and London
Companies and representatives
throughout the world

ISBN 0–333–62995–7 paperback

A catalogue record for this book is available
from the British Library.

This book is printed on paper suitable for recycling and
made from fully managed and sustained forest sources.

10   9   8   7   6   5   4   3   2
06   05   04   03   02   01   00   99   98

Printed and bound in Great Britain by
Antony Rowe Ltd
Chippenham, Wiltshire

Published in the United States of America 1997 by
ST. MARTIN'S PRESS, INC.,
Scholarly and Reference Division
175 Fifth Avenue, New York, N.Y. 10010

ISBN 0–312–12164–4

Contents

Preface to the
Second Edition

A number of books and papers on Kant's aesthetic theory have been published since the first appearance of the present book. This preface will discuss some of them; but since the discussion presupposes some familiarity with issues presented in the main text of this book, it may be best to consider the preface after reading the rest of the book.

John H. Zammito's book on *The Genesis of Kant's 'Critique of Judgement'* (1992) reconstructs a history of this philosophical text, presumably on the grounds that its history determines the text's meaning and use. In keeping with this guiding conviction, Zammito argues that the *Critique of Aesthetic Judgement* is structured by epistemic and moral or practical turns. Kant's lectures on Logic show that he had worked out the character of aesthetic judgements some time before he produced a deduction justifying their validity. By emphasizing the developments in his thought that occurred between the lectures on Logic and the deduction in the third *Critique*, Zammito maintains, he can explain something about the manner in which Kant came to construct the latter text; and, similarly, pointing out the moral and cultural engagements of beauty and fine art shows how he expanded the germ of his theory into a set of practical inter-relations. It underscores the 'fissures' that make the text interesting to some post-structuralist readings of Kant's aesthetic theory.

In the context of this kind of historical explanation of a text, Zammito's book is a detailed study, containing extensive quotations, eighty pages of notes, and fifty pages of bibliography and index. The book correctly identifies a cognitive turn that led Kant to explore the nature of reflective judgements and to incorporate his critique of taste within a critique of judgement. It is right also that Kant construes art as a part of culture, which he sees in terms of the construction of a morally satisfactory order. Some of us have argued for the latter association for some time; some may still resist it but it is unlikely to go away. The book also contains an interesting account of Kant's criticism of Spinozism.

Despite these strengths, and perhaps because its purpose is to explain the origins of the structure of the *Critique of Judgement*, the book fragments the text, leaving some of its philosophical issues unresolved. In identifying cognitive and ethical turns, for example, the author relates the latter to the nature and promise of art; he also suggests that Kant's discussion of taste principally concerns the nature of subjects' experience of beauty. We might expect that the author will also explain the inter-relation between these distinctions, especially as explaining how epistemic and moral turns shaped the text raises but does not answer the same issue, but it is not clear that the book provides this explanation; thereby it seems bound to leave the Third *Critique* in a fragmented state. Similarly, the book explains the nature of art by reference to a shared expressive and symbolic structure of products of genius and the sublime. But, given Kant's argument that the sublime does not need a deduction such as taste claims, too close an association between genius and the sublime will cost art its validity. And regardless of how detailed an account of symbolism and sublimity their association yields, it does not show how Kant can maintain that art *and* nature are expressive. A comparable problem occurs with the phenomenology of subjective consciousness and its concomitant conception of experience that the author uses to present the development of Kant's thought from his earlier works up to the Third *Critique*'s conception of aesthetic judgements: it does not clearly tally with Kant's own claim that the experience of pleasure that constitutes aesthetic judgements is not a distinctive kind of pleasure even though pleasure plays a distinctive role in aesthetic judgements.

At another point the author contrasts Kant's Enlightenment commitment to reason and universality with Herder's 'enthusiastic' and particularistic participation in the *Sturm und Drang*. He refers to Herder's *Gott* to explain the structure of parts of Kant's teleology and opposes Kant's rational and universalistic preferences to Herder's *Ideen zür Philosophie der Geschichte der Menschheit*. By so limning the differences between Kant and Herder, the book seems to obscure Kant's concerns with particulars, in which rationality and universality gain purchase through judgements. In Section 40 of the *Critique of Judgement* Kant says that subjects making judgements must think for themselves, from the viewpoint of others, and consistently. He does not describe the latter in terms of logic and a rational universality but conceives it, rather, in terms of the first two maxims of judging. This suggests that he wants to relate it to the particular engagements of human actors with their actual context rather than to a merely formal imperative. This call for consistency raises questions of how far reason can maintain a critical stance if its measure is what is acceptable within, in the sense of being consistent with the rules of behaviour of a particular social order. Kant's claim would be that Herder fails to provide any kind of critical stance when he values societies and social products for their uniqueness; therefore, for Kant, Herder also fails to explain value because he cannot take up a rational and universalistic perspective. Yet the viewpoint he himself promotes as consistency falls short of a rational universality. It is possible to work out a solution for Kant that allows him to escape the problem that afflicts Herder. But if the contrast between the two thinkers is cast as an opposition between the particularist villain and the universalist hero, it becomes difficult to give their due to the issues of consistency and engagement with particulars as they appear in Kant's work. Yet surely a history of the text should be able to clarify these philosophical aspects of the nature and kinds of judgements as they appear in the published text, where Kant resolves the fissures that may have been evident in its composition. An over-emphasis on the process of its construction fails to do justice to the theory presented in the text.

In his book on *Kant and the Experience of Freedom* (1993), Paul Guyer now maintains that Kant does seek to find a relation between aesthetic and moral value – indeed, he is tempted to say that this was Kant's principal reason for writing the Third *Critique*. The chapter in which the author examines crucial features of the relation more or less reproduces his paper on 'Feeling and Freedom: Kant on aesthetics and morality', which I have considered at pp. 184, 187–8, 189–93, and so does not need to be repeated here.

There are many other aspects of this book's tendentious readings of Kant that need comment, though it may be most useful for this preface to restrict itself to one issue: the distinction and relation between fine art and natural beauty. Guyer's explanation seems to assume that the 'Analytic of the Beautiful' is cast in terms of natural beauty. This assumption is not clearly warranted. Kant uses 'nature' in at least three ways: to denote objects which we experience according to the categories, to denote the complex and systematic order of our knowledge of Nature, and sometimes to contrast with grace or other divine actions. His explanations of the nature of beauty in the 'Analytic of the Beautiful' in the *Critique of Judgement* are principally in terms of the first use, which covers the objects of our experience. This would include both natural beauty and fine art, since both are objects of experience, subject to the categories, and capable of being explained by reference to their physical properties. This sense of nature as denoting objects of experience allows Kant's explanation of our experience of beautiful objects in nature to apply to 'natural' objects, whose occurrence we explain by pointing to the systematic order of our knowledge of Nature, *and* those of fine art, whose occurrence we explain by reference to the actions of some agent. Neither of them can make a greater claim to be the principal model for Kant's earlier considerations of beauty, and he can say of beauty generally that 'in the judgment of mere taste neither [natural beauty nor fine art] could vie for superiority over the other.' (KDU, Section 42, 300). In addition, despite this similarity between beautiful objects, there are differences between fine art and natural beauty that become important to Kant's theory when it turns to consider the origins of the objects. In this context we would identify objects either as natural beauty or as fine art by pointing to their 'construction' either in the order of our knowledge of nature or through the actions of human agents. And, as Chapter 6 makes clear, the distinctive origins of objects allow our experience of them to carry different interests.

Guyer's account of natural beauty does not address these distinctions and the passages in the *Critique of Judgement*, such as the one cited in the last paragraph, where Kant sets out further details of his theory. A useful corrective to his misreading of 'nature' is to be found in 'Art, nature and purposiveness in Kant's aesthetic theory' by Theodore Gracyk, in *Proceedings of the Eighth International Kant Congress*, edited by Hoke Robinson (1995). Further, when in his book Guyer criticizes an account of the relation between natural beauty and fine art that I have given elsewhere, then, perhaps because he assumes that natural beauty is the fundamental model for aesthetic judgements, he misconstrues my explanation of the distinctive interests and values we ascribe to fine art and to natural beauty: he mistakenly takes it to be an argument for the absolute superiority of fine art. Consequently his criticisms do not reach their target.

Two other books with significant sections on the *Critique of Aesthetic Judgement* are J. M. Bernstein, *The Fate of Art* (1992) and J. Luc Ferry, *Homo Aestheticus* (1993). Neither book is a straightforward commentary on Kant's text; rather, each takes up and engages with issues central to the text and to contemporary aesthetics, and both have very interesting things to say about the influence of Kantian thought on later writers, including Hegel, Theodor Adorno and Jacques Derrida. Another book, *Kant's Theory of Imagination* by Sarah Gibbons (1996), contains a worthwhile consideration of the role of Imagination in Kant's work. Two anthologies have been published recently: *Kant's Aesthetics*, edited by Ralf Meerbote and Hud Hudson (1991), results from a conference held at Rochester and contains six papers while *Kants Ästhetik*, edited by Herman Parret (Germany: der Gruyter, 1997), derives from a larger conference held at Cerisy la Salle. The first contains a useful introduction in which Meerbote characterizes the relation between Kant and empiricist and rationalist aesthetic theory and a searching paper by Peter Kivy that discusses Kant's reflections on music. The second contains contributions from a multinational collection of scholars, but centres on most recent Anglo-American readings of Kant. Most of the commentators considered in the present book as well as many others are represented in this collection.

Many more doctoral dissertations on Kant's *Critique of Judgement* are being written now than were even in the recent past. The wave of studies of this text does not show signs of abating, and we may hope that more books on it will appear in the future.

Acknowledgements

Some of the material in this book appeared in different versions in the *British Journal of Aesthetics*, the *Journal of Aesthetics and Art Criticism*, the *Journal of the History of Philosophy*, and *Kant Studien*. I am grateful to the editors of these journals for permission to use the material here.

Carl Hausman, Peter Iver Kaufmann, and Nabil Matar read earlier drafts of the book; their advice helped give it its present form. I am grateful to them, as I am to Jane Baston, without whom it would not have been possible for me to write this book.

I have again been lucky with editors: Sophie Lillington, Frances Arnold and Charmian Hearne at the publishers have been consistently helpful, and I am happy to thank them.

S. K.

1

The Background

This book will examine Kant's *Critique of Judgement*, and will be concerned with both historical and conceptual matters. Arguably that text is the first systematic study of aesthetic theory to be produced in the history of modern philosophy, and it raises issues which, if in somewhat changed form, still generate debate among aestheticians.

Kant was concerned with the distinctive nature, scope, and validity of aesthetic claims. When we say that things are beautiful, graceful, deformed, ungainly, pretty, prosaic, delicate, sad, or tragic, we usually intend these predicates to signify something that is more and other than a merely subjective liking or disliking. Rather, we expect that a claim that an object is beautiful can be acceded to by other subjects. Our claim is not just the expression of a subjective, idiosyncratic and merely personal preference, but is more like a claim about facts.

To explain this expectation, Kant clarifies just what sort of validity aesthetic claims can have; how they are like or unlike facts or moral demands; or how we know when someone has successfully made an aesthetic judgement rather than misunderstood what is merely an expression of personal preference. This leads him to consider other issues: what kinds of objects do we find beautiful? Does beauty depend on objects being of a certain kind? What makes them beautiful? For example, in the case of art: must we judge it beautiful in a way distinctive from our appreciation of natural beauty? How is art produced? What makes for creativity? What is genius in art? Or further, what is the value of beauty? How does it fit into our social, political, cultural and moral lives? Is the pursuit of beauty the most important task that can engage us? And so on.

THE KANTIAN BACKGROUND: THE FIRST *CRITIQUE*

At the time of the first edition of the *Critique of Pure Reason*, Kant believed that claims about beauty were subjective and could not have any general validity. Knowledge claims, for example, are true or false, and we not only expect that an assertion about events or objects will gain agreement from others, but also look for general principles or criteria for making such claims. By contrast, the claim that an object is beautiful is subjective because it is based only on feelings of pleasure that a subject has. These vary from subject to subject. Consequently, just as a subject would not expect others to like apples just because he happens to like their taste, similarly we cannot expect that our feeling-based assertion that a thing is beautiful *will* generate agreement from others. Nor will we have some rule or principle about how people should behave. If we do all behave uniformly, this is at best the result of a uniformity in ourselves.

In the past, philosophers attempted to provide rational principles for aesthetic judgements. But, as we shall see, Kant thinks their efforts were unsuccessful. The principles they put forward either turned out to be merely empirical generalizations about actual usage or did not apply to aesthetic claims specifically. Either way they could neither warrant particular claims about aesthetic value nor possess a justifiable validity.

As aesthetic responses are variable, subjective, and unruly, they cannot possess any valid principles. Consequently, Kant did not expect to produce a 'critique of taste', where the latter involves examining the scope and power of the rules or principles governing our rational capacity for appreciating beauty. Better then, Kant suggests, to reserve the term 'aesthetics' for a study of our sensibility and its operations, and to give up the search for a 'critique of taste' or any examination of the validity that any subject may claim for their appreciation of beauty. As he writes in a footnote to the *Critique of Pure Reason*, the 'Germans are the only people who currently make use of the word "aesthetic" in order to signify what others call the critique of taste. This usage originated in the abortive attempt made by Baumgarten, that admirable analytic thinker, to bring the critical treatment of the beautiful under rational principles, and so to raise its rules to the rank of a science. But such endeavours are fruitless. The said rules are, as regards their sources, merely empirical and consequently can never serve as apriori laws by which our judgement of taste may be directed . . .'.[1]

Yet some years later Kant rewrote this passage to allow for aesthetic validity. He also went on to publish a third *Critique*, whose first part, *The Critique of Aesthetic Judgement*, sought just those rules and justifications for our appreciation of beauty that he had earlier rejected. There is no inescapable contradiction between the two positions, however, but an increasing certainty on Kant's part that, in spite of the inadequacy of his predecessors' arguments, and despite his own earlier doubts, aesthetic validity was possible.

Nonetheless, we can understand why, in the first flush of the critical enterprise, aesthetics must have seemed too subjective and idiosyncratic ever to be rationalized. In the process of clarifying which distinctions, concepts, and operations are basic to correct reasoning, Kant also dismissed the conclusions of previous writers about the power and validity of reason. As those conclusions underlay their accounts of aesthetic validity, by implication Kant also rejected the aesthetic theory they sustain.

Kant initiated his account of correct reasoning with the *Critique of Pure Reason*. He begins by taking it for granted that we can have knowledge and resolve conflicting cognitive assertions. But he also wants to discover what warrants our certainty in this. We can clarify the need to discover the basis for such certainty by pointing out instances where reasoning seems to fail us. For example, it seems that a number of problems which engage us – about the eternity of the world, about the nature of the first cause, about the totality of the world – remain unresolved because we are not clear about the process of reasoning involved in thinking them through. This leads to antinomies – argument forms in which we can argue for mutually contradictory conclusions from the same premises. To resolve or escape such problems, Kant proposes that we should first carry out a *critique* of our capacity for reasoning, of the cognitive faculties we use, to see what are their strengths, how far they are reliable, and what kind of problems their use enables us to solve. Once we become clear about their power and scope, we can proceed to use reason in gaining knowledge, knowing which of our knowledge and other claims have a warrant and are reliable.

Kant's conclusions depend on the premise that the operations and nature of the mind structure our knowledge of the world. We can explain the latter by identifying four basic distinctions, which embody Kant's principal insights about the structure of our knowledge.

Kant's Conception of Reasoning

In the first basic claim, in the *Critique of Pure Reason* Kant insists that concepts are qualitatively distinct from the sensations, representations, intuitions, or impressions which make up the material content of our sensibility. Concepts are rules or tools for ordering and organizing our impressions, classifying these into appropriate groupings. The concept of 'chair', for example, allows us to classify objects of a certain kind together and to distinguish them from others. Only through application of concepts can we analyse, distinguish, and understand our mental content. 'Without sensibility no object would be given to us, without understanding no object would be thought. Thoughts without content are empty, intuitions without concepts are blind.'[2]

Kant's distinction between intuitions and concepts relates to one between faculties. The ability to respond to and have intuitions is a characteristic of the faculty of sensibility while that of applying concepts belongs to the understanding. These associations provide another way of describing our grasp of objects and events. Knowledge and experience consist in applying concepts to intuitions to conceptualize our experience of objects and events in the world or, in terms of faculties, in bringing sensibility under determinate concepts of the understanding.

Kant maintains also that conceptualization never occurs by itself but must always be expressed in a judgement. So, for example, a concept of 'umbrella' does not merely organize our experience of long, thin-stemmed, cloth-covered and openable spindles, but always does so by making an assertion of some sort. We never simply use 'umbrella' alone to denote an experience but always express judgements such as, for example, 'This is an umbrella' or 'Umbrellas stave off rain'.

The need to make an assertion is true not only of concepts used to organize particulars in experience but also of the association between concepts. This occurs in the form of a judgement that some relation subsists between the concepts, such that, for example, 'All umbrellas are black' or 'Not all umbrellas are black' or 'If all umbrellas are black, then all cats will be grey', and so on.

Clearly, all this makes judgement central to the discursive knowledge we have, and to understand our thinking and reasoning, we shall have to examine the nature of judgements.[3] For the present we may say, first, given that judgement is an activity of relating concepts or applying concepts to our intuitions, and, second, as concepts are supplied by the faculty of understanding while representations and intuitions are provided by the sensibility, then, third, in applying concepts we bring understanding to bear on sensibility under the governance of judgement. The judgement is a relation between the faculties of understanding, which yields concepts – or the formal, organizing or classifying principle or rule – and sense, which gains intuitions, representations, or the content of claims.

Kant also proposes an important role for the faculty of imagination. Imagination is reproductive when it brings to mind images or marks of the objects related in a judgement when the objects themselves are absent. It is this ability that allows us to talk and think of absent things. Further, the imagination is productive when it provides new and created images in judgements. This creative aspect will become important in his aesthetic theory.

By setting out the relations of faculties in assertions Kant provides an account of the functions of mind which are necessary for us to have the knowledge and experience we claim. This relates Kant's distinction of concepts from intuitions and understanding from sensibility to a second basic claim. He succinctly expresses it in the slogan that 'It must be possible for the "I think" to accompany all my representations . . .'. This must be true, Kant maintains, 'for otherwise something would be represented in me which could not be thought at all, and that is equivalent to saying that the representation would be impossible or at least would be nothing to me.'[4] That is, a self-consciousness of having impressions or intuitions is essential if that mental content is to play any part in a subject's knowledge and experience.

This claim subtends a more complex supposition that certain conditions must be satisfied for representations to belong to the subject's mind. Consciousness is not a merely unstructured having of representations, whose order and character depends completely on the objects of which they are representations. Instead, Kant insists, a subject is self-conscious of the content of his mind only because the elements of consciousness are combined in certain ways. In other words, for the content to become a content of self-consciousness, it must satisfy certain conditions or be combined in particular ways.

The claim has various implications, the most important of which, Kant thinks, overthrow any threat of scepticism about knowledge. This becomes clearer when he examines the conditions that must be satisfied for the 'I think' to accompany a subject's representations. Especially clearly in the transcendental deduction, he argues that we can have self-consciousness of our representations only if we can talk about those representations as experiences of events in an objective world existing independently of the subject having that experience.

One aspect of this argument may be made clear by contrasting it with another. Earlier theorists supposed that although consciousness itself is incorrigible, we can be mistaken about whether what we have in consciousness actually corresponds with reality. A consciousness of a black squareness of a certain kind leads a subject to infer that it is looking at a chalk board. But all such inferences from the content of consciousness to reality are always open to doubt because we could never be sure that our inferences were correct. The only way to be sure is to go beyond the content of consciousness and check it against a direct access to the object, from which vantage-point we might compare consciousness with reality. But as we cannot go outside consciousness, we cannot gain the vantage-point from which we could have certainty. So at one level, all our knowledge claims about the world – our claims that what we have in consciousness corresponds with the way objects actually are in the world – remain incapable of confirmation and certainty.

A consequence of this inability to grasp objects themselves, outside our consciousness, is that we cannot have any real grasp of causality, if this is understood as a power possessed by an object to bring about changes in other objects, or of the continued and distinct existence of bodies apart from our perception of them. The latter becomes a problem because if all we have is our consciousness, then we cannot infer from our consciousness and ideas of objects that the latter continue to exist even when we do not have ideas and perceptions of them in our consciousness. Hume maintained that we had no basis in experience for inferring from any regularity in ideas to the conclusion that objects continue to exist independently of our perception of them and are the source of those perceptions. Similarly, we might examine events in as much detail as possible, Hume suggested, but at no point can we point to an item in experience which is causality. From considerations such as these, by various steps, Hume came to deny the usual supposition that we had experience of a world of objects existing independently of subjects' perceptions and engaged in causal relations with each other.

Kant wants to argue against this kind of scepticism. But rather than justify inferences from the content of consciousness to the nature of the world, he prefers in effect to argue backwards. The reason why we can suppose that the content of our consciousness gives us access to the world of objects and events is that consciousness of experience and experience of an objective and causally governed world stand or fall together. We would not be able to have apperception – the consciousness of what is in consciousness or the 'I think' accompanying representations – unless we were conscious of the order and character of objects as causally determined and possessing various properties. In other words, we do not need to try to make an ever-fallible inference *from* consciousness *to* objects of experience because the objective order of experience *must* be *presupposed* if we are to have any consciousness of having representations. As we all agree that we have consciousness and apperception, and as the existence of the latter is now seen to depend on there being an objective order of experience, we may expect also that we have the latter. We can explain this more systematically.

The Deduction of the First *Critique*

The relations being proposed here are complicated but not difficult. Kant begins with the unity of apperception: for anything to be a representation for the subject, it must be possible for the subject to become aware of the representation as his or hers. Thus, first, the subject must be actually or possibly reflectively aware of having that representation, which is to say that the subject must be able to attach 'I think' to its representation. If a subject's representation is the assertion that 'The umbrella caused the clothes to stay dry', then it must be possible for the subject to say that 'I think that the umbrella caused the clothes to be dry'.[5] This assertion – and if we are to apply concepts at all, they must be put forward in *some* judgement or assertion – may be thought of as a *single complex thought* made up of simples – umbrella, clothes, dryness, etc. – in a particular relation. Further, the 'I' which has this single complex thought does not itself have any identifying characteristics by which it knows itself.

Now, second, Kant claims that the single complex thought must be had by a *single thinking subject* or it would not be a single complex thought. This may be made clearer by presenting the alternative: we could divide the single complex thought into its parts – this umbrella, the clothes, keeping dry. But if each of these parts were had by a separate subject, then it would cease to be a single complex thought. One subject would think the umbrella, another the dryness, and the third the clothes; none would think the single complex thought. Thus, for there to be consciousness of a single complex thought, there must be a single consciousness that thinks all the different parts of the thought. In other words, for the 'I think' to accompany our thoughts, it must be the same 'I' that accompanies all the thought.

Kant also argues, third, that it must be possible for the 'I' to be aware of its own numerical identity. He sees this as a necessary condition that must be satisfied if there is a single complex thought. To explain this, we must recall that the 'I' does not have any determinate identity of its own, independent of what it is conscious of. That is, the only way it can gain awareness of its identity is through the unity between the parts of the thought which it accompanies. Yet, it is necessary for it to be aware of its numerical identity, for in the absence of such identity there would be no single complex thought. If we look at what is involved in a single complex thought, we see that it must involve a synthesis of elements. This is because the single complex thought is constituted of an interrelation or synthesis between parts or elements. Only such a synthesis, and only consciousness of such a synthesis, allows us to have a single complex thought. But such a synthesis is only possible if all the 'discrete' selves attached to the different parts of the synthesis of the complex thought are themselves united or synthesized. As the 'I' has no criteria for identity beyond accompanying parts of the single complex thought, the only way it can become aware of its identity is by uniting the representations it has. But this involves more than just a unity between the 'I' that thinks of 'umbrella', the 'I' that thinks of 'dryness', and the 'I' that thinks of 'clothes'. It also involves awareness of their being united in a single consciousness. That is, the subject must be aware of not only thinking 'umbrella', 'dry' and 'clothes' but also of thinking of all three together in the same consciousness. If it did not think of them all together in the same consciousness, it would not be aware of its own consciousness of them. Unless it does so, it would not know that the 'I' which is thinking all three of 'umbrella', 'dry', and 'clothes' is the same as the 'I' thinking 'umbrella', and the 'I' thinking 'dry', and the 'I' thinking 'clothes'. This conclusion has other consequences.

If we must be conscious of some synthesis of the 'I' in order to have a single complex idea, then whatever is necessary for the single complex idea is also necessary for awareness of an 'I' as a synthesis. And what is necessary for the single complex idea is that its different parts be held in a certain relation proposed in a judgement. Accordingly, the unity of apperception is gained by the relations of the assertion or the judgement which is the single complex thought. Or, to put it the other way round, the judgement can be treated as the manner or relation in which those things we judge about – clothes, dryness, umbrella – can be brought to consciousness. The judgement is the manner in which those things are united in a single complex thought that, in turn, makes possible a single thinking subject and its apperception. Our judgement could be an assertion of a necessary relation between umbrellas and dryness of clothes, or the negation of this claim. In both cases, the judgement form disserts a causal relation between the umbrella and the dryness of the clothes. In any case, judgements and judgement forms are necessary for self-consciousness of the kind which, we all agree, can accompany our thoughts and representations.

This last claim points to something else. The issues it raises are numerous and difficult, but we may suggest briefly some of the conclusions Kant wants to gain. As we said, judgements are necessary for a reflexive awareness of having representations. This makes judgement central to having these representations, so that we must understand judgements and the rules they introduce in order to see how they make possible our reflexive awareness of having representations and the experience these portend. We know that every synthesis of representations involves a judgement; every act of conceptualization is also an act of judgement. Kant here talks of 'forms of judgement': briefly, these forms are the *ways* in which the judgement makes possible a synthesis or unity of representations, regardless of the particular content of any judgement.

Kant derives these judgement forms from textbooks on logic, which identify twelve forms as essential to reasoning. We may form a unity of representations, for example, by affirming or negating some feature of all of a class or some members of the class or of individuals. We could say that: 'All' or 'some', or 'this' umbrella(s) 'can' or 'cannot' keep clothes dry. Moreover, such unity may be categorical or hypothetical or disjunctive, so that we may assert categorically that 'All umbrellas can keep clothes dry' or do so in an hypothetical utterance: 'If all umbrellas could keep clothes dry, then . . .'. What these judgemental forms yield is a set of terms or concepts that refer to all the different ways judgements can be made and representations can be united.

Given that every conceptualization is a judgement, where these terms set out the different ways we make judgements, they also set out the ways we must be able to conceptualize our representations. Thus, to use a particular judgement form or to make a judgement using a particular form is to conceptualize in an appropriate manner. Consequently, the ability to conceptualize in the given manner is a necessary condition of the possibility of using these judgemental forms. Further, as it is through judgements that concepts are applied and objective claims are made about the character of items and events in the world, the ability to conceptualize in given manners is presupposed in making actual objective claims about the world. To speak loosely, the terms Kant uses to denote this 'ability to conceptualize in given manners' is 'category', and from what we have just said, it should be clear that our possession of a given set of categories is necessary for conceptualizing in judgements, and the latter, in turn, are necessary for our reflective awareness of our experience.

Kant develops his account of categories in a number of ways, to provide a critique of reasoning and resolve some of the issues raised by the antinomies. Such a resolution makes the bases of empiricist and rationalist aesthetics unacceptable. He explains the categories by associating the hypothetical form of judgement with the relation of causality and of ground to consequent.[6] To judge hypothetically is to assert a relation between two states of affairs such that if we can assume that the first state obtains, then we can infer that the second also exists. But to think of two events as such a sequence we must decide which of the two states will be our initial assumption and which will be the inference drawn from that. The rule by which we think this sequence is that of 'ground to consequent'. So, to make an hypothetical judgement, we must apply the rule that one of the two states related in the hypothetical judgement is a ground and the other a consequent.

Another similar development needs a number of other steps, but may be intuitively plausible. To think of one event as the ground for the other, so that the other exists or comes about through the first, can be to think of the two events as having a necessary connection. The latter is the relation of causality, where an effect cannot occur without a cause, and the two will always be thought of in their sequence. Thus, if the relation of ground to consequent can be shown to be homologous to that of cause to effect, then we must be able to think of, or judge, or assert that such a relation obtains if we can use the hypothetical judgemental form; and we must be able to use the latter if we are to make judgements; and we must be able to make judgements and synthesize representations if we are to have the reflective awareness of our experience which we all agree we have. Therefore, we must conceive of representations as representations of a causally governed experience if we are to have reflective awareness of experience.

Kant gives similar arguments for all those other forms of judgement and categories. His arguments depend on the need for 'time-determination': when we apply the twelve judgemental forms in our actual experience. Here Kant explains why we can and must describe temporal and spatial experience in terms of causality, substance, and objective determination. So far as his arguments are successful, they also validate our usual way of so describing the world of our experience, allowing us to make coherent and intelligible claims about objects and yielding a justifiable and rational knowledge of events. We order the world in terms of causality, substance, and other categories because we must do so if we are to make judgements, and we must make judgements if we are to have reflective awareness. The first two are a necessary condition for the latter and so are presupposed by the possibility of such reflective awareness of experience as we have.

Some Implications of Kant's Deduction

From these conclusions other claims follow. One of these is that the antinomies lead to mutually contradictory conclusions, about whether the world has a beginning in time or a limit in space, because the propositions are strictly beyond our ken. Given the conditions which must be satisfied for reflective awareness of experience, as we cannot escape the experiential world of causality, time, space, and substance, we cannot expect to grasp some point in the world but outside time from which the latter began or outside space but in the world at which it ends. Certainly we may *conceive* such states of affairs, but we cannot have any coherent knowledge of it because our mode of knowing is of one sort.

Another conclusion is this: the discovery of these categories is an *a priori* matter in the sense that we must presuppose that the categories obtain if we are to have consciousness of experience. For Kant consciousness has a structure, and for something to come to the mind it must have that structure. Second, as the structure determines the manner of our consciousness and experience of events and objects, our knowledge of that structure will be *a priori* rather than inductive or experiential. As only the deployment of the categories makes it possible for us to describe our experience, we cannot expect to *justify* their role and nature by abstraction from our experience. Instead, Kant begins with the logical forms of judgements generally, which are set out in textbooks on logic. If we are to apply these forms, we must have some way of knowing which judgements are appropriate and when – there must be some rule by which we relate abstract logical forms to the content of our experience. Thus, Kant moves from the nature of reasoning and the laws of logic to their engagement in our thinking about experience generally, and he does not need to generalize from our experience.

We must be clear also that justifying these categories yields restricted results. This is the third basic claim. The categories may tell us what order and structure our experience generally must have – it must be of objects, in causal relations; and so on – but they do not tell us which particular objects and causes will actually exist. We may know that every event must have a cause, but from this *a priori* conclusion we cannot infer empirical truths that heat will cause metals to expand, or that the attraction between bodies has an inverse ratio to the distance between them. To discover which causes actually operate between which objects, we have to rely on experience and must look to the world.

Moreover, we must examine the principles which order our *empirical* knowledge and must understand what guarantees its success. For this Kant calls on the power of the faculty of reason and its ability to govern the use of understanding by deploying

Ideas.[7] We use Ideas to develop a system of scientific knowledge that organizes our ordinary empirical claims into a unity. We may expect that questions of the nature of empirical scientific validity are distinct from questions of the *a priori* conditions for experience and knowledge.

The fourth basic claim is that Kant's theory of our experience and knowledge in the *Critique of Pure Reason* is distinct from questions about the moral quality and value of actions, and he easily admits that the latter need a separate and distinctive justification. By the account he gives in the First *Critique*, all our experience is causal. No event in our experience can be outside the compass of causal explanation. But if there is such a strict and comprehensive need for causality, then freedom of actions becomes impossible in our experience; and consequently morality, which presupposes such freedom, also becomes impossible in our experience.

Yet Kant *also* supposes that we have freedom. Even the account of scientific knowledge which he presents in the Preface to the Second Edition of the *Critique of Pure Reason* makes clear that scientists will conduct experiments in order to gain knowledge of natural laws, and that this requires our active intervention into natural causes to see what effect our manipulation has. He refers to Bacon, who put forward a model of an inductive experimental science, and to Galileo, Torricelli, and Stahl, all of whom were renowned experimentalists. He also speaks of 'constraining nature to give answer to questions of [our] reason's own determining',[8] and of reason using 'experiment[s] which it has devised in conformity with [its] principles', by which it approaches nature 'in order to be taught by it. It must not, however, do so in the character of a pupil who listens to everything that the teacher chooses to say, but of an appointed judge who compels the witness to answer questions which he himself has formulated.'[9] This role of reason and the task of experiment presupposes that the experimenter is free and able to formulate questions.

Similarly, if as knowing subjects we were ourselves subject to causality in all our thought and action, then it is not clear whether or how we could even begin to understand and reason about the world and so gain knowledge of it. If we must presuppose the existence of freedom, however, given that our experience is itself characterized by the form of causality, that freedom must exist outside experience. Therefore we must separate any validity for experience from the issues of validity involved in freedom. Thus, for Kant, questions of morality require a separate set of justificatory arguments, and so far as issues concerning knowledge and cognitive validity are construed as matters of theoretical reason while those governing justifications for actions are classified under the rubric of practical reason, the *Critique* suggests that the two are qualitatively different.

The result is a distinction between, on the one hand, scientific explanations of natural events according to the causal connections that subsist between objects and events in the empirical world and, on the other hand, subjective feelings, moral behaviour, and ethical systems. The former proceeds by reference to objective characteristics and events. Arguably it excludes the subject's feelings, moral judgements, and all the evaluative connotations that are involved in perfection from considerations of the truth, falsity, and coherence of knowledge claims. The fact that the observer likes pomegranates or thinks that the world is an imperfect place that should be made perfect, does not do anything to determine whether the fruit contains vitamins. But as Kant distinguishes theory from practice by reference to the nature of reason, we may also ask whether the division can be bridged by a deeper understanding of reason itself.

These items – the distinction between concepts and intuitions, the necessary conditions for self-consciousness of experience, the rules of science for successful knowledge claims, and the distinction of knowledge claims from feelings and morality – explain Kant's initial feeling that a critique of taste was impossible. He found that his four basic claims together demolished the theories of cognition and knowledge that underlay the aesthetic theories of his precursors among the rationalists and empiricists. As the latter theories constituted contemporary aesthetic theory, it is not surprising that in the First *Critique* Kant denied that a Critique of Taste was possible. We can clarify this by following some aspects of the earlier theories.

KANT AND HIS PREDECESSORS

Both Baumgarten and Hume thought taste and aesthetics were sensate matters, and supposed they were continuous with reason and ideas. Like other Rationalists, Baumgarten maintains that sensitive knowledge is 'indistinct' or provides 'obscure or confused representations',[10] because it depends on the body, while understanding knows 'distinctly'.[11] But unlike Leibniz and Wolff, Baumgarten ascribes a logic to each, that distinguishes the claims we make for and with the intellect from those we make with and for the senses. This move runs into its own problems, but we may first consider what Leibniz and Wolff have to say to clarify how their conception of ideas runs foul of Kant's distinctions.

Leibniz argued for a hierarchy of ideas and the knowledge they yield. At the pinnacle are adequate ideas, which give full knowledge of their objects, and are available only to God. Only He understands their perfection – their greatest diversity in the most comprehensive unity. Beyond adequate ideas Leibniz proceeds through inadequate ideas via distinct, clear, and confused ideas to end in obscure ideas and an absence of thought and knowledge. This route parallels that from rational knowledge to such confused knowledge as we gain through the senses. Leibniz associates clarity with the senses and so with the body as their source; but he also denies to the latter any capacity for grasping distinct ideas.[12] This renders sense knowledge imperfect but not qualitatively distinct from our clear and distinct or perfect knowledge of ideas and concepts. Its imperfection consists only in its confusedness or obscurity, and what we know only obscurely can be known more perfectly if we apply intellect and thereby develop clear and distinct ideas of the object.

Relying on a similar distinction, Wolff finds in cognitive knowledge a superior upper part and an inferior lower part. The first deals with clear and distinct ideas, the second with obscure and confused ideas. As we may expect, distinctness of ideas is a matter of intellectual comprehension[13] whereas, by contrast, the imagination and the sense yield at best clear but confused ideas. Further, for Wolff too, the distinction between the intellect and the senses is that they yield perfect or imperfect knowledge; it is not that one yields knowledge and the other something else; rather the difference between them is one of degree of perfection of knowledge.[14]

Both Leibniz and Wolff, then, assume a continuity between sense and reason. This coincides with the empiricists, like Hume, who also propose a continuity between sense impressions and concepts. They provide a genetic account of the manner in which vivid sense impressions lose their immediacy in the mind and begin to serve as ideas. Both impressions and ideas are still representational in important respects, while they also serve as rules;

but the empiricist stress on genetic explanations obscures their relation and distinction. And in this context, Kant's distinction between sense and understanding or intuition and concept reminds us of the role these faculties must perform but cannot if they are not properly distinguished.

The continuity of sense and reason also finds its way into the account Leibniz and Wolff give of aesthetic response. For them, the senses give us confused knowledge of the object. Aesthetic response was always a matter of the sense, and involved confusion either in judgement or in response. Yet precisely because it was itself confused, Wolff and Leibniz derived its validity from the clarity and distinctness available to the intellect. To eliminate doubts about whether a claim to beauty was justified, we were expected to clarify the response we had by showing how it approached but failed to gain distinctness. It was always an inferior kind of knowledge, which we always assessed by standards appropriate to perfect knowledge. Thus, for Wolff, if we understand the rules of construction of an object – if we have clear and distinct ideas about its purpose – such knowledge will increase the satisfaction we gain from responding to a work. In theory, satisfaction still depends on our responding to a sensate representation, but it becomes increasingly difficult to know how sensory ideas provide more than a formal basis or occasion for deploying all the clear and distinct ideas which constitute our understanding of rules and purposes.

Baumgarten proposed one possible escape from this problem through his 'logic of the senses'. By contrast with Leibniz and Wolff, he thinks sense and reason or intellect are species of knowledge, but of different kinds. He argues that in particular areas of our knowing, which do not depend on sensibility, we can expect 'distinctness', while in some areas, we expect only the order provided by sensibility.[15] He then proposes that sense and distinctness each have their own rules or logic. The senses still yield confusion for him, but he now understands the latter as a richness (*ubertas*) of content and as a vividness in appearance.[16] The senses are worth developing then because they have this richness; and for Baumgarten they work by a principle of association rather than by demonstrative, logical process. Elsewhere he lists the perfection of the senses as involving richness or abundance, magnitude, truth, clarity, certainty and liveliness, all working together.[17] There is a richness and unity which in some way gives form and truth. The most beautiful thought is that which perfectly represents perfection. Here, if the last is a list of perfections, then beauty consists of presenting those perfections together as well as possible.

This move allows Baumgarten to treat sensory representation without necessarily bringing in criteria appropriate to intellect. Nevertheless, he makes a questionable use of an association of ideas. He holds it is guided by wit, acumen, memory, imagination, etc. But this raises a number of issues, for it is not clear what wit, acumen, and so on are supposed to be: are they mental capacities we have in addition to the capacities for reason and sense? If so, then they have an application not only in sense knowledge but also in knowledge gained by the intellect. They form some sort of 'depth-structure' that may be used in either kind of knowledge. Indeed, the operation of this capacity for wit, acumen, etc., appears most clearly in gaining intellectual and perfect knowledge, from where, by analogy, we may identify it in application to sense knowledge. But for us to extend their application from intellect to sense, we need to know the limits and scope of their analogy – which common features of sense and intellect are significant, and why they are common only in certain respects. Yet any attempt to develop that analogy leads to circularity, because to know the limits and nature of the analogy we have to characterize the senses, their scope, and nature. We would have to show to what extent and in what ways the senses are such as can accept the analogy and operate in ways similar to intellect. But if we can do that, then we do not need to extrapolate from conclusions about the intellect in order to justify the validity of the senses, for we would already have an account of how the senses operate.

Baumgarten also makes other proposals. Underlying the senses, human beings have a natural aesthetic capacity. They exhibit it especially in play, when they associate ideas.[18] In effect this aesthetic capacity denotes the power and scope of the senses to make associations which are natural to sensate knowledge.

The procedure of association bears an analogy with reason and demonstration, but actually involves different things. It is based on: wit, the ability to discover resemblances between seemingly dissimilar things; acumen, which is the discovery of differences between similar things; memory, relating present perceptions to past ones; foresight, the ability to relate past to future through the present; imagination, to bring *phantasai* to mind when the object is not present; the ability to use signs, by which things are connected to signs and signs to each other so that knowledge is communicated; and the apprehension of perfection or deformity by taste.

If this tells us something of how the senses work, it also yields a set of odd prescriptions. Baumgarten claims that sensate representations will be better communicated if they are clear rather than obscure. We may expect, then, that poems with clear representations are better than ones using obscure representations.[19] But then he also claims that distinct representations, which are complete, adequate, and 'profound in every degree', are not sensate; consequently, they cannot be poetic.[20] Presumably, although a poem would in some sense be more perfect if its representations were clearer, nevertheless, if its representations become distinct, then they cease to be poetic. Consequently poetry must be as clear as possible in order to gain the fullest perfection that our sensate faculty is capable of, but must also be confused in order to remain a poem.

Nonetheless, Baumgarten goes on to explain, confusion plays a role. He contends that what the French call *le goût*, or taste, is a judgement of sense, which is a confused judgement about the perfection of sensation.[21] Confusion does not qualify the clear representation, which remains clear; it qualifies judgement: we have clear representations, but we make a confused judgement about them. To find something beautiful is, in part, to know confusedly something that is itself clear.

Given that sensory knowledge is perfectly clear, even if judged confusedly, and cannot owe its clarity to distinctness, it must owe it to something else. It seems that its clarity results from liveliness or vividness. But arguably such vividness attaches best to particular representations rather than to abstract concepts and ideas. The latter are not determinable in every respect, and therefore cannot sustain any great vividness. Baumgarten suggests that particulars best suit representations because all their details, which can be represented clearly, belong to and identify them; consequently, the more we seek sensate perfection, the more details about the particular we will and can represent. If we seek a sensate representation of an abstract or general concept, we cannot hope for sensate perfection because we could not represent many details without also turning it into a particular that was being represented. Consequently, since we can determine individuals in every respect, particular representations will be the most poetic.[22] This implies the artist should make his representations as similar to the experience of real objects as possible – even though his representations are only judged confusedly.[23] As Baumgarten then goes on to acclaim poetry over pictures because it 'contains more',[24] clearly he is not thinking of the particulars as visual items.

One of the perfections we must represent to gain aesthetic perfection has other consequences. The need for magnitude requires that the 'objects of thought be great'.[25] Greatness can be either natural or moral.[26] Most of Baumgarten's examples stress 'moral greatness', 'dignity', and '*gravitas*', suggesting we cannot realize that sensate perfection in beauty without some presentation of a moral greatness.

This introduces a moral element into beauty and aesthetic response; and although Baumgarten escapes the usual rationalist emphasis on reason and its commensurate derogation of sense, nevertheless the presence of that moral element also precludes the specificity or independence of the aesthetic. If he stresses the moral quality of the magnitude necessary to sensate knowledge and its operation by association, then of any work of art appreciated with the senses we may ask how well it satisfies the requirements of moral magnitude. Should it fail to have a morally satisfactory content, we can dismiss it even though it may satisfy every other requirement of taste and aesthetic perfection. Thus, the aesthetic becomes subordinated to a moral interest.

That relation between aesthetic response and the notion of perfection plagued rationalist aesthetics. For other rationalists like Wolff and Leibniz too beauty was almost always tied to perfection. As a result, taste or the ability to respond to beautiful objects was almost always caught in a similar conundrum. They argued that the relation occurred through the pleasure we usually associate with aesthetic response, which makes it difficult to separate out what is particular to *aesthetic* response from those other human capacities, etc., that we also possess. There is no longer anything distinctive about aesthetics, and our response to beauty seems no different from and is systematically mixed in with the appreciation of perfection and moral value.

Further, as aesthetic responses are indistinct, we cannot clearly know when individuals have correctly and successfully made those judgements because it is difficult to establish criteria for them. Finally, for Leibniz and Wolff sense and intellect yield knowledge of sorts that are continuous or a matter of degree. Neither faculty worked in conjunction with the other; each made its own contribution separately. On the other hand, where Baumgarten distinguished the different logics of sense and intellect, he ran into problems with characterizing the associational logic of the senses in terms of the rest of his theory.

As we proposed earlier, the lack of a clear distinction between sense and concept falls foul of Kant's distinction between intuitions and concepts and his reliance on the notion of judgement. For him sensate material has no significant rules of its own beyond, first, the mind's organization of it into space and time and, second, the order and validity it gains by being conceptualized and used in making assertions or judgements. If aesthetic responses are on a level with other sensual responses, and differ from the rule-giving power of the understanding and our capacity for applying concepts, then they are as arbitrary and incapable of validity as their sensate counterparts. Moreover, where aesthetic responses depend on feelings, there even if the sensate is a part of our knowledge, they prove arbitrary in another way because for Kant feelings are no part of knowledge claims and the conceptualization involved in cognition. At best, we must explain any uniformity present here by reference to its causes rather than to validity because the sensate has no independent validity.

Kant also emphasizes the role of judgement in relating sensibility to understanding. This underlines that there is no room for a purely sensate representation, for all representations must be rule-governed if they come to mind. Even if we leave aside issues of which concepts are involved, Kant holds that sensate representations always occur through the activity of the faculties of understanding and judgement. Kant later suggests that we can deploy judgements and recognize an order in our experience without being able or needing to say exactly what is the nature of that order and so without applying a *determinate* concept. This feature will become important when we consider aesthetic judgements, for the ability to discover order without being able to identify its determinate character is the subjective side of our use of faculties in making judgements. It is a side usually ignored in considerations of knowledge claims because it is irrelevant to their objective validity. Nevertheless, it is present in all the judgements we make, and comes to the fore when we consider aesthetic judgements of the beautiful and the sublime.

Sensate knowledge relates in Baumgarten's aesthetic theory to a perfection stemming from the diversity in unity of perfect divine knowledge. Against this account of sense, intellect, and perfection, Kant provides a justification of the validity of categories and of the objectivity of experience, articulating its necessary order without any reference to perfection or divine knowledge. The ordering he argues for is necessary only for a discursive intelligence like ours, and the more clearly he sets out its details, the more clearly he distinguishes it from the intuitive grasp of objects that God might possess. Consequently, Baumgarten's Leibnizian conception of adequate divine insight becomes inappropriate as a standard for human knowledge. The notion of a 'harmony of differences', where the latter bears references to God, becomes redundant, which robs 'perfection in knowledge' of its power to validate experience. This renders sensate perfection no different from the sensate component of experience. Therefore it gains validity without reference to perfection.[27]

The details I presented above show why Kant rejected the very bases of rationalist theories. Their inability to distinguish sense from reason and their tendency to provide empirical generalizations also led him to reject empiricist theories from the basis of his own distinction between intuition and concept and his recognition that validity was more than an empirical generalization about how we usually behave. This means he was also rejecting his own early work, *Observations on the Beautiful and the Sublime*, which relied on empirical generalizations about our responses to beauty and the sublime.[28]

However, if Kant dismissed aesthetics at first, in the Second Edition of the *Critique of Pure Reason* he was once again certain that a critique of taste is possible. Clearly, then, his demolition of aesthetics is not as total as his rejection of his precursors. And in the newer version of the relevant footnote he now argues that some indeterminate rule can be given for sensibility. That rule differs from the rules proposed in the first two *Critiques* and also from the rules he had dismissed in the First Edition preface.

However, Kant's earlier rejection of his precursors' theories of aesthetic judgements and response is so complete that he is now faced with a problem. To make good his new suggestion that there may be principles for feeling, and before he can justify *a priori* principles for aesthetic judgements, he has first to show that there can be such things. He has to characterize aesthetic claims while avoiding the problems which initially caused him to reject their validity and possibility. At the same time, he must show that they are things capable of being given a justification. This he proceeds to do by following the pattern of the *Critique of Pure Reason*, with some variations, while keeping an eye on the pitfalls he has just identified for aesthetic response.

2

The 'Analytic of the Beautiful'

Kant sets out his account of aesthetic judgements or judgements of taste in the 'Analytic of the Beautiful' of the *Critique of Judgement*. His procedure here cannot be similar to that followed in his earlier *Critiques*. There he took it for granted that we have experience and that we make moral claims, and then examined what conditions are necessary for our experiential and moral claims to be valid. So, just as the *Critique of Pure Reason* accepted that our search for causal explanations of events and objects seemed to work in the main, and sought to discover justifications for this practice, similarly, in the *Foundations of a Metaphysics of Morals*, Kant accepts our 'common moral knowledge' in order to understand what makes it legitimate. His search for justification leads him to formulate a supreme principle of morality, which embodies the only satisfactory model of rational behaviour, and so sustains the legitimacy of the moral demands we make of each other as beings capable of acting rationally.

But it is not clear that in the *Critique of Judgement* he can begin with our ordinary aesthetic claims in order to show why and how they are legitimately made. He has dismissed all previous aesthetic theories because they proved unsatisfactory both in themselves and by reference to his epistemological theory. Consequently, if he is at all to follow his usual procedure of accepting our claims in order to argue for their validity, in the case of aesthetic response he first has to explain what he is accepting.

JUDGEMENTS AND THE AESTHETIC

We saw that Kant treats assertions as judgements. To assert or claim that this is an oak table or that all bachelors are unmarried men is to make a judgement that 'This is an oak table' or 'All bachelors are unmarried men'. Similarly, he talks of our claims

23

about the beauty of objects in terms of judgements. These may not have all the qualities that make for knowledge claims, but they still have the form of judgements or assertions. We saw also that in his epistemology Kant gives a distinctive and vital role to judgements. If he can show how claims about beauty borrow from and develop that role, he will have gone some way towards incorporating these claims into his larger theory about the rational and feeling character of subjects.

Kant also thinks of our judgements on the beauty of objects as judgements of *taste*. The empiricists spoke of a 'sense' of beauty. This sense – taste – was an ability to respond to beauty that was comparable to our other senses. The rationalists too identified taste as a sensitivity for beauty.[1] By talking of our claims about the beauty of objects as judgements of taste, Kant is adopting part of their vocabulary. Judgements of taste denote our capacity for responding to beauty, and by explaining the nature and scope of these judgements, he can set out the nature of that capacity.

We usually classify claims about beauty as 'aesthetic'. In part we do this because of the influence of Kant's work; but he did not take that association for granted. Instead, he thinks we need to justify thinking of judgements of taste as aesthetic. The latter has an older meaning, owed to classical Greek usage, that refers to anything that deals with sensibility, whether in cognition or in feeling. And in the first section of the *Critique of Judgement*, Kant proposes that judgements of taste are aesthetic in this older sense because they have to do with feelings of pleasure and displeasure.[2] Accordingly, if we are to talk of our claims about beauty in terms of judgements of taste, we must account for the connotations of validity that *judgement* has while also showing how judgements of *taste* are distinctive.

Kant associates judgements of taste with sensation and feeling because, first, he has an argument that despite their subjectivity they are capable of validity. Second, their subjectivity constitutes their distinctive nature. To ensure that subjectivity and distinctiveness, to preclude all objective determinant aspects from taste, Kant claims that judgements of taste are pleasurable. This preserves the subjective aspect of judging because pleasure is entirely subjective. Pleasure tells us nothing of objects; its occurrence tells us about the subject only. Whereas 'any reference of presentations, even of sensations, can be objective (in which case it signifies what is real [rather than formal] in an empirical presentation); excepted is a reference to the feeling of pleasure or displeasure – this reference designates nothing whatsoever in the object, but here the subject feels himself, [namely] how he is affected by the presentation.'[3]

Even the sensations we experience – colour or other secondary properties, for example – refer to the object as their origin. We might describe an object in terms of its capacity to bring about sensations of blue in subjects and can proceed to explain away instances where the sensation fails to occur by bringing in *ad hoc* hypotheses – the light was bad, the subject was not looking in the right direction – or by referring to abnormalities in the subject – he is drugged, and so on. We might be tempted to treat pleasure like a secondary quality and to describe an object as having the capacity to bring about pleasure in subjects. But such a claim seems inappropriate because a reference to the object would not warrant any expectations about subjects. Whether or not they feel pleasure has to do with the subjects and their state, and is arbitrary to the object. In the case of *any* object, whether a feeling of pleasure results depends on the subject: in some it will, in some it will not; and so the 'ability to cause pleasure' does not serve as a predicate of objects. It makes little sense to try to explain away instances where pleasure fails to occur as if they were anomalies in what should have been a standard response caused by objective properties when such a response is not standard. Rather, feelings like pleasure are entirely subjective in having their basis in the subject.

In this context, given Kant's claim about pleasure, our explanation of the formal properties of judgements of taste must affirm this subjectivity. And to see how this subjective nature of judgements can claim validity, we must return to Kant's talk of judgements in the *Critique of Pure Reason*.

As we saw, he held that judgement was central to our knowledge, having determinate forms governed by the categories. This application of concepts in judgements having these forms yields knowledge of objects and events. Usually we focus attention on the latter, but there is also a subjective side to objectively valid claims, for they denote subjects who make and understand them. When examining the nature and legitimacy of knowledge claims we tend to ignore the subject's role, but it remains important; and we can explain it in the following ways.

Kant identifies judgement as the ability or 'faculty for subsuming under rules; that is, of distinguishing whether something does or does not stand under a given rule'.[4] The understanding provides concepts or rules for ordering our mental content, the sensibility provides the material of that content, and judgement seeks out the appropriate form of relation of the concept to relevant material. By correctly relating concepts to sensibility or to other concepts – different parts of our thoughts – in logically coherent ways, judgement allows us to think intersubjectively valid and complex thoughts about objects and events – and also allows us to make judgements about or to have thoughts about thoughts and judgements themselves.[5]

Their part in finding appropriate rules for given materials makes judgements peculiar in an important respect. Kant brings out this distinctiveness by saying that 'judgement is a peculiar talent which can be exercised only, and cannot be taught. It is the specific quality of so-called mother-wit; and its lack no school can make good.'[6] The suggestion is that judgement itself has no rules for its application. It relates concepts as rules to sensibility, and if we tried to 'give general instructions how we are to subsume under these rules, that is, to distinguish whether something does or does not come under them, that could only be done by another rule. This, in turn, for the very reason that it is a rule, again demands guidance from judgement.'[7] And so on indefinitely. A concept is a general rule, so that we might use 'umbrella' to classify all the objects with long spindles covered with waterproof material which we open to stave off the rain. It is possible here to ask for other rules which tell us what 'spindles', 'waterproof', and so on are; but it might also seem that once we have reached an appropriate level of simplicity and clarity about what 'umbrellas' are, we can also ask for a rule telling us when to apply this rule 'umbrella'. But if there were such a rule that could be supplied, then we could also ask of the second rule that there be a rule for *its* application; and if there were a third rule, we could ask for the rule for applying the third rule, and so on *ad infinitum*.

The possibility of this infinite regress leads Kant to conclude that if we do make judgements in which concepts are related to sensibility, it cannot be on the basis of rules for judgement, but on the basis of some native talent or mother-wit. We do it spontaneously in the sense that we are not following rules but, in all particular instances, are exercising an ability to bring a given content under an appropriate concept. We may do this well or badly, and a person who usually does it well may in certain instances make a mistake and propose an inappropriate concept for the given material; but in every case, the act of bringing the concept as a rule to its appropriate material is not itself a matter of following a rule. And to instruct others in the act of judgement, the best we can do is to put forward examples in the hope that they will discover from these models what needs to be done. In this sense, for Kant, 'examples are . . . the go-cart of judgement; and those who are lacking in the natural talent can never dispense with them'.[8]

In those who possess this natural talent – which includes anyone able to ascribe concepts to material to yield descriptions of objects and events – judgement must operate in a particular way. For example, it must be spontaneous and creative because there are no rules governing the application of rules to material. It must also involve some sort of direct and immediate relation to the material, that does not itself depend on any prior conceptualization. Yet it is capable of allowing concepts as rules to be brought to bear on the material, and so it must involve *some* kind of appreciation of order which, since it is not as yet cognized, must be indeterminate but also, because it can accept a concept, be capable of general validity. In serving as examples, these judgements demonstrate what can be done. Without establishing general rules, they exhibit how others may follow them in their own attempts to bring material to rules. And in some instances these judgements may be exemplary because they are especially valuable as models.

The activity of judging described here provides some sense of how subjects find concepts appropriate and bring them to bear on material so that we gain thought about experience. In the *Critique of Pure Reason*, Kant does not develop any detailed account of the act of judging. He argues that our thoughts are capable of objective validity gained through concepts and that these depend ultimately on general concepts and judgement-forms such as causality, substance, and so on. But the subjective element remains present, for all these applications of concepts depend upon the subject's non-cognitive and conceptually indeterminate but direct appreciation of the material's order. Here it does not matter whether the material in fact already possesses order, for only through the *subject* appreciating that order through judgement can the concept be brought to bear. And even if by bringing the concept to bear it becomes possible to fit the particular experience of material into the comprehensive order of all our knowledge of nature, nevertheless, only by the subject's appreciation of order through judgement can we link that experience to the system of knowledge.[9]

In a sense, then, our understanding of objective knowledge remains vulnerable until we understand the activity of judging in some more complete detail. One motive Kant had for writing the *Critique of Judgement* was to explore the nature and power of judgement as our pre-cognitive, order-appreciating, and creative, spontaneous, or rule-free activity. We can develop this aspect of judgement by noting that Kant introduces a distinction between determinant and reflective judgements.[10] Briefly, in making determinant judgements we both possesses a material and have a given concept which provides a rule for that order. There are cases of judgement, however, in which the concept may not be given or be immediately obvious although judgement is able to discern some order in its material. In this case, the judgement may be said to possess a particular – the material – for which it lacks but seeks a universal or concept. Kant calls these judgements 'reflective' to mark the need to search out the rule appropriate to the particular. Now, in a sense, given that the activity of judgement generally was said above to be a talent for bringing concepts and material together, every exercise of judgement is reflective in some measure because it brings material to its universal. But the distinction as Kant makes it, while it attends to this activity of judging and emphasizes the absence of a given concept, commensurately also stresses the subject's non-cognitive awareness of an order. This concern for order indicates the presence of something which we may describe as a pressure towards articulation that leads judgements in a search for a universal, even though one is not obviously available for applying to the order discerned by judgement. Kant's emphases become important because by grasping this 'attending to order' and its pressure to articulate even in the absence of any determinate concept or determinant judgement, and by making clear what it involves, he provides us with a location for aesthetic judgements. For aesthetic judgements are a variety of reflective judgement.

Given this background, we can see better why Kant wants to look at judgements to describe the aesthetic. Judgements denote the subject, and introduce a subjective yet valid sense of order which we ascribe to aesthetic judgements.[11] In addition to looking at judgement to explain the aesthetic, Kant also examines aesthetic judgements because these reveal the mechanics of the operation of judging. He maintains that our perplexity over the nature of judgement, over whether it follows objective or subjective principles, 'arises mainly in those judgements, called aesthetic, which govern the beautiful and the sublime in nature or in art'.[12] Because this issue appears in its most acute form here, 'a critical inquiry [in search] of a principle of judgement in [these aesthetic judgements] is the most important part of a critique of this power [of judgement generally].'[13] In aesthetic matters the activity of judging appears clearly and for itself, separated out from its use in relating objective events and objects. And so our examination of its exercise there can serve as a 'propaedeutic to all philosophy',[14] for the subjective validity which aesthetic judgements claim is one that also underlies cognition. As Kant reminds us, the objective determinant judgement 'that is universally valid objectively *is always subjectively so too'.*[15]

ANALYZING JUDGEMENTS OF TASTE

Kant examines the nature of aesthetic judgements in the 'Analytic of the Beautiful'. First, he uses the judgement forms of the First *Critique* heuristically to analyze the form of aesthetic responses. Our judgements of taste may be subjective, and the activity of judging may involve grasping order without applying a determinate concept, but they are still judgements and will have the same forms. In other words, judgements of taste do not differ from, say, cognitive claims in being any less judgements; rather, they are a peculiar kind of judgement; and, as judgements of *some* kind, they will share in the rubric of categories which Kant has identified in the *Critique of Pure Reason* as the forms of all judgements. They too must have Quality, Quantity, Relation, and Modality, and Kant refers to this rubric of categories to exhibit their distinctively aesthetic nature.

Second, given Kant's intention of showing that there can be such things as aesthetic judgements or judgements of taste – that the distinctions developed in his epistemology have not made impossible any distinctively aesthetic claims – and commensurate with his interest in the power and activity of judging, he starts with the *practice* of making aesthetic claims in order to clarify conclusions about the formal properties of judgements. This is to say he exhibits the formal nature of our aesthetic response by looking at our ordinary way of talking about and responding to beautiful objects. In this activity, pleasure plays a prominent role.

And while he wants to show that the precritical conceptions of aesthetics can be dispensed with, mostly he hopes to make clear that the failure of empiricist and rationalist aesthetics lies in the *explanation* it gives of our ordinary usage of pleasure in characterizing aesthetic response. He can now show this inadequacy by clarifying our ordinary usage from the perspective of his own theory. Further, because he is considering the practice of making aesthetic claims or the activity of judging aesthetically, in which pleasure plays the central role and functions like an assertion about an object, he begins with Quality rather than Quantity 'because an aesthetic judgement about the beautiful is concerned with it first'.[16]

A consequence of the subjectivity of judgements is that, third, Kant cannot use the rubric of categories merely mechanically. Instead, he uses the rubric to draw out four Moments or declarations in a kind of phenomenology of aesthetic judgements. He begins with the central characteristic of aesthetic judgements – their subjective, pleasurable nature – and proceeds to show that in relation to his theory of knowledge, mind, and morality, certain other formal and phenomenal qualities must be true if that characteristic is to hold; and those other qualities invite yet other forms and qualifications, and so on. Thus his first Section sets out the claim that judgements of taste are aesthetic because they have to do with a subjective experience of pleasure occasioned as a response to the mind's grasp of the object. Certain other factors must hold true for aesthetic judgements to remain subjective. For example, the judgements cannot be subjective *and* subject to determinate concepts as ordinary cognitive judgements are, for by imposing concepts we make the judgement objective rather than subjective. And so on.

This exploration of subjectivity is not immune from all references to objects, and because he has begun with the activity of making aesthetic claims, fourth, Kant turns his attention to the objects involved in those claims: the subject who makes the judgement and the objects referred to through the judgement. Of course, in order to preserve the subjectivity of aesthetic judgements, the relationship to the object will be of a particular sort, as we shall see, but as the activity of judging involves discovering order in some material or object, the latter cannot be ignored.

In the Analytic Kant wants to explain this distinctive aesthetic relation between the subject and the object by developing a phenomenology of aesthetic judgements. Throughout the Analytic he considers either the mind involved in making judgements or the object being judged. Both the First and Third Moments concern the object, while the Second and Fourth consider the mind. Of course, the other is not excluded from consideration in any of these sections. In the First Moment, for example, Kant focuses on our relation to the *object*, but does so in order to clarify that beauty is really a claim about the *subject* rather than the object. While in the Third Moment he considers the object, but this too is to show that subjects attend only to certain features of it in aesthetic judgements. In other sections of this Moment he raises yet more issues about the way the object is sometimes taken to determine aesthetic responses, but again he wants to indicate how the subject brings about such responses. So in neither case is the object alone the matter of the Section. Later in the text, after the Analytic has set out the formal properties of aesthetic judgements, Kant once again turns to the object, to consider the nature of natural beauty and fine art and to present some conclusions about their role in our activity of judging generally.

In any case, by following the four Moments, Kant eventually exhibits the formal properties of aesthetic judgements. But because he wants to show that by his theory there are such things as aesthetic judgements at all, and, in considering the activity of judging, is concerned with examples of the actual practice of making judgements, fifth, his analysis does not always clearly distinguish their transcendental features from what is true of their actual empirical instances, and his complete arguments are often scattered in different parts of the *Critique of Judgement*. For example, at Section 8, Kant shifts between the transcendental conditions for aesthetic judgements and the problems of actual judgements without making clear that two different kinds of issues are involved. Thus, he talks of what is *postulated* – that the actual judgement takes it for granted that aesthetic judgements generally are universally valid and *possible* in a transcendental sense because their necessary conditions are satisfied – and links this with the need for confirmation from the agreement of others – which is a criterion for the success of our actual judgements rather than an issue of the transcendental conditions for judgements generally. That Section thus makes clear what the relation is between transcendental possibility and criteria for success in actual judgements, but Kant does not present these clearly as involving the two different kinds of issues.

As another example, this time of Kant relying on parts of his theory that are made clear later in the text, we may cite his argument against the realism of aesthetic judgements.[17] This is important to earlier parts of the text because it puts forward some of the theoretical reasons Kant has for some of the positions he sets out there. Similarly, his account of expression and the use of indeterminate concepts appears late in the text, though it is crucial to fully understand his rejection of the use of determinate concepts earlier in the Analytic.

Moreover, as Kant raises the issue of the formal properties of aesthetic response as part of a concern with our aesthetic activity generally, clarification of its formal nature is far from being the whole explanation of our aesthetic activity. We must remember that the activity of judging aesthetically is at issue. In understanding this activity we will analyze its formal properties, but must also consider other issues. Kant refers to these issues of pleasure, understanding, objects, and morality, and they take us beyond the analysis of the forms of judgements alone. For example, knowing that aesthetic responses are subjective, and denote the subject rather than the object, we must clarify the role played by the object. One issue raised here turns on showing that responses result from distinctive concerns with objects. Our concern is not with objects of nature as they are determined by the system of natural laws but is with some other of their features and order. And, here, although we can explain this relation of objects to subjects and thereby clarify the formal properties of subjects' responses, once we see judgement as an activity, then we also raise the wider issue of the role of objects in relation to this activity – as the objects of this activity: that is as fine art and natural beauty. One way Kant deals with this matter is by distinguishing fine art as the product of human activity. And his explanation raises other issues about genius – construed as an activity conducted by the rational will which 'underlies all our actions'[18] – about beauty, their relation, and so on. We shall examine these wider ranges of Kant's aesthetic theory in more detail later. For the present, it is as well to remember that the Analytic's formal analysis of our aesthetic judgements is only a part of a more general theory.[19]

THE FOUR MOMENTS OF THE 'ANALYTIC OF THE BEAUTIFUL'

Kant presents the four declarations in the Analytic as:

1. *'Taste* is the ability to judge an object, or a way of presenting it, by means of a liking or disliking *devoid of all interest.* The object of such a liking is called *beautiful'.*[20]
2. *'Beautiful* is what, without a concept, is liked universally'.[21]
3. 'Beauty is an object's form of *purposiveness* [form of *finality*] insofar as it is perceived in the object *without the presentation of a purpose* [*end*]'.[22]
4. 'Beautiful is what without a concept is cognized as the object of a *necessary* liking'.[23]

The First Moment or declaration wants to argue that talk of the beauty of objects is really best understood in terms of the subject and its feelings of pleasure. Although we usually talk of objects being beautiful, suggesting that beauty is a property of some existing objects that generate pleasure in us, Kant wants to maintain that such is not the case. And he puts forward this negative claim in terms of a contrast between an 'interest' we have in the existence of the objects which cause us pleasure and the disinterested pleasure which he thinks typical of aesthetic response. This needs to be explained further.

The First Moment

The First Moment begins with a definition of taste as 'the ability to judge the beautiful'.[24] Possession of this faculty allows us to seek a critique of it in order to establish its nature, scope, and validity. For the more clearly we exhibit its distinctiveness, the less we will mistake it for sensate knowledge, perfection, and so on. Kant explains this reference to the faculty of judgement, saying that when we consider 'whether anything is beautiful or not', when we say 'This object is beautiful', our saying only seems to be about the object. In fact, the important feature of this saying is not about the object, neither the character it has as a result of its particular position in the nexus of determinate causes and natural laws, nor the purposes it can serve. Rather, the judgement 'The object is beautiful' is really an appraisal of the way the *subject's* faculty of taste is satisfied. The object 'is referred only to the subject, namely to his feeling of life, under the name feeling of pleasure or displeasure'.[25] Every aesthetic judgement, then, of the form 'This is beautiful', is really a disguised expression of the subject's feeling of pleasure or displeasure or 'of life'.

The consequence of this association with pleasure is that the judgement of taste *'cannot be other* than *subjective'*.[26] Kant wants to maintain this, we saw, because of his concern with the subjective aspect of judging. But to explain this claim further we must first consider his assertion that aesthetic response has to do with pleasure or the feeling of life. He is not the first to assert this connection with pleasure. It is frequently made in classical writings on poetics, in the theories of poetics produced in Arabic philosophy, both before and after Islam, and is generally accepted in medieval Europe and in the Enlightenment. It also tallies with our own conception of aesthetic response in that whatever else may be involved in appreciating a poem, novel, or other object, certainly pleasure is also present, and comes from appreciating their various features.[27]

The best defence of this association does not necessarily lie in finding some more basic feature from which we draw the association of pleasure and beauty as a conclusion. Rather, accepting the connection, we may develop Kant's theory and show how, on this basis, it is much more comprehensive than other theories because it gives a coherence and unity to our diverse conclusions about beauty and aesthetic judgement. In a sense, the association's worth is proved by its usefulness in organizing the gamut of our intuitions about the subject and in providing a basis for assessing other theories of aesthetic response. If aesthetic judgements are pleasurable, what Kant says about them will apply to any subjectivist theory, whatever concept of subjectivity they involve. Similarly, where others propose a more objective account, the comprehensiveness and strength of Kant's theory will provide a counter-instance against which they will have to argue.[28]

Kant explains that the association between pleasure and subjectivity in aesthetic responses is 'independent of all interest'. Pleasure does not occur only in aesthetic response, but in the latter case it is qualified by being *free* of interest.[29] Only a disinterested pleasure is entirely subjective, he holds, and so it alone can constitute aesthetic response – 'one whose determining *basis cannot be other* than *subjective'*.[30] To understand this, we must be clearer about interest. Kant defines interest as a pleasure or liking 'we connect with the presentation of an object's existence'.[31] The suggestion is that we are pleased that an object exists when it is something we desire. The desire arises when we value the object either because it causes us pleasure or because we think it is good. For Kant, 'good' includes moral worth, instrumental worth – as when the object serves as a means to satisfy some end we have – and the 'perfection' of an object – as when it satisfies some ideal and so is a 'good' object of its kind. But as all these have in common the ability to serve an end, we may consider them all under the rubric of 'good'. Thus, in the case of desire, we value the object for the purpose – moral or sensual – it serves, and the fact that it exists is itself an occasion for delight because it can satisfy our purposes. In the one case, it must exist to cause pleasure in us and in the other case it must exist to satisfy its purpose and so be good. In both cases, then, the existence of the object is crucial if it is to play any part in satisfying our desires, and so the very fact of its existence is an occasion for delight in addition to any pleasure it may cause.

To use the vocabulary Kant favours, we can label the first value one of sense, and maintain that it involves a judgement about what is agreeable (because it gratifies our senses); the second we can label one of morality, using this word loosely as 'good', and can maintain that it depends on a judgement of what is good because it satisfies our moral reasoning. For Kant, these are the only kinds of interest there can be. Further, given the delight we can feel in the very existence of an object, and that interest is this pleasure connected with the existence of the object, we can express the nature of interest by saying that 'interest allows us to give *reasons* for our delight in judging or seeing that an object exists'. So when we judge an agreeable object to exist, this judgement about its existence itself gives us pleasure or delight for the reason that we know the object causes us pleasure. Similarly in the moral case, we judge that something is morally good and then, when we find that the object or event exists, we are pleased for the reason that it exists and can satisfy our moral purpose. In both these cases, our delight is interested because it is based on a conception of the purpose that can be served by the object. That is, our 'liking' is 'determined not just by the presentation of the object but also by the presentation of the subject's connection with the existence of the object'.[32] Thus, 'what we like is not just the object but its existence as well'.[33]

By contrast, Kant wants to maintain, aesthetic responses are pleasurable without interest. Pleasure is only that which is the experience of beauty. Our liking depends only on the presentation of the object. In a painting it is not, say, the *actual* house represented that concerns us but the representation itself; and similarly in poems, novels, or music. The physical properties of the oils, canvas, papers, or so on are not germane to our appreciation, nor do the events related have to exist for us to appreciate their order in a novel or painting. We point to the structure, complexity, expressiveness, balance, coherence, unity, etc., of the object, perhaps pointing out the features by which it gains a unity that we grasp with pleasure and characterize as beautiful. Our concern with articulating our response, where it relates to the object, is merely with the object for itself and its order. We do not have an interest in the existence of the beautiful object *for reasons of* the use to which we will put that object, whether moral or agreeable, nor for its relation to other objects within the system of scientific knowledge. In terms of reasons for pleasure in existence, aesthetic responses are pleasurable for no reason at all, and no further use to which we might put an object can explain our aesthetic pleasure.

The above shows us that aesthetic pleasure is disinterested. If we call an object beautiful, we consider it only for its suitability to that disinterested pleasure. Talk of beautiful objects cannot then be about objects as such. If our pleasure is to be entirely subjective, it must be disinterested, for else it would involve reference to the real existence of objects; but if pleasure is disinterested, it is not really about the object at all, in the sense of attaching to or being caused by its objective properties, but about the subject and the quality of its relation to a particular.[34]

An objection to this way of distinguishing aesthetic from other pleasures is that it is difficult to apply in practice. We often make mistakes about our own motives, and may think we cannot give reasons for our pleasure only because we are deluding ourselves about the interest we actually have. Nothing in our experience of pleasure itself shows it is different in the cases of the agreeable, the good, and the beautiful, and so we can easily confuse them phenomenologically. Kant suggests no remedy for this, yet if we cannot clearly apply the distinctions he has proposed, they are surely unsatisfactory.

In reply we may argue for Kant that his distinctions are not intended as phenomenological ones. Pleasure is pleasure, for Kant, and does not have diverse qualities in experience that identify it as aesthetic or otherwise. If there were such phenomenological properties, then an analysis of the judgements would be unnecessary because their nature would be obvious and clear immediately. Instead, Kant provides an analysis because he recognizes that pleasure occurs on other occasions as well as in aesthetic judgements, and wants to clarify the different ways we treat pleasure in these occurrences in terms of how we behave – the rules we follow – rather than in terms of an impossible merely introspective intuition. In effect, Kant is pointing out that our feelings do not simply occur naively. They are always part of a theory and set of distinctions. In particular, they are instances of judgement rather than variable causal responses.

This still leaves open the possibility that we may mistake aesthetic pleasure for something else. Kant accepts that possibility: the judgements are corrigible; but by setting out the different ways we treat pleasure in its various occurrences, he also sets out what the appropriate standards of success are. A disinterested pleasure cannot involve reasons for the pleasure, and we may have to probe to discover whether a putative instance is disinterested. This kind of openness is intrinsic to Kant's philosophical method, which relies on gaining agreement between subjects, and so has to leave open a space for debate and interaction between them.[35]

In any case, from these claims about taste and the role of disinterested pleasure, Kant thinks we can arrive at the Second Moment, of Quantity, because a disinterested judgement 'must contain a basis for being liked [that holds] for everyone'.[36]

3

The Second Moment

Kant's 'deduction' of universality from disinterestedness has a particular sense. It is not an analytic truth that disinterested pleasure is also universal. In part, by proposing that there is need for argument, Kant reminds us that he has no complaint with the concept of disinterestedness as it was developed by British thinkers like Shaftesbury and Hume.[1] What he does reject, though, is their assumption that by uncovering the disinterestedness of aesthetic claims, they have also successfully defended their validity. Kant's deduction of universality from disinterestedness clarifies that, despite its subjectivity, nothing about pleasure intrinsically excludes it from being shared. This will give taste an especial universality, which is comprehensive over subjects, rather than over objects; but the fact that it can be comprehensive at all needs to be defended. We can begin by examining the role of concepts in disinterested pleasure.

As always, Kant's argument explores the nature and limits of a subjective pleasure. He looks first to the logical form of the judgement. Having established its quality in the First Moment and shown this to be a matter of subjective disinterested pleasure, he turns to quantity. The *Critique of Pure Reason* has shown that judgements must be Universal, Particular, or Singular in their Quantity.[2] Logically universal or particular judgements are claims about objects with determinate properties. They either make general claims about objects of a given kind or about an object with given properties, and in both cases depend on applying determinate concepts to objects. By contrast, Kant wants to show that aesthetic judgements are subjective and therefore must exclude determinate concepts. Given that he wants to conclude from the Second Moment that aesthetic judgements are 'liked universally' yet 'without a concept', it must seem at first that he wants to exclude all concepts altogether.

To show that disinterested and subjective aesthetic judgements must exclude determinate concepts, Kant develops the notion of disinterestedness as follows. In order to ascribe an interest we must identify the object as of a class or kind that is causally related to the subject because it gives rise to pleasure or serves some intention or purpose. For Kant, to identify an object is to make an assertion about that existent object. So, every recognition of interest must involve a determinate judgement in which the object is brought under some given concept in the form 'This X is Y' or 'All Xs are Ys' and related to the subject's desires. We cannot generate interest without applying determinate concepts to identify the object, its nature, the characteristics it possesses for being of its type generally, its effect on the subject, and all the other properties it has to have in order to be the object it is. In these cases, we need to arrive at generalizations that apply to objects and must consider them all as items in the field of causal connections.[3] Now, conversely, if this is a correct picture of what is necessary for expressions of interest, then one way to guarantee the disinterestedness of pleasure is to exclude a necessary condition for interests – the application of determinate concepts. A subjective pleasure that occurs even in the absence of the concepts necessary to establishing interests must be disinterested.

These moves are open to at least two objections. The exclusion of determinate concepts does not clearly show that our pleasure is disinterested. There are at least a couple of reasons for this: first, we may be mistaken in the particular instance where we think we have excluded interests by excluding concepts. This is because of a more general problem: we lack clear criteria for distinguishing a disinterested pleasure from one whose causality is known. And if we lack general criteria for this distinction, we are likely to be mistaken in the particular instance too.

It may seem that we have already resolved this problem by arguing that the distinction between aesthetic and non-aesthetic judgements will not show itself in our phenomenological experience, as a characteristic of the experience of pleasure itself. The lack of general criteria just bemoaned by the objector may be simply an inability to discover those non-existent phenomenological differences. But the objection has a deeper ground, for it is suspicious of any claim that we have excluded interests if all we have excluded are the concepts through whose application we identify objects and interests. All that may be happening is that, because we are ignorant of the causes which in fact still continue to operate and serve our interests, we delude ourselves into thinking that certain occurrences of pleasure are disinterested. In fact, the objector may argue, all our pleasures are causal because all events are causal and this one must be so too, and disinterestedness at best is only a confession of ignorance. The second objection is that even if this exclusion yields disinterested pleasure, it may neither exclude all interests nor be the only way to do so.

Although we cannot answer either objection fully here, both indicate that Kant's claims depend on the rest of his critical theory. Of the second objection: Kant holds there are only two sorts of interest, those arising from sense – the agreeable – or those arising from moral or other intentions – the good. This depends on his distinction between practical and theoretical reason, whose implications for morality, cognitive knowledge, science, and ourselves as natural animal beings capable of action and understanding, all underlie his identification of interests. But it is inappropriate to question that basis here. Insightful analysis of the underlying critical theory will best wait on first displaying how the theory sustains Kant's account of aesthetic judgements. And, in the present context, we can clarify the latter by, say, identifying the interests that we cannot incorporate into either the agreeable or the good.

Another expression of this objection is that Kant's distinction of aesthetic response from the agreeable and the good is inadequate because we could develop an interest in beauty. If so, then aesthetic judgements would be associated with an interest. Kant wants to argue that our aesthetic responses can be neither determined by an interest nor be the basis for any interest.[4] But, surely, the critic might argue, even if we accept that no interest determines a pleasurable response to beauty, we may have a moral or other interest in beauty. Perhaps we value beautiful objects because they promote moral sensitivity or because they serve a social interest.[5] Accordingly, we may propose a need for beauty.

Fortunately, this claim does not work as an objection, and Kant's essential point about the disinterestedness of aesthetic pleasure remains undamaged. As he himself argues later, we may possess a need for beauty, and by our justification of this need, we ground an interest in beauty. Thus we may argue that we have an interest in natural beauty[6] or may develop a social interest in fine art,[7] but these interests do not determine the disinterested aesthetic judgement by which we find the object beautiful in the first instance. The interest we have in beauty does not decide which objects we will find beautiful, if any; for a reason for seeking beauty is not a reason for finding some one particular object or type of object beautiful. Nor is it a reason for finding something beautiful rather than thinking it aesthetically uninteresting. By contrast, a reason for seeking something pleasurable is a reason for finding some one object or particular type of object agreeable. Their agreeableness determines which objects we will find of interest and which we will dismiss. Thus, the objection fails to show that Kant is confused about the role of disinterestedness.[8]

In any case, we began with two objections, and have dealt with one that says excluding concepts does not exclude all interests because there may be other interests than those of the agreeable and the good. Another objection was that we think our pleasure is disinterested merely because we cannot see any causal connection between an object and our pleasure. In fact, this objector holds, every occasioning of pleasure must be causally related to objects and there can be no such thing as a disinterested pleasure. This objection too raises more issues than can be answered in considering only the Analytic of the Beautiful, but it is worth pursuing here because of what it shows us of Kant's approach. For his defence against this objection involves reiterating his stand on idealism,[9] and suggests other features of the critical task and his attempt to discover a justification for aesthetic responses.

Kant's answer refers us to his general theory. He can concede the causality, holding that our very seeing, hearing, and so on must involve causality at some level. However, the objection maintains that there is a direct causal relation between the object and the experience of pleasure which is our judgement of beauty. By contrast, Kant argues that beauty and taste depend on our exercise of mind: the latter may seek to grasp a particular object, but our aesthetic pleasure is a result of the operation of the mind and is not a direct response to the object. The objector seems to forget the need for that operation and seems to take up a stance which Kant has attacked elsewhere. He argued that empiricists mistakenly assume that the world of experience is distinct from our experience of the world. By this construal, we may have a set of ideas in consciousness but cannot know whether these coincide with objects in the real world.[10] The natural end of this beginning, Kant holds, is scepticism, and in later sections of the *Critique of Judgement*, he argues that those who propose that there may be some as-yet-unknown cause operating to bring about the pleasure we mistake as aesthetic – these he now labels as realists – must take up a similar theoretical stance. They must suppose that even if we do not know what cause is operating, there must be some cause, arising from objects, which results in the feeling of pleasure we have – and this because all events need causes.

Against this Kant argues that the realist position is essentially no different from the empiricist one. It maintains that there is some as yet unknown cause outside us; and it expects that is the real basis for our feelings of pleasure. But such a realist position suffers the fate of scepticism. Because of its starting-point, which begins with something outside the mind and seeks to find for it a correspondence in the mind or vice versa, the realist position will never be able to get off the ground. If a realist aesthetic relates nature generally to a particular exercise of the mind, it must identify that exercise by reference to the 'form' of objects judged beautiful. But this identification could not even begin. First, to judge the beauty of an object we suppose that *our judgement* of beauty has some validity. This cannot itself be derived from experience because that would make it a merely contingent generalization about the uniformity of human nature, and while the latter can claim to be true, it cannot give the activity of the mind – the judgement of taste – any validity. Thus, realism would have to presuppose the validity of the principle of judgements of taste in order to begin to discover the causal connections between the object and the mind. But in trying to substitute causal principles, realism is also trying to deny the principle which gives aesthetic judgements their validity. The realist would have to use that principle to identify the experience of disinterested pleasure which is beauty and whose causal relations he is trying to identify and, at the same time, he would have to deny that principle because he wants to substitute causal relations for it. But if he is going to deny that principle, there is no experience of beauty which he can identify in order to begin substituting causal connections, for if we deny the principle of judgements of taste, then our experiences of pleasure will become no different from agreeable or moral judgements: that is, there will be no such things as aesthetic judgements, and so the realist will be unable even to begin to identify the instances of aesthetic pleasure for which he wants to find causal connections. Consequently, the realist ends up in the position of the sceptic who can never, because of his starting point, get out of his circle. Only by accepting idealism do we get to aesthetic judgements, and so we cannot expect to substitute causal connections for the occurrence of judgements of taste. And for Kant idealism is tied up with such distinctions between theory and practice, reason and sense, as make it usual to distinguish only two kinds of interest – in sense and morality.

A critic may object that both these defences are inadequate because at best they show how Kant relates a set of distinctions, between interest, disinterestedness, and subjective universality, to other parts of his theory. They do not ground his claims independently, and so do not constitute any real defence of the theory. However, a theory is supposed to show the interrelation of elements and issues, and its comprehensiveness is a measure of its success; so Kant's interrelation of these concerns is a mark of his success. Yet the objection is sensible – for a successful attack on a fundamental part of the theory will be debilitating, and it will be of no advantage to point to that part's coherence with the whole theory. Thus, while we may deflect the above objections by showing their relation to Kant's theory, nevertheless they also identify the fundamental features we may attack eventually.

In any case, we were considering the claim that to preserve the subjectivity of aesthetic judgements we must exclude concepts because their use introduces interests. Against this the critic argued that an exclusion of concepts does not ensure the disinterestedness of judgements because we could still be subject to interests. By arguing against the realist we have suggested why this argument is unsatisfactory. We may develop this by arguing now that we can sustain the subjective disinterested pleasure of aesthetic judgements not by excluding concepts altogether but by excluding them only when they bring in interests; if they do not, then we may continue to use concepts in a particular way. Kant suggests something like this when he explains how we can articulate the order in an object of judgement without using determinate concepts. The issue is worth pursuing at some length because it makes clear features of the structure of judgements of taste.

Although the Second Moment seems to suggest that we must exclude concepts to gain a purely subjective experience, available to all, because interests, the determinate nature of objects, our physiology, or the determinations of morality, all depend on using determinate concepts, later in the *Critique of Judgement* Kant seems to recognize that the exclusion of interests does not need anything so drastic as expunging all concepts altogether. For in those later passages he suggests that our aesthetic responses involve concepts but that their basis in feelings of pleasure gives them a special character. Kant writes of 'the exhibition of the concept' to which there is linked a 'wealth of thought to which no linguistic expression is completely adequate'.[11] Here 'no language can express [the thought] completely and allow us to grasp it', Kant says, and talks of what is presented as 'surpassing' concepts, of 'expand[ing] the concept itself', and of the imagination as 'creative',[12] or of thoughts being 'conjoined with a given concept',[13] or of 'multiplicity of partial presentations' through which we 'add to a concept the thought of much that is ineffable', that is 'over and above harmony with the concept'. Concepts here are not so much excluded as added to and extended beyond their ordinary use in cognitive judgements and knowledge claims because aesthetic judgements induce 'so much thought as can never be comprehended within a *determinate* concept'.[14] As a result of this abundance, we 'expand the concept itself in an unlimited way'.[15] Given this extra-cognitive use of concepts in their non-determinate form, we may distinguish an aesthetic use of concepts from a cognitive or moral use, and understand Kant's apparent exclusion of concepts in the Second Moment as an exclusion of concepts in their determinate – moral and cognitive – use.

Earlier Kant had written that in judgements of taste 'the cognitive powers brought into play . . . are engaged in free play, because no *determinate* concept restricts them to a particular rule of cognition' and that judgement works 'without presupposing a *determinate* concept'.[16] So far as determinate concepts operate by giving us experience of objects possessing a nature which, in turn, we explain by pointing to their location in the causal nexus, the disinterestedness of aesthetic responses will be compatible with the use of indeterminate concepts.[17] He can then distinguish determinate from indeterminate concepts by saying that the former depend on causes and rational connections to gain objective knowledge of experience, are universal, based on given properties, and have uses we can specify and order in science to have precise application. Indeterminate concepts depend on associations of ideas,[18] are singular in that they organize only the material they are used to inform, cannot always warrant any general inferences about the nature of their object,[19] and have a poetic, metaphorical, or idiomatic order.[20]

Disinterestedness and Expression

Kant identifies this imaginative and aesthetic order as an expression of aesthetic ideas. The products of the imagination – the non-causal associations we make and the new nature we create out of given material – outstrip the understanding and its application of determinate concepts, and can only be ordered by ideas of reason. Kant calls 'such presentations of the imagination' *ideas* because they 'strive towards something that lies beyond the bounds of experience, and hence try to approach an exhibition of rational concepts (intellectual ideas), and thus [these concepts] are given a semblance of objective reality. Another reason, indeed the main one, for calling these presentations ideas is that they are inner intuitions to which no concept can be completely adequate.'[21]

While Kant's discussion of the expression of aesthetic ideas occurs mainly in relation to the powers of mind that constitute genius, it is plain that regardless of how they are produced, these indeterminate concepts or this aesthetic use of concepts must enter into judgements of taste irrespective of whether these are on works of fine art or objects of beauty. Kant cannot bring them to bear when explaining fine art without also, so to speak, making room for them in the formal properties of the judgement of taste itself. Indeed, there is good reason for supposing that natural beauty too is expressive in a manner parallel to the expressiveness of fine art.[22] And Kant affirms that 'we may generally call beauty (*whether natural or artistic*) the *expression* of aesthetic ideas'.[23]

We may further explain this aesthetic use of concepts to develop themes (or aesthetic ideas). In a play, for example, the entire causal history of any event is not necessary to understanding its meaning. A handkerchief appears in the play as an instrument the villain uses to incite the rage of a jealous and suspicious husband. The causal history of the cloth is not important; it does not matter whether such a handkerchief really existed; nor need the events in the play follow necessary determinate laws before we can find them plausible. Instead, we take elements from reality or nature, and rearrange them to suit our purpose of making this meaning clear. The piece of cloth has connotations in the play, which it derives from its role in the events represented on the stage, that it does not have outside the plot. In effect, its meaning is limited to the play. The singular use does not determine the properties of handkerchiefs outside the play in that other writers may give those pieces of cloth other uses in their own works, whether they talk of 'flannel waistcoats and moral pocket handkerchiefs',[24] of 'snuffle and sniff and handkerchief',[25] of 'Holding the Pocket Handkerchief Before his streaming eyes',[26] of 'the handkerchief of the Lord',[27] or of knitting 'my handkerchief about your brows, – The best I had, a princess wrought it me'.[28] Those singular connotations and individual meanings, Kant's claims suggest, seek validity not from being made part of a system of natural scientific explanation with its determinate placings of clearly defined concepts, but from the universalizable pleasurable response of our aesthetic judgement. The latter considers the events represented on the stage in terms of the order of the play rather than of the relation between the events and the systematic causal nexus.[29]

Kant sometimes talks of this use of indeterminate concepts – this aesthetic use of concepts – as the free play of faculties.[30] The latter attends to the mental operations involved in this use of concepts, affirming that we cannot issue any kind of judgement at all, whatever its epistemological status, unless there is a supporting operation of the mind. The last claim follows from the definitions he gives of faculties – like understanding, imagination, and reason – as capacities subjects have to carry out certain rule-governed activities. The understanding provides concepts and is the capacity for ordering and classifying objects according to rules; the imagination provides the sensible material for this ordering, and is our capacity for reproducing images of absent particulars and for reordering and manipulating them; reason is our capacity for the most general order, including rules we discover for employing the understanding.

The close relation between faculties and the claims we make allows Kant to characterize the former in the latter. A cognitive judgement, which applies a determinate concept to an object, Kant suggests, depends on a fixed and determinate relation between the faculties of understanding, which supplies the concepts, and imagination, which brings us the absent particular. As a result of the activity of these faculties we can say that 'Some roses are red' or that 'Copper expands on heating'. If we order the latter statement into the system of scientific knowledge, then we turn to reason for a principle by which we can give it a determinate location in the science of metals and chemical structures. The precision we demand of concepts in their determinate use is reflected in the fixed relation between the faculties providing those concepts, images, and order.

Conversely, the indeterminate use of concepts sustains a free play of faculties. These concepts proceed by associations of ideas, metaphor, metonymy, and catachresis, and do not follow causal determinations, ordered into a system of scientific knowledge, as a standard. Rather, we use reason to guide the associations into a theme – an aesthetic idea – which we explore through the association of ideas. No exactness according to causal factors or 'particular rule of cognition'[31] is at issue here, though we may refine and direct associations of ideas to their theme.

In the free play of faculties, Kant maintains, we are no less rational than when we make cognitive or moral claims. The faculties we use, our thinking and reflection, in that free play are still ratiocinative; but rather than assess them by reference to the knowledge of objects they yield, we consider them in aesthetic judgements for their positive mutual relation. In this free play of faculties we engage in thought and reflection for themselves rather than to gain knowledge of the world or moral certainties.

Here it is Kant's insight that our experience of this mutual positive relation of faculties gives rise to a 'feeling of life' – a positive and healthy sense of our own power to think and act. He talks of the faculties in their free play being in harmony when they relate positively by promoting each faculty's intrinsic power in balance with the others. By contrast, in cognitive judgements, our power for thought and reflection is constrained to grasping the object and its determinate properties in order to explain the latter's genesis and nature. In aesthetic judgements, our thought and reflection are free to pursue their own extent and power. An association of ideas proceeds as the power of thought develops in relation with the powers of imagination and order. If we use the image of a handkerchief, we may relate it to a number of other images and concepts, but these will not exceed the meanings we can plausibly give to these pieces of cloth. The latter excess is a disharmony between faculties. Another arbitrariness in the relation between faculties may result from associating ideas in ways irrelevant to a given theme. The work then fails to express an aesthetic idea and becomes nonsensical.

These examples suggest that attaining a harmony between faculties is an art, requiring a fine judgement that the order of ideas, images, and theme is appropriate and balanced. The important point at present is that an harmonious relation of faculties, a well-formed work, which reveals aspects of our power of thought

and reflection for themselves, generates pleasure, as a species of
the feeling for life, because we enjoy this fact of the operation of
the mind. This is the pleasure of aesthetic judgements, whose
experience is beauty.

In summary, then, our reading novels, watching plays, and
looking at paintings gives rise to pleasure in our understanding of
their meanings and order. This pleasure Kant identifies as a feeling
for life, and explains as the result of our exploring our capacity for
thought and reflection for itself. This insight relates aesthetic
judgements to pleasure – our ratiocinative activity to feelings.[32]

If we now look back at the Second Moment, we see that Kant's
conclusion, that aesthetic judgements are 'liked universally', even
'without a concept', need exclude determinate concepts only. The
singular aesthetic uses of indeterminate concepts are sufficiently
removed from the natural causal nexus intrinsic to interests and
the satisfaction of desires to be usable in disinterested judgements.
Now from, first, this exclusion of determinate concepts and from,
second, the singularity of aesthetic judgements using indeterminate concepts, we may also be able to argue for the universality of
our pleasurable subjective responses.

Disinterestedness and Universality

Initially Kant seems to suggest that the universality of aesthetic
response follows from excluding interests. The latter depend on
factors which vary from person to person. If the person happens to
like looking at pictures of elongated male and female figures, he
may have an interest in Ingres' works. But those who do not share
this preference cannot share his interest, and the attendant
pleasure cannot be universalized. Similarly, the achievement of an
intention which is desirable or good – even morally good – may
give rise to pleasure, but only someone who shares that end will
share that pleasure. If a subject's pleasure with Manet's *Olympia*
(1863) results from its usefulness in covering a discoloured patch
on the drawing-room wall, it is unlikely to be universalized. If the
subject has a moral intention, then everyone should share that
end; but, first, since that sort of end does not necessarily give rise
to or depend on pleasure, we cannot expect it of all subjects; and,
second, even if moral validity were the basis of pleasure, then
again the pleasure would depend on how each moral agent felt

about the achievement of a moral end. In all these cases, the pleasure each subject associates with an object is variable, and this arbitrariness precludes pleasure from being universally shared. Where a pleasure is disinterested, on the other hand, since pleasure is not based on any interest, it will not be particular to the individual, who may expect that the basis of delight in him is something which all others may also have.[33]

The last remains a *non sequitur* and is not Kant's whole claim. But it does clarify why Kant wants to deny universality to interested judgements. His positive thesis about universality turns on the basis of aesthetic judgements in the free play of cognitive powers or faculties.

We may approach this claim from another direction, to clarify some related issues. The availability of judgements of taste to all subjects possessing rational faculties points to another feature of them, which Kant suggests later through talk of 'imputation'. This indicates the expectation we have of pleasure in aesthetic responses. With interests, 'everyone is allowed to have his own opinion', and we do not expect others to share in ours; with disinterestedness, our expectation is of an agreement from others because our own pleasure is more than an expression of merely personal preferences. In Kant's terms, disinterested pleasure claims universality or a 'general validity' that is still subjective; and by saying that an object is beautiful we maintain a second thesis that our predication of pleasure 'extend[s] . . . over the entire sphere of *judging persons*'.[34] When we call an object beautiful, 'we believe we have a universal voice, and lay claim to the agreement of everyone'.[35]

At other places Kant also finds moral connotations for such imputation or uses cognates of such compulsion. More immediately for our present purpose, the reference to subjects and universality points to a factor we have not explained: the role of the object. It was said that disinterested pleasure excluded determinate concepts because by introducing the latter we brought in considerations of interest. This claim is not a psychological one, requiring us to exclude any thought of the nature of the object and its causal relations. That would be a curious task, even if we could achieve it by great concentration. Rather, the proposal invites us to complement the denotation of subjects in aesthetic responses, expressed by saying 'This object is beautiful', with a claim about the logical form of this reference to the object. An interest of sense depends on understanding how an object of such and such a type has a given effect on the subject. From the fact that oranges satisfy a desire in me, it is possible to infer that objects of a certain type will satisfy certain desires in me. By contrast, Kant wants to suggest, the logical form of the aesthetic judgement is singular and does not sustain a generalization about objects of such and such a kind. At best, we might say 'This rose is beautiful', denoting a subjective response and referring to an object as the subject of a logically singular judgement, but we cannot generalize from that to the claim that all objects of this kind – all roses – will be beautiful. The grammatical subject serves only as a means for identifying the object, and does not denote its determinate class-properties. 'The object to the left of the sheet music on the piano' could identify the beautiful rose and so be substituted for 'the rose' in the aesthetic judgement. Similarly, we may explain in detail the process of production in order to identify an object, but the explanation will be redundant to appraisal of and response to the particular object.

This ostensive use of explanation, description, and so on need not be arbitrary. Kant writes later that we can use examples and illustrations to identify the object and direct attention to its features.[36] Comparison with familiar examples of poems or pictures can indicate relevant features of the object to others, perhaps exhibiting a pattern in a painter's work, and allowing other people to appraise the object in a specific way. They can then share in the subject's disinterested pleasure in the object.

In these cases, then, the object plays a distinctive role as the subject of a singular judgement. We consider it for itself, as it appears, rather than attend to explanations of its nature. The latter apply determinate concepts to locate the object within the system of scientific knowledge, and not only treat the object like any other element in this system of explanation, but explain it as an instantiation of a causal generalization over objects. By contrast, the subject responding aesthetically appraises the object for itself, disinterestedly, without regard for that empirical nature, for an application of determinate concepts, or for its place in the nexus of causal explanation. And as the response is universalizable, though it treats of a particular object the judgement claims universal validity.

The discussion of the last few paragraphs shows that Kant is not simply assuming that a disinterested pleasure must be universal over all other subjects or must have a subjective general validity. Their disinterestedness is crucial to the universal validity of judgements of taste. For if the judgement is disinterested, then it does not involve any determinate concepts. This implies that the judgement form is neither universal nor particular in quantity but is singular, referring only to the individual beautiful object – this rose, this tulip, this painting, etc. – which occasions pleasure, rather than to objects of a given kind. However, because it is a judgement of taste, the subject judges 'not just for himself but for everyone';[37] therefore his singular but subjective judgement must yet have a wider scope than its quantity. As the judgement is a subjective one, its scope will extend over the pleasure or feeling which makes up its subjective quality, and will claim a subjective universality by doing so. Thus, if the subjective judgement is to have any validity, which it must if it is to be a judgement, it will have a subjective universality – or will be comprehensive over subjects.

We can develop these claims by contrasting aesthetic judgements with both the agreeable and the good. Judgements of the agreeable are merely subjective, in that everyone will be 'of a mind of his own, no one requiring others to agree' with his own claims because in effect we suppose that these claims are by nature 'true only for me'. By contrast, Kant wants to claim, where we think something beautiful, we 'require . . . agreement from everyone',[38] and think our judgement is more than just 'true for me'. Another consideration distinguishes judgements of taste from moral claims. With the latter, we expect objective agreement: if we have correctly identified the morally valuable object, then we expect agreement from everyone because of the object's moral quality. By contrast, while aesthetic judgements demand agreement, they do not base it on any concept of what the object is supposed to be or the moral quality it exhibits but instead rely on a subjective felt pleasure. 'No one can use reasons or principles to talk us into a judgement on whether some garment, house, or flower is beautiful'.[39] That kind of argument might work in the case of moral judgements, but in judgements of taste, which depend on our feeling of pleasure, 'we want to submit the object to our own eyes, just as if our liking of it depended on that sensation. And yet, if we then call the object beautiful, we believe we have a universal voice, and lay claim to the agreement of everyone'.[40]

Even if we accept this universal validity, the subjectivity of these judgements leads to the problem that we need to consider carefully the criteria for their success. As Kant complains at the end of

Section 8, the subject ought to be able to separate out 'whatever belongs to the agreeable and the good from the liking that remains . . . after that'. He 'would under these conditions [always] be justified in this claim, if only he did not on occasion fail to observe these conditions and *so make an erroneous judgement of taste*'.[41] But he does make mistakes, so that his internal reflection on the nature of pleasure remaining is always corrigible and open to the danger of confusing charm, emotion, sensation, etc., with what should be a disinterested judgement. Consequently, although the subject 'postulates' a universal voice for his actual particular judgement, in that he supposes that his aesthetic response has a general subjective validity, he cannot suppose similarly that everyone agrees with his judgement. While he expects in good faith on the basis of his own judgement that everyone will agree with him, his judgement may be mistaken. Indeed, because it is a subjective disinterested judgement, it cannot expect confirmation except by agreement from others, when they too feel the same pleasure as he does in his judgement.[42] Consequently, the success of a judgement of taste is not measured by the subject's own fallible reflection but by its being confirmed by other subjects' experience of pleasure.

This raises two issues, one about the process of judgement and another about the confirmation we can expect. The issue about judgement is this: if we are to reflect upon our judgement to assess whether it is universally valid or merely determined by charm, emotion, or sensation, we are really being asked to make two judgements. Or, perhaps more precisely, the activity of judging aesthetically involves a double process. In the first we reflect upon, estimate, or appraise the singular object, where such appraisal occasions pleasure; in the second we reflect upon or assess whether that pleasure is disinterested and universalizable. That is, these judgements are concerned with their own origin and their own application, consisting of both a pleasurable estimation of a singular object or representation and a reflection on the source of that pleasure.[43] Kant usually distinguishes between the two processes, calling the first 'simple' or 'mere' reflection or 'estimation' and the second a judgement of taste,[44] but does not seem to use them as technical terms. Nevertheless, if we fail to recognize that there are two processes at work, a number of the theses Kant goes on to develop will fail to make sense.

Given that there are two processes, the second issue we need to raise here is how we can expect to confirm our judgement of taste and its implicit claim that the pleasure we feel is universally valid. Our second reflection is fallible, and so we need confirmation. For Kant, such confirmation comes from other subjects, not from applying concepts to make objectively valid judgements. But this raises a further problem, for we cannot confirm our judgement merely by the fact that another subject agrees with us. The other subject too will want to submit the object 'to his own eyes', and his own self-reflection is corrigible. Moreover, as he too has only the feeling of pleasure as the basis of his judgement, it is possible for two subjects to agree that a work is beautiful on the basis of feelings of pleasure which are dissimilar. The 'confirmation' we would gain through such agreement is surely false. To circumvent such a possibility, Kant insists that 'universal communicability' is crucial. We gain confirmation truly when subjects communicate their feelings of pleasure and, on the basis of that communication, agree about the beauty of an object. Thus, 'it must be the universal communicability . . . which underlies the judgement as its subjective condition, and the pleasure in the object must be its consequence'.[45] Pleasure arises out of communication because to communicate a pleasurable judgement of taste is to enable another subject to experience the same feeling of pleasure.[46] That is, success in communicating aesthetic judgements consists in bringing another subject to have the same feeling of pleasure and so to making the same judgement and thereby confirming the first subject's judgement.

This explanation of the role of communication shows now that the subjective universality of aesthetic judgements which we argued for above is a universal communicability through which we confirm the subjective judgement. However, this does not impose any new requirements on the necessary conditions for the judgement of taste. By explaining subjective universal validity by reference to universal communicability we are not suggesting that aesthetic judgements must be both subjectively valid *and* universally communicable and that these two involve separate requirements which must be satisfied in two different ways. Rather, both universal validity and communicability are satisfied by the same conditions. He indicates the latter by explaining the source of the subjects' pleasure when judgements of taste claim universal subjective validity and communicability.

That explanation occurs in Section 9, entitled 'Investigation of the question whether in a judgement of taste the feeling of pleasure precedes the judging of the object or the judging precedes the pleasure'.[47] As he maintains that the 'solution of this problem is the key to the critique of taste', it behoves us to look carefully at the issue and its resolution, even though we have considered some crucial features of this argument above and may have to repeat some matters here.

The material of the first two Moments prepares the reader for this way of expressing the problem only indirectly. We know that the distinctiveness of aesthetic judgements lies in their subjective but universal pleasure, and as we saw, this experience must be 'universally communicable'. In Section 9 Kant explains that if the universally communicable pleasure gained through appraisal of an object in a singular judgement constitutes aesthetic response, then this pleasure could not be antecedent to the appraisal. A pleasure that precedes all appraisal of the object must be due entirely to sensation, for a pleasure of sense need not depend on reflection in order to be felt and is not universally communicable. It 'has only private validity, because it would depend directly on the presentation by which the object is *given*'.[48] By contrast, the universality and non-sensuality of pleasurable aesthetic responses follows from or is coincident with appraisal.

Kant's argument in Section 9 is tied up with other factors. To consider what mechanism allows aesthetic universality, Kant compares aesthetic with cognitive judgements – with 'cognition, as well as presentation insofar as it pertains to cognition'.[49] For all their objectivity, these judgements have a subjective side, which includes the state of mind, representations, sensations, and so on which enter into cognition. Now Kant proposes a close relation between knowledge and a state of mind – between judgements made and the activity of cognition involving representations. He maintains that both the true objective judgement and the subject's state of mind have a universal validity and are communicable. He has not as yet identified or defended what that communicability is and how the state of mind can be communicated, but the association Kant is making is clear. And if cognition or its state of mind are alone what have been granted universal communicability, then, if pleasure is universally communicable, it must be because it is associated with a state of mind. That is, only an association with a state of mind would give pleasure a universal validity.

Further, only association with a state of mind that does not involve cognition or determinate concepts will be able to preserve the subjective and disinterested character of aesthetic response. Kant identifies the state of mind by reference to our faculties. If cognitive judgements are instances of a determinate relation between the faculties of understanding, providing concepts, and of imagination and sensibility, providing the materials of present or absent particulars which come to be ordered, then judgements of taste are said to be instances of the 'free play' of those faculties because, although their materials are ordered and the faculties are in harmony, the relation of faculties does not depend on a determinate concept. In aesthetic judgements, accordingly, the appraisal of the object which results in a universally valid and communicable but subjective pleasure – this 'merely subjective (aesthetic) judging of the object' – depends on a free play of faculties. The estimating or appraisal of the object must 'precede[ ] the pleasure in the object and is the basis of this pleasure, [a pleasure] in the harmony of the cognitive powers'.[50] That is, the appraisal of the object, the judgement which this appraisal consists in, is itself pleasurable. So, if a subject can ascribe pleasure to the operation of the mind, understood as a play of faculties, without also applying determinate concepts, and so in the absence of interest, etc., then because this state of mind is universally communicable, we may expect it of other subjects also. In much the same way a cognition and its state of mind were expected of others. Thereby a subjective experience of pleasure, because it results from a state of mind capable of validity, can be 'imputed' to others.

By arguing that the source of aesthetic validity must lie in the free play of the mind, Kant provides the key to the Critique of Taste because he makes clear what we must justify to make good all these claims about taste. We can justify the validity of aesthetic responses because this subjective experience of pleasure depends on a state of mind which has certain conditions and possibilities. Pleasure does not simply rest on sense. The conclusion of the Second Moment is that the beautiful is that which, apart from (determinate) concepts, pleases universally. The deduction must show that this state of mind can claim universality or validity. And in order to do that, it must also argue that the state of mind accompanying a communicable judgement is itself communicable.

Earlier, in Section 8, Kant permitted himself a programmatic statement in which he used the vocabulary of critical theory and transcendental deductions to outline the conclusions he wants to justify. The issues already dealt with suggest that now 'we can see . . . that nothing is postulated in a judgement of taste except such a *universal voice* about a liking unmediated by concepts. Hence all that is postulated is the *possibility* of a judgement that is aesthetic and yet can be considered valid for everyone. The judgement of taste does not itself *postulate* everyone's agreement (since only a logically universal judgement can do that, because it can adduce reasons); it merely *requires* this agreement from everyone, as an instance of a rule, an instance regarding which it expects confirmation not from concepts but from the agreement of others.'[51]

Although the whole sense will not be clear until much later, some of the distinctions Kant makes here mark the limits of any transcendental deduction, but also, in this text, leave open a number of other issues. For example, his talk of postulation refers to the First *Critique*, where to postulate is to take a proposition as a premise for reflection. In making an actual judgement of taste, we postulate that in some cases pleasure is capable of being universally valid and that the subject's pleasure is one which claims such validity. To rely on such a postulate we must suppose that the deduction of taste has already justified the universal validity of judgements generally – that aesthetic judgements claiming this kind of validity are possible because we are justified and rational to make them. But the deduction of these judgements will at best tell us that we are justified generally in making these judgements. It has little or nothing to say of the further conditions which must be satisfied for us to know that a particular actual judgement is successful. We could know through the deduction that aesthetic judgements are possible, that some occurrences of pleasure can claim universal validity because all the necessary conditions are satisfied, but that will not tell us how to decide in the case of a particular actual claim that it is a successful aesthetic judgement. For the latter case we need separate criteria.

Further, we need to understand the role of the singular object we appraise. Kant treats this issue in the Third Moment. Of the poles between subject and object, the Second Moment clarified the role of the subject and its state of mind as the source of pleasure. But while aesthetic responses denote the subject, they also bear reference to an object, and we need to understand how this reference manages to maintain the subjective nature of universal validity.

4

The Third and Fourth Moments

Kant begins the Third Moment by defining purpose or 'end' and abstracting from that to a *finality of form* or purposiveness as to form.[1] That he should then go on to talk of a *form of finality* or form of purposiveness is not mere carelessness, for he is here specifying the relation between the subject and the object by characterizing how the reference to the object is made. Kant begins by considering ends to distinguish them from finality. The distinction relies on a contrast between an object and a state of mind. He defines an end as 'the *object* of a concept insofar as we regard this concept as the object's cause (the real basis of its possibility); and the causality that a *concept* has with regard to its *object* is [finality] *(forma finalis)*'.[2] An end is an object whose nature and the conditions for whose existence cannot be understood except as being determined by a particular concept – as if the concept were being followed by a causal agency, and the object, with its parts ordered in the given way, were the realization of a determinate intention. Where the concept of the object is necessary for the object to be realized, as when various materials are brought together *in order to construct* a watch, there the concept of a watch is essential to, or the 'real ground of the possibility' of the object. Hence, we think of an end 'if we think not merely, say, of our cognition of the object, but instead of the whole object itself (its form, or its existence), as an effect that is only possible through a concept of that effect'.[3]

For an object to be an end, we must be able to do two things. First we must know what it is generally to conceive of objects so that they could be the result of concepts: we must be able to compare elements, treating them as parts of the whole, analyzing the relation of elements or the structure of a whole. In other words, we must be able to analyze the relation of parts by reference to their suitability to the whole – Kant calls this their finality. Through such analysis we could know how to recognize a particular sort of causality – that of 'a concept with respect to its object'. So, in

particular cases, where a given concept can be seen as the cause of
the object, we classify the whole as of a particular class, and ascribe
to it a definite teleological history – a *nexus finalis* – that ends with
the particular object. More simply, we must recognize and appreciate designs and also show what concept-determined design occurs
in a particular instance. The first is the ability to make a certain
kind of judgement generally, in which we sense order; the second
is an ability to apply a particular concept to a particular object as a
result of that initial estimation. The second is to identify the object
as an end; the first judges finality.

While an end depends on an operant finality, for Kant we may
appreciate finality without identifying a particular end. Talk of
ends is native to our conception of the will but it is possible also to
talk of the will as having a finality or purposiveness. We 'call
objects, states of mind, or acts purposive even if their possibility
does not necessarily presuppose the presentation of a purpose; we
do this merely because we can explain and grasp them only if we
assume that they are based on a causality [that operates] according
to purposes, i.e. on a will that would have so arranged them in
accordance with the presentation of a rule'.[4] Even where we do not
act for a given end, we can still think of the will as having
purposiveness or finality just because we know that it is the
capacity to act intentionally, towards some end. Kant is suggesting
that certain objects or activity may be seen as rule-governed and
ordered, even though we cannot identify the order by reference to
a particular given end, because they involve the activity of a
rational will. This presence of rule and order Kant calls purposiveness or finality,[5] and he holds that it may exist apart from a
particular end or purpose, 'in so far as we do not posit the causes
of this form in a will, and yet can grasp the explanation of its
possibility only by deriving it from a will'.[6] This last possibility
needs to be explained further.

Kant's suggestion is that some order can be thought of as having
a 'finality of form'. Its contrast is with a finality of ends. Finality of
form is an order and organization of parts for the sake of a whole,
where the whole is undetermined by concepts. The parts are
related to each other in the service of the whole, and we may talk
of their order as purposive or directed towards maintaining that
unified whole. In possessing this undetermined order, the relation
of parts is merely formal for its order is not defined. By contrast,
the finality of ends is an order and relation of parts that is directed

towards and determined by a given end. The parts are organized for the sake of a whole where the end is defined and their order derived from that end. So the parts of a mechanism are ordered so that they allow the instrument to tell the time, and the parts therefore have a finality gained from the fact of it being a watch. The parts are then directed towards an end.

However, as Kant proposes that the parts gain order from that end, it is not clear how a finality of form is possible. Kant writes as if a finality of *form* should be intelligible because the finality of *ends* is straightforward and presupposes the finality of form. Because we understand the basic mechanism involved – the will – and know that, as it is active, even if directed at a particular end in one case, we know we can also direct its activity at gaining an order for other ends; and we assume also that we can direct the will gaining order even though there is no particular end. Later in the text Kant develops this claim further, proposing that if we recognize order and design, and even if we cannot identify any particular end from which we derive that order, the presence of such order suffices for us to invoke the presence and operation of the will.

In that later context Kant treats the order or finality of form as a mark of rational activity. He writes that if we were to perceive a geometrical figure in an uninhabited country, as we 'reflected on this figure, working out a concept for it, reason would make [us] aware, even if obscurely, of the unity of the principle [required] for producing this concept'. That is, even before we had found a concept for this figure, while we were 'working out a concept for it, reason would make [us] aware, even if obscurely', that it would be inappropriate to 'judge that such a figure is made possible by the sand, the adjoining sea, the wind, or even animals that leave footprints familiar to him, or by any other non-rational cause'.[7] Rather, we would be tempted to seek the operation of a rational will constructing this order.

This reference to the will complicates the picture, and before it helps to solve the problem, Kant will have to make a number of qualifications explaining why not every perception of purposive order leads us to infer that a will is operating to produce the object. If he fails to do so, then we will be forced to admit the will in every instance where there is such order. In any case, where there is order in the absence of a particular end there we find the finality of form, and though we need to justify the assumptions underlying this claim, we may accept it for the moment with the promise to

clarify later how the finality of form ties up intimately with con-
ceiving of some objects, in the 'territory' of the phenomenal world,
as the result of human action. Thus 'we may at least observe a
finality of form, and trace it in objects . . . without resting it on an
end (as the material of the *nexus finalis*)'.[8]

Talk of the finality of form does not show what it is, in the object,
to which the aesthetic response attends or refers, which still
preserves the subjective aspect of judgements of taste. Kant raises
the issue in Section 11 by claiming that the 'judgement of taste is
based on nothing but the [FORM OF FINALITY] of an object (or the
way of presenting it)'.[9] The switch from 'finality of form' to 'form
of finality' needs to be explained. Kant's position seems to be this:
finality of form may be thought of merely as finality so long as we
oppose it to the finality generated by an end. That is, we use
'finality' for 'finality of form'. We know also that 'form' refers to an
absence of ends which can be specified. A finality of form is just
such an order, in which the parts seem directed towards sustaining
a whole, even though the whole is not identified by a concept or an
end. Now, our larger concern has been with the relation of the
object to the subject and its response. These responses must be
disinterested if they are to be aesthetic, and they will be disinterested if they do not involve the application of determinate
concepts. This constraint also excludes ends, so far as these are
gained by applying determinate concepts. Thus, our aesthetic
concern with objects and their order can refer only to the finality of
form or to finality and not to the finality of ends or to the object
considered as an end.

But, in addition, we cannot direct the finality of form at the
subject without qualification. The subject cannot appraise it by
reference to a particular end which the subject has. But if it cannot
serve an end for the subject, then it must eschew considerations of
the determinate concepts that may be applied to it. Its suitability is
to the free play of the faculties or their harmony, which, because it
is not determinate, is formal or has a finality apart from any end.
So far as the finality of an object consists in its ability to generate an
aesthetic response, it must address only the form – the 'concept-
less' order of faculties – and will only have a finality of form rather
than a finality of end. This Kant now describes as a FORM OF
FINALITY, meaning that the judgement denotes in the subject a
suitability of the object – a finality – which is merely formal because
it has an order but does not have a determinate end. The only 'end'

it can satisfy is the formal and conceptually indeterminate one of a harmony of faculties in free play. Its suitability to the subject, which is the basis of the subject's appraisal of the object, is therefore a matter of being the 'form of finality of form': its success lies in suiting the disinterested and non-conceptual, therefore 'formal', relation of faculties, through its order apart from any ends or determinate concepts – as having a finality of form and not a finality of an end.

Here then, as earlier, preserving the universal but subjective nature of aesthetic response depends on accepting certain restraints. Not only do we restrict the subject to disinterested judgements, but we must restrict appraisal to a consideration of the formal properties of the object. 'Therefore, the liking that, apart from concepts, we judge to be universally communicable and hence to be the basis that determines a judgement of taste, can be nothing but the subjective [finality] in the presentation of an object, without any purpose (whether objective or subjective), and hence the mere form of [finality], . . . in the presentation by which an object is *given* [to] us'.[10] From all this Kant concludes that '*beauty is an object's* [form of *finality*] insofar as it is perceived in the object *without the presentation of an* [*end*]'.[11] That is, beauty denotes a harmony of faculties (the form of finality) which we refer to an object (it is 'in an object'), but only to the finality of form in the object – by contrast with, and so 'without the presentation' of an end and its appurtenant finality.

From this a number of consequences follow, which clarify the distinctiveness of aesthetic response: that the finality of an object and its suitability to the form of finality in the subject do not depend on any charm and emotion we may connect with the object; that perfection plays no part either, because it depends on some concept of the perfect object or 'what sort of a thing it is to be' – which also needs determinate concepts in both the subject and its reference to the object; that consideration of what the object is meant to be, even if such consideration suits only a form of finality in the subject, still renders the appraisal impure; that the notion of an Ideal for beauty, against which we may measure the form of finality in the subject, is also illicit and lacks necessity because it sins against both the form of finality and the finality of form.

In the following sections of the text Kant argues against other theories of beauty. Many of these conceived of beauty in terms of its ideal object or its ideal purpose. Such theories are not much less prevalent now, and Kant's work has been used to derive alternative conclusions about the role of perfection and the ideal of and for beauty. We shall consider these further later.

The Fourth Moment

Having considered the manner in which the object enters consideration in the pure judgement of taste, and having in the following sections shown why certain other approaches are misguided, in the Fourth Moment Kant goes on to clarify the modality or necessity of these judgements and to show, again, which features he will justify in the deduction itself. As he suggested in the programmatic statement disserted earlier, the deduction will defend the general possibility of making aesthetic judgements. It cannot justify criteria for success in the actual judgements we make.

Kant does not make this clear immediately. He first sets out the nature of aesthetic judgements by distinguishing their necessity from moral or cognitive judgements and so from interests in the agreeable, the good and, with some structuring, in perfection. As the agreeable is contingent, its pleasure cannot claim universality. By contrast, pleasure in the beautiful is universal because we expect every subject can share it. Nor does this universality depend on causal necessity, by which objects of that type cause pleasure in every subject, for the aesthetic judgement is logically singular and comprehensive over subjects, not objects. Nor can moral compulsion determine aesthetic judgements: it does not always evoke pleasure, and, where it does, will depend on an interest.

To explain that subjects can share pleasurable aesthetic judgements, Kant argues against one kind of sceptical doubt. This doubt emerged in our discussion of the Second Moment: is the state of mind accompanying a communicable judgement also communicable? Kant maintains that unless this were true, no knowledge or communication of even the most objective claims would be possible.

In this context, we might raise the issue in the following way. It may be that we all make the same objective judgements even though we cannot be certain that the accompanying inner experiences we have are precisely the same. For example, we may all apply the concept 'red' at appropriate moments when there are red things in our sight, and so know that we are all applying the concept correctly. Yet it may be that the inner sensation that a subject feels when he applies the concept 'red' is not identical with the inner sensation another subject has when she applies the concept 'red'. Although each has the same subjective sensation on every occasion when each sees red things, it may be that the inner sensations accompanying those objective and correct applications of the concept which each one has differ from those had by the other. This raises a problem for subjective judgements of taste because the sensations and inner feelings which result from judgements need not be the same in all subjects. Such differences apparently had few consequences for objective judgements because, in spite of any differences in sensations and feelings between subjects, judgements remained testable and successful in application to actual objects. In the case of aesthetic judgements the matter of sensations and feelings is much more important, for if there is no way of ascertaining what the feelings are, then there is no way of knowing that communication has been gained; and if there is no way of knowing that we have communicated our judgements, we do not know that we have correctly judged aesthetically. All we would have is a 'merely subjective play of the presentational powers, just as scepticism would have it'.[12]

On the other hand, if we argue against the sceptic's doubt that the inner sensations and feelings accompanying the presentations are universally communicable, we will have deflected an objection to the universality of aesthetic claims. The rejection of doubt is straightforward. The sceptic questions whether the sensations and feelings accompanying representations can be identical; he can raise the issue only if he can make sense of comparing such sensations and feelings, to show that they are the same or different. But it is difficult to see how he can compare sensations. His only access to others' sensations, except for getting inside their feelings, is through asking them and seeing what they do. In these cases, it seems that we do all make the same claims, for if the sensations and feelings accompanying presentations are relevant to the communicable judgement we make, then the fact that we make judgement successfully suggests that the accompanying representations must be the same. If they were not, then their differences would show themselves in the judgements we make. As there do not seem to be any such differences, we may suppose that the accompanying sensations and feelings are the same.

The similar inner sensations, feelings, and so on which accompany presentations, Kant labels 'common sense'. This common sense, as we shall see, is the basis of one kind of necessity that Kant ascribes to judgements of taste. Before we turn to that issue, we must describe the necessity Kant discovers for judgements of taste in the Fourth Moment.

Kant combines the singularity of taste with its universality or comprehensiveness over subjects to infer that the necessity of judgements of taste is exemplary. The subject's response to the finality of form of a singular object is an example of a universalizable pleasure. We cannot generalize from it, as if it were true of all objects of that kind; we cannot generalize from it as a moral rule, setting out what we should do; but it does serve as an example of the pleasure we can gain from the 'finality of form of finality' where we share with others the ability to respond in this way.

Kant then identifies the necessity of aesthetic judgements as something more than an imputation or expectation. Although his vocabulary has consistently implied binding or compulsion, so that even if these judgements are exemplary, they are imputable to or can justifiably be expected of all others, he now says that 'who ever declares something to be beautiful holds that everyone *ought* to give his approval to the object at hand and he too should declare it beautiful'.[13] Rather than simply ascribing validity to a subject's own pleasure, which imputes agreement to others, Kant expects in the sense of *justifiably demands*, an agreement from others. He then qualifies the demand, saying that the *'ought* in aesthetic judgements . . . is still uttered only conditionally': the *demand* also depends on the conditions whose satisfaction allows us to *impute* judgements to others. But the 'oughtness' of aesthetic judgements is not identical with, even though it depends on, the imputation which is characteristic of aesthetic judgements. Nor can we derive it solely from this imputation and the requisite data.

Kant clarifies this distinction further when he says 'we solicit everyone else's assent' – or, in Meredith's nice phrase: 'we are suitors for agreement from everyone else' – because 'we have a basis for it that is common to all'. The imputation is a necessary condition for 'oughtness' because we cannot make a demand that cannot be realized, but, still, satisfaction of these necessary conditions only 'makes us suitors', it does not necessarily mean that our suit is accepted. Indeed, we 'could count on that assent', and justify the 'ought', 'if only we could always be sure that the instance had been subsumed correctly under that basis, which is the rule for the approval'. But whether or not a particular putative universal pleasure actually is a judgement of taste does not depend only on knowing that aesthetic judgements generally are possible. While we could demand that other subjects accept our suit if we knew an actual judgement was an aesthetic one – because we were 'sure that the instance had been subsumed correctly under that basis, which is the rule for the approval' – the fact is that we can be mistaken. We may impute pleasure to other subjects, and can justify making aesthetic judgements, but we need some additional criteria by which to know that our particular actual judgements are correct, and can *demand* agreement.

We suggested that the distinction between imputation and demand is between the universal but subjective experience of pleasure, which is a judgement of taste, and an additional justification. Kant shows that a universally valid but subjective experience is 'possible' in the sense of transcendentally justified in the way that cognitive judgements are transcendentally justified, by reference to common sense.[14] The common sense underlies the harmony of faculties in free play that is the 'form of finality' in the subject. We have yet to examine this claim, but even if we were to accept it, we would still have to justify the necessity ascribed to the actual judgements we make. We will know that generally they are possible – that they are transcendentally possible because certain necessary conditions are satisfied – and so may accept that there can be imputations of a subjective experience of pleasure, but yet be unable to say of any particular actual judgement that it is necessary in the sense that we *ought* to agree with it. In other words, there is a distinction between the transcendental and the empirical realms at work in Kant's discussion of necessity, and the deduction, the transcendental justification, even if successful, will support the general practice of imputing agreement to everyone on the basis of our own experience of universalizable pleasure, providing a necessary *condition* for making a demand of other subjects, but will not justify the demand we make on the basis of an actual particular judgement.

We shall return to this distinction between actual and transcendental claims when we consider the autonomy of judgements. First we must return to the sceptical doubt to provide a more positive account of the claim that we have a common sense. So far in the Fourth Moment Kant makes clear that the imputations involved in aesthetic judgements carry a necessity. He argues for this necessity by pointing to our possession of a sense common to all rational, thinking, and feeling beings such as human beings. In Section 20, he associates the common sense with the form of finality as the basis of aesthetic responses. Now, in Section 21 he defends the postulate of a common sense. The form of finality is the harmony of faculties or indeterminate relation of faculties which appraises the form of the singular object. As we argued above, we may expect that the feelings associated with this use of the faculties must be communicable. For there to be such communicability, we must possess the feelings and use of faculties in common – that is, there must be a common sense underlying these judgements, possessed by all subjects. If such a common sense were absent, then it would be impossible to refer to objects existing independently of individuals. For Kant our objective experience is made up of subjective 'inner' experiences. Here, without a common sense, each of us would make judgements about objects, have an individual and distinctive subjective experience of them, but be unable to identify the object in others' descriptions because their descriptions of their experiences of the object would be distinctive and need not bear any similarity to our own. Instead of a communicable experience of objects, then, cognition would consist only of 'a merely subjective play of the presentational powers, just as scepticism would have it',[15] where the play of the powers of representation would be the individual possession of each subject. If we are to have cognitions which can be communicated to other subjects, Kant holds, 'then the mental state . . . must also be universally communicable'. And as communication does obtain, including the communication of a feeling, we are right to assume the existence of a common sense which underlies aesthetic judgements.[16]

By this argument we are justified in assuming that the common sense which is essential to the argument does exist; but it is not yet clear that its existence justifies the validity of judgements of taste. However, having clarified the need for and possibility of the common sense, we have also clarified where we must look to justify our practice of making subjectively universal or valid aesthetic judgements. In turn, this points to the transcendental deduction, which argues that as necessary conditions are satisfied, we are justified in supposing that we make aesthetic judgements.

But the distinction of transcendental necessity from empirical necessity we introduced when considering Section 19, by which we could satisfy the conditions necessary for imputation but still face scepticism over actual judgements and their success, points to another meaning of common sense. For Kant we may identify this meaning as the *sensus communis*. He proposes it in Section 22, when explaining the move from imputation to 'ought' by reference to a distinction between subjective and objective necessity. The section title concludes that the 'necessity of the universal assent that we think in a judgement of taste is a subjective necessity that we present as objective by presupposing a common sense'. The common sense which justifies objective necessity cannot simply be the necessary condition for making aesthetic judgements at all. The latter common sense is necessary even for 'subjective necess-ity' – for individuals to suppose their experience of pleasure is universalizable. In the paragraph following, Kant clarifies that there is a different meaning of common sense at play by saying first, that our concern is with actual particular judgements rather than with the transcendental conditions for aesthetic judgements generally. Actual judgements, of course, contain an 'ought', which goes beyond the general possibility of their justification.[17] Second, we put forward particular actual judgements of taste as examples of common sense. For this it must be that 'common sense . . . is a mere ideal norm'.[18] *This* common sense or *sensus communis*, then, is an ideal for the success of actual judgements, rather than a tran-scendentally necessary condition.

We have set out these distinctions as if they were clearly pre-sented in the Fourth Moment. In fact Kant presents a number of ideas in train, without arguing for them clearly, and ends with a host of questions. In presenting the above distinctions, we have also accepted various answers to questions without indicating exactly which these are. It was necessary to do this, in part, because scholars often ignore the different senses Kant gives to 'necessity' and suppress a range of issues by seeing the Fourth Moment as only a rehearsal for all the issues Kant will sort out in the deduction. For example, following the deduction Kant turns immediately to consider taste as a *sensus communis* and to clarify issues engaging actual judgements. Such a move would be un-necessary if the transcendental deduction answered all the issues of necessity. Kant's move suggests that he distinguishes between two kinds of necessity, and finds in the *sensus communis* the criteria for success in actual judgements. So, when he concludes the Fourth Moment with the assertion that the beautiful 'is what without a [determinate] concept is cognized as the object of a *necessary* liking', we must see necessity as ambiguous between transcendental and empirical realms.

What these four Moments yield, then, is an account of aesthetic responses that shows what is involved in their being purely subjective judgements within the terms of Kant's theory of mind and knowledge. He develops the account between the poles of subject and object, disinterest and interest, determinate concepts and form. He begins with the assertion that judgements of taste are aesthetic and conducts what is more or less a phenomenological analysis to exhibit its characteristics and their coherence by saying that certain conditions must be satisfied if that initial claim is to be true within his system. In clarifying these conditions in the vocabulary of his own critical idealism and theory of mind, he has shown first, that there are such things as aesthetic judgements; second, what they are; and third, what we need to argue for in order to show that they are legitimate. These judgements of taste are aesthetic and generally valid, being based on the experience of feeling for life or pleasure that we gain from appraising the suitability of a form of a singular object to a state of mind. Kant defines the state of mind as a free play of faculties, where we may not only impute this experience to all other subjects on the basis of supposing that they share the common sense which makes for that state of mind, and so suppose it universally valid for all subjects, but also may go on to demand of other such subjects that they assent to the judgement of taste by gaining the same pleasurable state of mind for themselves. Having seen how validity depends on the supposition that there is a shared state of mind, the deduction will justify the supposition. Once Kant proves its validity, showing that we can legitimately ascribe that experience of pleasure to all subjects, it will become possible and necessary to show what further demands we can justify for this experience.

SOME IMPLICATIONS OF THE ANALYTIC

We shall pursue the issue of the Deduction of Taste further in the following chapters. First we may establish this account of the Analytic by considering some of its implications. One claim often derived from the Analytic emphasizes Kant's conception of disinterestedness as a means for distinguishing aesthetic from all other judgements. Arguably, this emphasis was developed in New Criticism in the 1940s to argue that our appreciation of a work must consider the poem, novel, picture or other work alone and for itself. If a work is found aesthetically pleasing, the argument goes, it should be because of what is present in the work itself. We must exclude extraneous features such as the intention of the artist, the social background of the work, and the particular psychology and interests of the critic.[19] All these involve interests for they treat the work not for itself but for its being an effect of or for facilitating the pursuit of other ends, and so as serving an extraneous purpose.

Knowledge of an artist's intention can only interfere with our appreciation. First, artists often fail to understand their own work, just as people often misunderstand their own actions. Second, if the artist has understood and realized his intentions, then these will be present in the poem or picture, and we will already have grasped these by understanding the work. As anyone can see what is in the work, the artist is not any more privileged than anyone else in understanding the picture or novel. Similarly, if critics try to bring in social and cultural factors to explain pictures, novels, and other works, these attempts to 'contextualize' the object are also attacks on its aesthetic specificity.

The notion of aesthetic specificity or autonomy involved here arguably has its source in the Analytic of the Beautiful. Kant proposed that aesthetic judgements must be disinterested and cannot be determined by purposes or by notions of perfection. If aesthetic judgements are to be pure,[20] as we should surely all wish them to be, they cannot involve any determinate concepts, but will consider only the object for itself.

A stress on disinterestedness seems to underlie Derrida's more recent rejection of Kant's aesthetic theory and project. In *Truth and Painting* Derrida examines the distinction between art and the theory of art, using Kant's claim that the 'frame' of a work serves to focus our attention on the object of beauty.[21] The frame itself should not be attended to, for it only marks off the work from its surroundings. It is not a part of the picture even though it is an essential condition for our grasp of the work.[22] But Derrida asks how the frame succeeds in separating out a work from its surroundings; and he uses the difficulties in the way of making clear any such distinction between what is 'in' the work from what is 'outside' to raise issues about the supposed aesthetic autonomy of art. The status of the frame raises questions about grasping the work. The frame is necessary to focus our attention on or 'define' the object of our attention, and so is necessary to our aesthetic response, yet it does not seem to be a part of what we attend to. If we cannot identify the object without the frame, then what counts as a frame and what as a work is itself a matter of consideration – of theory – and it becomes difficult to see how we might claim autonomy for art except by invoking some theory. But where the latter is essential to distinguishing aesthetic from other objects, the inescapable need for a theory infringes on any claim to autonomy, for we cannot separate aesthetic response from its theory and the former fails to be autonomous in any sense of having a purely aesthetic space.

Derrida strives to make clear the impossibility of such a framing and purity, from which he goes on to argue the need for an extra-aesthetic but neither 'theoretical' nor 'practical' understanding of art on the basis of a *passage* between theory and art.

However, two kinds of response are available to us here. First, Derrida fails to see that Kant's account of the specificity of aesthetic judgements cannot and is not intended to establish a pure, necessary, and essentially aesthetic space *per se*. Kant avoids ascribing some permanently valuable aesthetic essence to objects, for he argues instead that an object's beauty is its suitability to universally pleasurable judgements made by the subject. But even in characterizing these judgements Kant does not commit himself to that purely aesthetic space which Derrida seeks to ascribe, for the very structure of the act of judging is one in which the subject seeks confirmation from other subjects. In a sense, it is a matter of a constant negotiation between the individual and the community for warrant to have made aesthetic claims. As we explained with reference to universality, judgements involve a concern with their own origin and application, consisting in both a pleasurable estimation of an object and a reflection on the source of that pleasure to see whether it might be universalizable. In this second reflection we cannot be sure that our response is an aesthetic judgement unless we see that it is universalizable; but this reflection is fallible, and so we need some other criterion by which to confirm our reflection and so claim success for our judgements of taste. As judgements are universalizable over subjects, for Kant such confirmation must come from other subjects, by communicating our judgement to them and enabling them to make the same pleasurable judgement. The community of taste is essential to confirming the subject's actual judgement of taste, and the very structure of judgement therefore is a constant negotiation between individual and community; and given that the community is constantly developing – that the ideal is 'always in progress' – that search for universality and communication is constantly changing with the community.

Beauty depends on a feeling we have, to be sure, but first that feeling must be confirmed by other judgements; and second, our possession of a capacity for feeling does not make for or constitute an aesthetic essence. Even though we have a capacity for pleasure, aesthetic judgements do not constitute that pleasure. Rather, aesthetic judgements only constitute the universal validity of some experiences of pleasure; but, as we saw, that only involves us in treating the community of subjects as rational and feeling beings like ourselves. And that, in turn, leads us to develop and change as our relation to the community changes. That is, our aesthetic responses develop as our relation to each other and the community changes. No 'frame' is intended to be permanent in this sense, we may argue, and changes in the frame, developments in what is art, are a part of a larger process of a developing humanity and community of subjects.

Kant argues for a permanent value in this context,[23] but he does not rest this on some aesthetic essence. This is because the specificity of the aesthetic prevents it from hypostasizing or making essentialist claims about the nature and character of art. The aesthetic is always caught in the relation of individual to community and is ever in process, for the individual's autonomous judgement is always in search of a warrant from the community, which is itself always in a process of development. If Derrida is arguing for a *passage* between theory and art, then Kant provides just such an account, in which the 'aesthetic' does not stand on its own, separated out from all context and independent of all other considerations. Instead, for Kant beauty and the aesthetic subtend a relation between subjects that is constantly in progress and so is always being 're-framed'. Of course, Derrida also rejects the references to 'anthropology' and to 'subjectivity' that are involved in Kant's theory, but that rejection is a different issue, and Derrida's own claims for 'desire' and 'subjectivity' are highly questionable.[24]

The aesthetic essence which Derrida seeks is not clearly identifiable in our understanding of Kant's theory, where we have stressed the conception of subjective universality rather than the notion of disinterestedness. In thinking that Kant wants a purely aesthetic space, which he explains as the *autonomy* of the *aesthetic* by reference to disinterestedness, Derrida may be accepting uncritically the reception given to Kant's *Critique of Judgement* in France, when it was incorporated in the search for *art pour l'art*. But that was never all that the Third *Critique* was about, and there is no reason to understand it in that way now. The Analytic contains an understanding of the particular problems we face in explaining the act of judging aesthetically, that sustains a stress on the universality of aesthetic judgements, where the *autonomy* of the *subject* judging aesthetically plays a crucial role, and precludes us from ascribing to Kant some search for an essentially aesthetic space. Indeed, a stress on universality is so clearly appropriate to the *Critique of Judgement*, that we need to explain a stress on disinterestedness. In his own understanding of aesthetic judgements and their deduction, Kant makes clear that there are two central characteristics of judgements. These he calls 'logical peculiarities' of aesthetic judgements: one is the universality of judgements of taste. We can argue that disinterestedness appears in this context only as a secondary characteristic of the other peculiarity – that it is impossible to prove a judgement of taste objectively because aesthetic judgement does not depend on determinate concepts. And to understand further Kant's account of aesthetic judgements, we may turn to consider how he develops these logical peculiarities of aesthetic judgements as a prelude to deducing them or justifying their validity.

5

Judgements of Taste and Their Deduction

Kant proceeded from our actual experience of pleasure in judgements of taste to describe these judgements. To be valid, aesthetic judgements must be entirely subjective – being based only on a feeling of pleasure or displeasure; must be disinterested – free of determinate concepts, including determinate ends; must be singular – and so seek confirmation through other subjects; must be universal – in being based in ourselves on something we share with others; and are necessary – we can demand others' agreement. In the process Kant rejects various other conceptions of the 'aesthetic' and defends his own claims. For example, he dismisses the sceptical claim that we cannot rely on pleasure as the basis for any validity, by showing that unless our 'inner experience' were similar, we could not communicate our objective experience.

This argument depends on a notion of a 'common sense', which he thinks we have reason to suppose in all subjects. In putting forward this claim, Kant oversteps the limits of the Analytic, understood strictly, in that he not only clarifies the conditions necessary for aesthetic judgements, but also argues for or justifies these conditions by reference to the common sense. However, if this is to overstep the strict limit, it is neither great crime, nor his only infringement. He also breaks bounds when talking about universal validity and confirmation, because the latter depend on an as-yet-unargued distinction between transcendentally possible and actual judgements. In any case, although expressed positively, to say that we have reason to suppose a common sense, in the Analytic his defence is a negative argument against a sceptical doubt and he does not conclude that the existence of the common sense guarantees the possibility of judgements of taste.

He will argue positively in the Deduction of the *Critique of Judgement* that the conditions which aesthetic judgements must satisfy to be subjectively valid are indeed satisfied. But that argument is complicated by a number of factors, including the dual structure of judgement – the initial pleasurable estimation of the object which we affirm by communicating to other subjects – and the implications of his Analytic of the Beautiful. Kant draws out these implications of what the Deduction will legitimate in the passages following Section 30. He argues that two 'logical' peculiarities of judgement provide the basis for the features identified in the Analytic; and by arguing for the latter, he will show that the former are possible.

Kant presents these logical peculiarities in Sections 30 onwards, and in a sense they are not unexpected. He is merely emphasizing some implications of the description he gave in the Analytic. For example, as a judgement does not depend on any concepts, if it is universal and able to claim validity for itself, then it is comprehensive over subjects rather than objects. Its logical form is not like a standard generalization about objects, which asserts that any member of one class will also belong to another. The generalization that 'All duck-billed platypi lay eggs' asserts that any member of the class of duck-billed platypi will also belong to the class of things that lay eggs. This kind of claim is comprehensive over objects and therefore also comprehensive over all subjects. If an assertion is true of all platypi, then every subject must accept that assertion. Similarly, any valid claim derived from this assertion must also gain assent from subjects. A subject would show himself mistaken or irrational were he to accept the evidential grounds for a claim and the validity of the process of an inference or deduction from those grounds, yet reject the conclusion that followed from these grounds. Each subject making cognitive judgements must accept that because his claims are about objects in the world and their nature, 'others may see and observe for him, and even though what many have seen the same way may serve him . . . as a sufficient basis of proof for a theoretical and hence logical judgement'.[1] Consequently, we may dismiss a subject's claims as false on the basis of another's experience of the evidence because we know the evidential basis of the first subject's claim. The latter is public in the sense that the object is available to all, and subjects are bound to agree because of the nature of the object.

By contrast aesthetic judgements are comprehensive only over subjects, yet are autonomous. This follows Kant's explanation in the Analytic: if aesthetic judgements depend on feelings of pleasure and displeasure, then they are entirely subjective and free of all determinate concepts. But feelings of pleasure are entirely subjective also in the sense that they belong to particular subjects. No one else can experience this pleasure for a subject, and so far as a judgement of taste is a pleasurable experience, even if it is valid for all others, it must be one which a subject makes for itself. His experience of pleasure cannot determine her judgement of taste because only her own experience of pleasure is the ground for her judgement. Similarly, her inability to feel a pleasurable response is not evidence for the inappropriateness of pleasure in his own case. If pleasure were associated with concepts, then perhaps the occurrence of a concept would generate pleasure directly or mediately through satisfaction of an interest, and the occurrence of pleasure could serve as evidence for other subjects' reactions. But such determination is absent in aesthetic judgements, and no such 'evidence' can constrain a subject's appreciation of a work.

For Kant, the subject plays this role in every genuine exercise of taste. 'This is why a young poet cannot be brought to abandon his persuasion that his poem is beautiful, neither by the judgement of his audience nor by that of his friends; and if he listens to them, it is not because he now judges the poem differently, but because, even if (at least with regard to him) the whole audience were to have wrong taste, his desire for approval still causes him to accommodate himself (even against his judgement) to the common delusion. Only later on, when his power of judgement has been sharpened by practice, will he depart voluntarily from his earlier judgement, just as he does with the judgements which rest wholly on reason.'[2] Because of the nature of taste, 'other people's approval in no way provides him with a valid proof by which to judge beauty; even though others may see and observe for him, and even though what many have seen the same way may serve him who believes he saw differently, as a sufficient basis for proof for a theoretical and hence logical judgement, yet the fact that others have liked something can never serve him as a basis for an aesthetic judgement'.[3]

Accordingly, aesthetic judgements, so far as they are subjectively valid, are pleasurable. If they are pleasurable, then, because of the entirely subjective nature of pleasure or displeasure, which only the subject can experience for himself or herself, the judgement of taste, which is assent to another subject's judgement, can only be made by the subject for itself. Kant describes this by saying that 'we demand that [a person] judge for himself: he should not have to grope among other people's judgements'; and the latter leads him to conclude that 'Taste lays claim merely to autonomy.'[4] This autonomy is the first peculiarity of judgements of taste.

Clearly proofs are either inadequate here or are very distinctive. Proofs usually begin with generally accepted premises, asserting that certain relations hold between concepts and, from these, on the basis of various inferential rules, draw relevant conclusions. If we accept the premises and the validity of the argument, then, unless there is a mistake, we must accept the conclusion. In some sense, our agreement is compelled, for a dissenting individual's claim will be dismissed as false – because it does not tally with some part of the premises; or as irrational – because it cannot tally with any proof of procedure. Disagreement is still possible, because premises are questionable and proofs may be inadequate. But such arguments and conclusions are objective and universally valid on the basis of given procedures. Agreement between subjects does not determine the truth of cognitive claims; rather the truth of judgements depends on the nature of objects and their relations in the world.

Such is not the case with aesthetic judgements; and this is their second peculiarity. They depend on the subject's experience of pleasure. Assent can only be *given* by the subject on the basis of his experience of pleasure. No manner of pointing to the truth of premises or the validity of objective proof procedures will do. Whereas the conclusion of an objective proof is logically tied to, or dependent on the relation of concepts to each other, such is not the case in aesthetic judgements. If pleasure is the conclusion, it cannot be generated by the relation of concepts. If a proof shows why given premises necessarily lead to a certain conclusion because of the concepts and proof procedures involved, then such a proof cannot have the experience of pleasure as a conclusion. Pleasure may be attached to attaining a conclusion for reasons external to the proof – perhaps the prover is freed to attend to his lunch – but the proof itself will not have as its conclusion the experience of pleasure because 'there is no transition from concepts to pleasure'. The concepts are not pleasurable in themselves or for their role in a proof.

However, there is another sense in which, in aesthetic judgements, an indication of appropriateness serves as an analogy of proof. Even if this does not have the necessity of logical and evidential proofs because aesthetic judgements are autonomous, Kant talks of this 'proof' as providing 'examples and illustrations'[5] to lead another subject to appreciate a work. We use examples and illustrations to emphasize particular features of an object. And although we cannot compel a judgement of taste as if it were a conclusion required by the fact that the object possesses relevant features, and even though subjects must make only their own judgement on the basis of their own experience of pleasure, nevertheless we may suggest what they might look at in making their judgement. Someone who does not appreciate Cézanne's *Vase* may be brought to understand that the artist distorted its shapes in order to recapture in two dimensions the three-dimensional experience of an object; that he was motivated by a particular conception of creativity, in which objects were 'found' rather than simply constructed; and that he rejected Impressionist technique and self-understanding.[6] This illustration by examples serves to direct attention to certain features of the work, suggesting what is significant to judgement. Yet this directing does not constitute a proof another subject must accept, for these interpretative proposals may still fail so far as the subject cannot make a pleasurable judgement by attending to the features made significant in this interpretation.

The possibility of this kind of failure is built into the process of demonstration by example and illustration. This procedure of interpretation does not deal with an object defined by determinate concepts. First, interpretation attends to the particular object and relies on a singular judgement, not on a universal one. The judgement does not seek to classify an object under a generalization to explain its behaviour and relation to other objects in the world. Where a viewer judges that a tulip is beautiful, his judgement is not a generalization about all tulips, as if every tulip will be beautiful because this one is. The beauty of the particular tulip results from our pleasure in appreciating its particular qualities, not from the objective properties it must have to be a tulip.

Second, the indeterminate aesthetic use of concepts will have a distinctive power. The concept of the object yields no inferential rule. By grasping the general nature of platypi we can infer conclusions about a particular platypus. Because platypi lay eggs, we can derive other general properties which belong to the class of platypi. But from a judgement that a particular platypus is beautiful we cannot infer that every platypus will be so: this one may be beautiful for the particular texture and colour of its fur, the variations of yellow and orange in its beak, fur, and webbed feet, and the particular proportion of the angle of its beak to its body. Nor does the judgement of its beauty follow from its possession of those particular properties. The judgement of taste rests on the subject's pleasurable and autonomous response to the properties of the object. Concepts, even those which describe the particular qualities of the platypus, are not determining of the judgement, and their use in pointing out what is significant about this particular platypus or this painting of this vase, etc., does not have objective force. Instead, if concepts are used at all, they point to the balances and relations in a work, perhaps recommending the focus of a judgement, but unable to exert any objective compulsion. Further, the indeterminate concepts we use are indeterminate because, among other reasons, of what is 'added to' the objective use. We grasp their particular occurrence through illustration and comparison but with an inexactitude appropriate to the absence of cognitive concepts and to the basis of judgements in a subject's own experience of pleasure.

At best interpretation brings other subjects to gain the pleasurable response by indicating what is significant in the object. This procedure of demonstration by example and illustration involves a relation between subjects. Kant associates this autonomy of aesthetic judgements closely with our expectations of *others'* autonomous judgements. The individual's response to a work arises from factors that are present and available to all subjects, and therefore it can serve as a standard and example for all other subjects. In effect, the relation to the object is mediated through the subject's relation to another subject. The relation between subjects is a communicative one, in that judgements attend to subjects who appreciate a work by grasping the object in their own aesthetic judgements. Even if the pleasurable response cannot be proved, as it is not the conclusion of any argument, and although it involves only a logically singular judgement about a particular, nevertheless the subjective response arguably has a general validity or universality, 'extend[ing] its claim to *all* subjects, just as it always could if it were an objective judgement that rested on cognitive bases and that [we] could be compelled [to make] by a proof'.[7]

This emphasizes the paradoxical nature of judgements of taste. Because they are subjective, singular, concept-independent, and autonomous, we would expect that aesthetic judgements must be idiosyncratic and arbitrary, varying from subject to subject as a

result of differences between the latter. Agreement between subjects would, at best, be a coincidence and entirely subjective. But
Kant maintains also that we do seem to expect agreement from
others. The judgement of taste is other and more than a matter of
personal preference. And he resolves the 'two peculiarities' of
these judgements – their autonomy and their universality – by
showing why in these instances we can expect that pleasure is
capable of universality or subjective general validity.[8] The autonomy and universality of aesthetic judgements are not mutually
exclusive, even if they seem opposed, because the source of
pleasure is available to all subjects.

Here, it is necessary to labour a point: that Kant is in the process
of trying to constitute aesthetic judgements, to show that they are
transcendentally possible because the conditions necessary for
them do obtain. But in doing so, he is not constituting pleasure:
pleasure already exists. Rather, he proves or constitutes the universality of pleasure itself. There is not a specific kind of pleasure,
that can be phenomenologically distinguished from others, whose
constitution will legitimate making aesthetic judgements.[9] Hence
'it is not the pleasure, but the universal validity of this
pleasure, . . . that we present a priori as [a] universal rule . . .
valid for everyone'.[10]

In summary, in this chapter we proposed that the description of
beauty and judgements of taste yielded by the Analytic has implications for the logical or epistemological nature of those judgements. Kant describes these implications as the logical peculiarities
of their autonomy and universality. By identifying these traits,
Kant makes clear that the justification of these judgements, and
the arguments which he will give to show why they are legitimate,
address their distinctive logical and epistemological status.

The other characteristics of judgements of taste that Kant presents in the Analytic will be considered later, for his explanation of
their role, nature, and legitimacy depends on the central argument
of the Deduction of Taste. In any case, the Deduction will not
prove that we can ascribe a distinctive kind of pleasure to all other
subjects. Pleasure is primitive and we cannot clarify it further in
any other terms; nor is there a phenomenological ground in
pleasure for distinguishing a universal one from other subjective
kinds. Instead, Kant will defend the legitimacy of supposing that
in some instances we are justified in expecting that an experience
of pleasure can be available to all.

KANT'S DEDUCTION OF JUDGEMENTS OF TASTE

Kant identifies the problem of justifying the validity of judgements of taste in terms of explaining how a judgement is possible 'in which the subject, merely on the basis of his *own* feelings of pleasure in an object, independently of the object's concept, judges this pleasure as one attaching to the presentation of that same object *in all other subjects*'.[11] Our expectations of the judgement depend on how the mind is involved in making such judgements, not on empirical evidence.

To explain Kant's argument we shall present his account, then raise some objections; third, we shall examine some implications of these claims and, fourth, relate the latter to issues in the Sections following the Deduction.

Kant's Presentation of the Deduction

Kant explains the validity of aesthetic judgements in one paragraph of argument.[12] His central claim remains that subjective experience is universally communicable.[13] In Section 38, titled the 'Deduction of Judgements of Taste', Kant sets out his reasons for this claim, and in the following Sections draws out its implications. To understand his argument, we must begin by looking at an earlier Section.

In Section 35, Kant clarifies that in aesthetic judgements our concern is with the activity or power of judging. He wants to conclude by elimination that since aesthetic judgements are indeterminate, their necessity or universality cannot be a result of applying determinate concepts, and so must relate to the very ability to judge. Logical or determinant judgements, we saw, compelled agreement from other subjects because they made claims about the way the world was. Aesthetic judgements cannot depend on this compulsion because that would destroy their subjectivity by bringing in interests. Their validity must, then, result from some other source. For Kant there are only the objective and subjective components of judgement. If validity cannot rest on the objective nature of objects, it must arise from 'the subjective formal condition of a judgement as such'.[14] But the latter, being neither the set of merely subjective and arbitrary feelings and sensations accompanying an objective judgement nor the determinant judgement that results, must be our very ability to engage in the activity of judging. This is the formal subjective condition.

Kant expands on this claim in Section 38, in the footnote to that Section, and in the Comment following. In the last, he explains that the deduction of taste is easy because 'all it asserts is that we are justified in presupposing universally in all people the same subjective conditions . . . that we find in ourselves'.[15] He has already made such a claim in a number of ways, and it may be as well to relate those instances. Kant has proposed that the subjective condition for judging involves the power of judging. He did not stress this power or activity in the First *Critique* because his concern was with determinant judgements and their conditions rather than with the power of judging as such. However, there are occasions when the power of judging comes to the fore. In the passages discussed in Chapter 2 above,[16] he considers the activity of judging for itself, apart from the judgements which result from its exercise. His claim is that the subjective condition for making judgements, our ability to judge, must be present in all judgements. It is a formal condition in that it is not identified with any particular subject and his or her subjective identity, and clearly it is necessary for us to make any judgements at all. It becomes important especially when we talk of cognition *and* of communicating our experience of objects. This is because, for example, to explain what is necessary for a subject to have experience – to be conscious of what he is experiencing – it is not enough to say that the categories must be applied. Instead, for us to make judgements which deploy the categories, we must have a unity of consciousness in which concepts subsume representations. In other words, for subjects to make any judgements or claims about objects, for us to have any coherent experience of objects, we must suppose that those different components or aspects of our experience are all had by a single experiencer – that these aspects are united in the consciousness of a single experiencer or else they would not be any kind of coherent experience. Upon this unity 'rests the very possibility of the understanding'.[17] Unless there is this unity of consciousness, no representation or collection of representations would ever 'become an object for me'.[18] For these representations, which are the subject's experience, must come together through the subjects' consciousness of having them if the subject is to construe representations as an experience of an object. If this condition of the unity of consciousness were unsatisfied, we could not have experience which we know as the experience of an object.

The claim may be obvious; it is also significant. The conditions necessary in a subject for him or her to have cognition in general are necessary for anyone making that judgement. The unity of consciousness must occur in whoever makes that judgement. It is a formal identity, necessary for any subject who is to make a judgement. Moreover, it involves the use of the same faculties, for these are necessary for the unity of every single consciousness. Kant clarifies this by saying that 'the "I" . . . is [an] absolute (although merely logical) unity'. It is not itself an experience but is a 'formal condition'; and the 'I think' here 'belongs to and precedes every experience and as such it must be taken only in relation to some possible knowledge, as a merely subjective condition of that knowledge'. It is a 'formal condition, namely the logical unity of every thought',[19] and in justifying the possibility of making claims to validity, we begin with consciousness, treating 'I think' as the 'vehicle of concepts',[20] though the subjective conditions have a wider role than in cognition alone. And it is only because we can make judgements at all, because the subjective conditions for cognition in general are satisfied, that we can use categories which claim objective validity. Consequently, we can use a common set of categories because the same subjective conditions for judgement occur in all subjects. And the latter must be satisfied, for unless they bore some relation to 'actual or possible experience', judgements 'would yet be without objective validity'.[21] These subjective conditions then are necessary for communicating our knowledge, for without them either concepts are empty or we have nothing but 'a rhapsody of perceptions'.[22]

The subjective formal condition for the unity of consciousness relates to the subjective condition for making judgements – our ability to judge – because the ability to judge and have experience is present in objective judgements as the unity of consciousness. In a sense, the 'I think' embodies the act of judging, and is the subjective formal condition for all judgements because it is the component in any judgements that signals the subject's act of judging. If so, then the subjective conditions for judging must be present in all subjects because it is the act of judging, and this must be the same in all subjects because without it objective validity and knowledge claims would be impossible.

Kant's Deduction of Taste and Some Objections

Kant develops this claim further in Section 38 and in the footnote following, when he argues that the aesthetic judgement, because it is subjective, addresses the conditions for making judgements rather than to any claim about objects. The 'power of judgement', he maintains, 'can be directed only to that subjective [condition] which we may presuppose in all people (as required for possible cognitions as such)'.[23] If aesthetic judgements depend on the power of judging, which must be the same in all subjects, then aesthetic judgements must be transcendentally possible, for they rely on faculties that others also possess because these are necessary for objective validity and knowledge claims.

Kant also wants to infer from this claim that 'we must be entitled to assume *apriori* that a presentation's harmony with these conditions of the power of judgement is valid for everyone. In other words, it seems that when, in judging an object of sense in general, we feel this pleasure . . . we must be entitled to require this pleasure from everyone.'[24] He explains in the footnote that all we need 'for laying claim to such universal assent to a judgement of the aesthetic power of judgement, which rests merely on subjective bases' is that 'in all people the subjective conditions of this power are the same as concern the relation required for cognitions as such between the cognitive powers that are activated in the power of judgement; and this must be true, for otherwise people could not communicate their presentations to one another, indeed they could not even communicate cognition'.

Kant's claim then is that certain conditions are necessary for us to make aesthetic judgements. These include possessing similar cognitive faculties. A certain relation between faculties is pleasurable, and so far as other subjects possess those faculties, then they too are capable of experiencing that pleasure. He argues that we can know that the necessary condition of possessing similar cognitive faculties is satisfied because of our apparent ability to communicate our knowledge of objects and events. Given that knowledge of objects consists in our conscious objective experience of them, then to communicate our knowledge of objects we must be able to communicate our experience of objects. But for others to understand a subject's description of his experience of the object, they must recognize something similar to their own experience. If they could not recognize something in their experience as 'squareness' and 'redness', they would be unable to grasp a subject's claim to be looking at a red flag.

As a subject's own claim or judgement about an object depends on using the categories and bringing faculties to bear, we may expect that other subjects too must use the same categories and faculties. This claim may seem too ambitious, for it may seem that subjects' 'wiring' may be entirely different from each others' yet they could make the same true knowledge claims. Two computers with different circuitry and languages could both agree that 2 + 2 = 4. Similarly, we might suppose that our experience and knowledge are true to the objects of which they were experiential claims without depending on the same faculties and circuitry.

Kant's claim is not defeated by this kind of counter-example. His claim depends on the communicability of our knowledge. By the analogy with wiring, the two different computers could not tell each other that 2 + 2 = 4 unless they shared a common language and could recognize the other's claim in their own experience. If they can share these experiences and claims, then differences in circuitry become merely idle because they are irrelevant to shared meanings and claims. Thus, either those faculties or that circuitry are necessary to understanding and communicating meaning and experience or they are not. If they are not relevant, then pointing to differences in circuitry does not serve to explain or destroy claims to meaning because the differences are irrelevant to meaning. If the circuitry and faculties *are* relevant to having and communicating knowledge, then they would have to share relevant features for communication to occur at all, for if they were relevant but different, then subjects with different faculties or circuitry would not recognize the same truths in each others' expression and description of them. Further, even if we think of circuitry in more physical terms, such as brain structure, as it happens our circuitry seems to be identical, and we are able to communicate our knowledge claims through our description and grasp of experience, which depends on using the same categories and faculties.

Moreover, if pleasure accompanies a general relation of faculties, and this makes up our judgement of taste, then we can justifiably suppose that the conditions for such experiences of pleasure are satisfied where others possess these faculties. This suggests not that others *will* feel the same pleasure but that the conditions necessary for them to feel pleasure are satisfied, so that they *can* do so.[25] But this assertion too may seem too strong. Even if we grant the universality of subjective conditions accompanying judgement, we accept that where we make objective judgements, there the subjective conditions, such as the relation of faculties, sensations, and 'inner experiences', must be the same for us to recognize each others' descriptions of our experience of objects. Here, the act of judging must operate in similar ways in different subjects, allowing them to discern the order of an object. But it does not follow from this that pleasure is shared, for pleasure accompanies a non-cognitive judgement in the aesthetic case. Where we could argue that pleasure was shared if it were one of the subjective features accompanying an objective judgement, the fact that it accompanies a subjective judgement causes problems. It makes it difficult simply to extend to non-cognitive judgements a claim made for cognitive ones.

But this objection too fails to work against Kant. Given that judgements are communicable and that their subjective conditions are also communicable, then the subjective conditions which generate pleasure must also be communicable for something like the following reasons. Those objective judgements which we think are communicable must have a subjective side consisting not only of the sensations, relation of faculties, 'inner experiences' and so on, but also of the very activity of judging. This activity of judging is instantiated in the 'I think' as a formal condition necessary for having conscious experience. Both the objective determinant judgement and this subjective side of the act of judging must be present if we are to communicate our knowledge. In other words, the fact that we communicate knowledge suggests that we all possess the ability to judge and the faculties involved in making the judgements.

The activity of judgement, we saw, is spontaneous and creative because it does not have any given rules it can follow in its activity. It must also involve some sort of direct and immediate relation to the material, but that relation cannot depend on any prior conceptualization because judgement has yet to bring the material to concepts. Yet, because the order it discerns is capable of allowing concepts as rules to be brought to bear on the material, it must involve an appreciation of order which, since it is not yet cognized, must be indeterminate but also, because it is capable of accepting a concept, must be capable of a general validity. In serving as examples, these judgements demonstrate what can be done. Without establishing rules, they exhibit how others may follow them in their own attempts to bring material to rules.

Further, for Kant, the pleasure of aesthetic judgements arises from the harmony between faculties. The condition necessary for such pleasure is the possession of those faculties and the ability to make judgements – both these are presupposed in our ability to communicate knowledge claims. If we make determinant judgements and communicate our experience, it must be because we can make judgements generally – that we can participate in the activity of judging. It is just this activity that is necessary for making aesthetic judgements, for we feel pleasure in the harmony of faculties and such a relation of faculties is gained by an act of judging. If we can judge by discerning order and thereby can gain experience and communicate knowledge, then we can judge by discerning order and can gain a harmony of faculties. As Kant describes it, our apprehension of the harmony of faculties 'occurs by means of a procedure that judgement has to carry out to give rise to even the most ordinary experience. . . . [The resulting] pleasure must of necessity rest on the same conditions in everyone, because they are subjective conditions for the possibility of cognition as such. . .' .[26]

Of course, all this leaves open the issue of criteria for success in actual judgements of taste. If the explanation of the role of pleasure as an instance of a feeling of life is acceptable, then Kant has gone some way towards justifying the possibility of making judgements of taste. However, in terms of the distinction between expectation and demand, because judgements are subjective in the way made clear by reference to pleasure, and so are autonomous, we cannot *demand* agreement. In other words, we may know generally that aesthetic judgements are possible, but we do not as yet know which if any actual instances *are* judgements of taste nor how they demand agreement.

To know that they are possible generally is not to know which actual cases are cases of judgement; nor does the general possibility of judgements tell us how we assess particular cases. In the Deduction Kant is not considering particular actual judgements and how we must treat them, but is concerned with the *a priori* conditions for judgements of taste generally. His conclusions about these conditions are bound to determine features of the actual judgements we make, but the latter have properties *in*

addition to those general *a priori* conditions, which we must understand.

To consider these issues further, we must return to some of the
distinctions Kant presented in the Fourth Moment of the Analytic
of the Beautiful. We must compare the conclusion – that judgements of taste are possible – with what Kant has to say of necessity, for it is not clear how the deduction relates to the Fourth
Moment's distinctions between subjective and objective necessity
or the *sensus communis* as presupposition or postulate and ideal.
Once we understand his argument in these cases, we can explain
our distinctions further and can go on to compare this account with
what other commentators have proposed.

Judgements of Taste, Success, and the *Sensus Communis*

In the Fourth Moment Kant examines the *actual* judgements we
make. He makes this clear from the beginning. For example, he
notes that the 'necessity . . . thought in an aesthetic judgement . . .
can only be *exemplary*, i.e. a necessity of *everyone* to *a judgement that
is regarded as an example* of a universal rule that we are unable to
state'.[27] Such an exemplary necessity can only attach to a particular
actual judgement – to a *given example* which we construe in the
required way. It does not attach generally to objects we treat
merely as instances of a general kind, but attaches to the actual
particular. Similarly, in Section 19, Kant must be talking about the
actual judgement, which he says 'requires everyone to assent', for
he adds that 'we could count on that assent[] if only we could
always be sure that the *instance* had been subsumed correctly'.[28] It
is the actual instance of a judgement on an object that is found
necessary, and its justification is a warrant of why we 'ought to
give . . . approval to *the object at hand* and . . . declare it beautiful'.
In the following Section 22, having argued that we need some Idea
of a common sense to provide a principle for aesthetic judgements
generally, Kant again exhibits a concern with actual judgements
rather than with the *a priori* conditions for the possibility of aesthetic judgements generally. He writes that 'whenever we *make a
judgement declaring* something to be beautiful, we permit no one to
hold a different opinion'.[29] Once again, his attention is directed at
the actual particular judgement or declaration we make, not at
the *a priori* conditions for judgements generally. Moreover, this

Section makes clear another aspect of his concern with actual judgements of taste. For it now appears that the necessity of taste is a matter of the demand we make of other subjects that they agree to our particular actual judgement. We think of the actual judgement as an exemplary instance, and thereby 'demand universal assent insofar as agreement among different judging persons is concerned'.[30]

These Sections of the Fourth Moment, which issue in Kant's characterization of aesthetic judgements as necessary, suggest other conclusions about the relation of the possibility of judgements of taste to their necessity. If necessity as a demand for agreement attaches to the actual judgements of taste we make, then we should distinguish this issue from that of the universality of aesthetic judgements. The latter is our expectation that, despite their subjectivity, others can make the same aesthetic judgements because the conditions necessary for making any such judgements at all are satisfied. If judgements of taste were not universalizable, they could not be valid as judgements at all but would be merely agreeable claims, which have no validity over subjects.

Nevertheless, the fact that we can make judgements of taste at all does not explain all that needs to be said about the expectations we can have of our actual judgements. Certainly in claiming that particular actual instances are judgements of taste we postulate or take it for granted that the conditions necessary for making them generally or at all can be satisfied. But that does not guarantee that a particular case is an aesthetic judgement. Given that it is subjective, it does not tell us how we deploy our general expectation that others *can* make the actual judgements, or what justifies us in *demanding* that others shall agree with our own judgements. For knowing that aesthetic judgements generally are possible does not tell us how we should deal with their actual instances and the additional criteria of success involved here. Although we know that judgements of taste are possible generally, even though they are subjective and depend on a feeling of pleasure, nevertheless just because they are subjective we do not as yet know how to confirm in *any actual instance* that ours is an aesthetic judgement. Our reflection might be mistaken, and we need some criteria, in addition to knowing that they are possible, by which we can confirm actual aesthetic judgements. In this context, the deduction tells us only that the minimal necessary conditions have been satisfied, and while these will determine what our maximal expectations can be, they do not determine them completely. 'What we say of cognitive judgements (about things in general) also holds for aesthetic judgements: *a posse ad esse non valet consequentia.*'[31]

The distinction between the possibility of making judgements of taste at all and the demands we can attach to actual instances of such judgements suggests that some approaches to the deduction have misconstrued Kant's intentions. Some critics have argued that Kant identifies universality and necessity; as the deduction justifies the universalizability of taste, they hold it also thereby explains the necessity of taste.[32] In a sense, this is quite true, for the deduction proves the universality of aesthetic judgements and thereby shows that certain necessary conditions have been satisfied such that we can expect a subjective experience of pleasure of others. Given the distinction between possible and actual judgements, however, we should accept that while the deduction justifies the universality of aesthetic judgements, making them more than expressions of a merely personal preference, we also need to justify the necessity of *actual* instances of such putative judgements. Here, while issues of confirmation and communicability are not essential to justification of the possibility of judgements of taste, they may serve as criteria for justifying the compulsion of actual aesthetic judgements.

Kant himself suggests this distinction when he separates the Moments of universality and necessity or identifies the two as separate logical peculiarities of aesthetic judgements and then links necessity with a consideration of the actual judgements we make and with the demand we may make on their basis. 'We permit no one else to be of a contrary opinion' in our judgements and 'demand universal assent',[33] holding that 'everyone ought to give . . . approval to the object at hand and . . . should declare it beautiful'.[34] Later he says that feeling in a judgement of taste is 'required from everyone *as a duty*, as it were. . .' .[35]

Given that distinction of universality from necessity and the proposed association of necessity with actual judgements, we might relate actual judgements to subjective and objective necessity in the following way. For Kant, the actual judgements we make have a subjective necessity so far as they occasion a feeling of pleasure which the subject thinks is universalizable. In identifying his own pleasure as an aesthetic judgement, the subject first takes it for granted or postulates that judgements claiming such validity can be made because the deduction has shown that they are generally possible. Second, he claims that his is such a judgement – that the pleasure he feels is one that is universalizable and valid and so might be claimed from other subjects. He ascertains this by reflecting that his experience of pleasure is free of interest, independent of charm, etc. In some ways, this judgement resembles an objective one. The latter carries a necessity because it cannot be denied by any other subject. It sets out how the object is, and *must* be accepted by every other subject because of the nature of the object and our attempt to grasp its truth. Similarly, even though the aesthetic judgement is a universalizable experience of *pleasure*, the expectation is that it cannot be denied by any other subject. This is not because it is entirely subjective so that no other subject can compare it with his own judgement and find it wanting. Rather, it is undeniable because our pleasure constitutes an aesthetic judgement which, according to the deduction, is valid for all subjects. Yet it is subjective, because it turns on feelings, and autonomous, and must be made by each subject for itself. Rather than assuming that every subject's experience is the same, the subject can only impute to others the capacity for making such judgements, and cannot make the judgement for them but must wait upon them to make their judgements for themselves. So, on the basis of their own experience of pleasure in a harmony of faculties, subjects expect that all others can make the same judgement – that it has subjective necessity.

Unfortunately, this subjective necessity remains problematic. Aesthetic judgements involve a dual process of reflection, first gaining a pleasurable assessment of the object and second reflecting on the source of this pleasure to see whether it is universalizable. In claiming subjective necessity, the subject both postulates that aesthetic judgements are possible and, of the actual aesthetic judgement, maintains that it can be universalized. That is, if pleasure must satisfy certain conditions to be universalizable in our aesthetic judgement, then the claim is that the actual particular instance of pleasure in question does satisfy those conditions. These conditions may be spoken of as a *sensus communis* – a common sense which is our common possession of what makes possible a shared 'inner experience' and pleasure. However, subjective necessity rests on reflection by the subject on his own experience – and that reflection is fallible.

Kant writes that 'whether someone who believes he is making a judgement of taste is in fact judging in conformity with that idea may be uncertain . . . [At times] he fails to observe [the necessary] conditions and so makes an erroneous judgement of taste.'[36] Kant suggests that we make mistakes, confusing the pleasure of aesthetic judgements with charm, emotion, etc. In such mistakes, instances which we suppose are judgements based on the common sense are not so in fact. Hence necessity is subjective not only because it is the subject's felt experience but also because subjects' reflections are fallible. They think they have a universalizable pleasure where in fact they have failed to grasp a judgement based on a common sense and so have an experience of pleasure that is merely subjective. By contrast, if they could be assured that they had correctly grasped a judgement of taste based on a *sensus communis*, then they could claim an 'objective necessity'. This judgement would have 'objective necessity' not because it did not depend on the subject's experience of pleasure, but because, by contrast with subjective necessity, the judgement was in fact based on – or correctly assumed – the common sense.

But this raises again the problem we left earlier. How do we confirm that subjects have correctly assumed a common sense and so made an actual aesthetic judgement? In other words, how do we warrant the claim that our judgements have correctly assumed a common sense and that the concomitant necessity of the judgement of taste is objective? It seems that Kant has already proposed an answer in saying that confirmation is gained from other subjects, not from objects. The only way to gain confirmation, it seems, is by bringing other subjects to make the same judgement – to confirm in *their* judgements that the subject's experience of pleasure is an aesthetic judgement. But this requires something more – for if our self-reflection is fallible and our judgement can only be confirmed by other subjects, then it seems that to confirm our own judgements we must develop a mechanism for bringing others to make *their* own judgement, thereby confirming our claim to have made an aesthetic judgement claiming aesthetic objective necessity. But this leads to a paradoxical claim that, among other things, the activity of judging aesthetically must itself be found necessary in some way so that by satisfying the necessity of pursuing this activity subjects will make the aesthetic judgements that confirm the objective necessity of the subject's aesthetic judgements. In effect, to assure ourselves of the modality of aesthetic judgements, we must explain why judging aesthetically is an important activity.

To explain these senses of necessity and the extra compulsion by which Kant wants to generate confirmation from other subjects to a judgement of taste, we may look at the *sensus communis*. Kant uses this term in a number of senses, three of which are important to explaining universality and necessity. One sense, which is not vital, includes what we generally call 'common human understanding'. It follows no consistent principles, and is the least we may expect of human beings. As the lowest common denominator, it bears a connotation of vulgarity.[37]

Of the other uses of the *sensus communis*, we are already familiar with the one, involved in the deduction, which Kant refers to in Section 20, where he treats it as a subjective principle whose possession allows us to suppose that our own response is universally valid. He proposes that if we show that we possess a ground in common with other subjects, that is the source of pleasure, then we may be justified in believing that others too can have the same subjective experience. However, when in Sections 38 and 39 Kant provides his deduction of taste, he does not mention the *sensus communis* as such; nevertheless he still points to our common possession of the 'same subjective conditions of the power of judging',[38] whose similarity he warrants by arguing that without a similarity in these subjective conditions we should never be able to communicate our knowledge claims.[39] Although Kant does not speak of this common ground as a *sensus communis*, it does the work which the latter was supposed to do in making possible or justifying the possibility of judgements of taste.

But Kant also introduces a second use of *sensus communis* in Section 20 when he adds in parentheses that the *sensus communis* 'is not to be taken to mean an outer sense but is the effect arising from the free play of our cognitive powers'.[40] As the effect of the free play of the harmony of faculties is the 'feeling of life', we must understand the *sensus communis* as the feeling that results from a relation of faculties which we may expect from every subject. This use of *sensus communis*, as the *effect* of the free play of the harmony of faculties, clearly depends on the first use, which involves the common possession of the faculties or the subjective conditions of the power of judging. But the second use is not reducible to the first. For one thing, it is the *effect* of the play of subjective conditions that is at issue here, not the conditions themselves. By pointing to the latter as the basis for judgements, we warrant our expectation that others can make the same judgement; but the effect of the play of these subjective conditions is a different matter because, first, it concerns not *a priori* conditions but empirical or actual experiences; second, we may be mistaken about our experience and so about the validity of our putative actual aesthetic judgements.

To explain this further, we may begin with the second point: in the actual judgement we make, Kant says, 'whether someone who believes he is making a judgement of taste is in fact judging in conformity with that idea may be uncertain'.[41] We may be confusing the judgement which is a harmony of faculties with one which expresses merely that we have an interest in the object, or are charmed by it, or think it satisfies a moral need. So, because we are dealing with this actual case, we need to consider not only the general validity of such judgements but also the success of the particular case. We must consider whether an instance is actually an instance of a judgement of taste: and for the latter we need criteria for the success of these actual judgements. Second, as we are dealing with the actual cases and criteria for their success, the latter must take account of the possibility that 'the feeling for life', the effect of the harmonious play of faculties, can take different textures in diverse individuals. The subjectivity of this 'feeling for life' exacerbates this problem, for it is not clear how we might compare them. Further, all such criteria must also be cognizant of the first point – that the concern is not with *a priori* conditions but with claims about how we might grasp and deal with particular actual judgements, given that judgements generally are subjective and possible.

In the programmatic statement from Section 8, Kant writes that aesthetic judgements seek confirmation not from concepts and their determinate relation to objects of experience, but from other subjects.[42] Because of this, it was proposed earlier, we may suppose that particular judgements of taste are successful when they are confirmed by other subjects. They are confirmed by other subjects when they are communicated to them, and they are communicated when subjects successfully make the same judgements for themselves. As the judgements are autonomous, they can only be confirmed by other subjects giving the same response. Yet, as they are subjective, it may happen that two subjects' responses to the same work are thought to be similar, and so to confirm each others' judgement, when in fact they are similar responses to different features of the object. That is, they are two different judgements of taste which issue in similar feelings – say of pleasure – and so are mistaken for the same judgement of taste. To circumvent such a confusion, it may be suggested, we must be able to communicate judgements of taste to other subjects so that their subjective response is not only the same as the first subject's but also something more than a mere coincidence of responses.

There are a number of things to be said about this need for confirmation through communication. The need for communication introduces a third use of *sensus communis*. Whereas the second use construed the *sensus communis* as the feeling that was an effect of the free play of the harmony of faculties, Kant talks of the third sense as 'the idea of a sense shared [by all of us], i.e. a power to judge that in reflecting takes account (apriori), in our thought, of everyone else's way of presenting [something]'.[43] The *sensus communis* as an idea is now presented as the ability to judge or reflect that the feeling is shared – as a power to consider the success of the judgement of taste by assessing whether the particular actual feeling is shared. Indeed, Kant goes on to say that taste can be called a *sensus communis*, and he defines taste as 'the ability to judge something that makes our feeling in a given representation *universally communicable* without mediation by a concept'.[44] It seems, then, that the *sensus communis* is an idea that guides our reflection on a feeling which we know, from the deduction, *can* be shared if it is the effect of the free play of the harmony of faculties. If our reflection gauges that the feeling *is* communicable, then we take that feeling to be a judgement of taste and that instantiates the *sensus communis*. It is an actual particular case in which we have rightly assumed the common ground, and where the feeling is the effect of the free play of a harmony of faculties, and so may be demanded of others. Where such certainty obtains, where the *sensus communis* is satisfied, we no longer simply solicit everyone else's assent but feel a stronger warrant. That is, the *sensus communis* in this third sense, which is exemplified in the actual judgement of taste, 'is a mere ideal standard. With that standard presupposed, we could rightly turn the judgement that agreed with it . . . into a rule for everyone. For although the principle is only subjective, it could still be assumed as subjectively universal (an idea necessary for everyone); and so it could, like an objective principle, demand universal assent insofar as agreement among different judging persons is concerned.'[45]

Kant is arguing that if the standard of the *sensus communis* in this third sense is satisfied, then we can demand universal assent. But, as we saw, our attempts to satisfy this standard face various problems. Kant points out in Section 22, in the footnote to Section 38, and in the Comment immediately following Section 38 that we can easily make mistakes in our own reflection. He admits that we could demand assent 'insofar as agreement among different judging persons is concerned, provided only we were certain that we had subsumed under [the idea of a common sense] correctly'.[46] But at Section 38, in the footnote, he says that we might mistake a judgement which is 'mingled . . . with concepts of the object [or] with sensation . . .'.[47] for a judgement of taste. And in the Comment following he notes that our supposing 'we have subsumed the object correctly . . . involves unavoidable difficulties . . . so that the subsumption may easily be illusory'.[48] The occurrence of actual errors does not militate against the possibility of making subjectively valid judgements at all, but it suggests that our actual judgements stand in need of some criteria for success that do not simply depend on our own fallible reflection on their communicability. Rather, we need to confirm our judgements also by seeing that they are communicated. Only through such communication can we confirm our judgements and thereby demand agreement because we know that the common sense is rightly assumed and the idea of a *sensus communis* is satisfied. Without such confirmation, relying only on our fallible reflection, our demand for agreement will ever remain powerless.

At this point we might raise three issues. One concerns our ability to communicate a 'feeling for life' where this is the subjective effect of a harmony of faculties. From what we have seen of Kant's claims it seems that the judgement of taste excludes determinate concepts but remains communicable. Kant has explained this communicability by reference to 'demonstration by illustration and example', by talk of indeterminate concepts, and of 'adding to' concepts a subjective resonance they do not possess in actual experience. He develops these references later in the text by reference especially to the expression of ideas. By this account, the subject can articulate his or her aesthetic response to the object in idioms, images, and metaphors, which 'enable[] us to communicate to others, as accompanying a concept, the mental attunement that those ideas produce'. In order to 'express what is ineffable in the mental state accompanying a certain representation and to make it universally communicable . . . we need an ability [*viz.*

spirit] to apprehend the imagination's rapidly passing play and to unite it in a concept that can be communicated without the constraint of rules (a concept that on that very account is original, while at the same time it reveals a new rule that could not have been inferred from any earlier principles or examples)'.[49]

Kant is pointing out how communication occurs. His account applies to the artist's relation both to his work and, through his work, to the audience of subjects to whom he communicates. The mental operations involved in all these contexts remain the same, so far as our concern is with both expression in and communication of judgements of taste. As Kant reminds us, that which 'is ineffable in the mental state accompanying the representation' is made 'universally communicable' by using these devices.[50] Where we articulate the feeling through expression, indeterminate concepts, subjective resonances, illustration and example, and understand it through the array of available critical tools, thereby successfully communicating our judgements of taste, there we have also attained that 'one attunement' which Kant thinks is 'most conducive' to a judgement of taste.[51]

The second issue concerns the possibility of confirmation from other subjects. We may object to Kant's account that it neither provides the confirmation we seek through community nor warrants any claim to the beauty of objects by its reference to community. Kant may talk of the need for 'communicating' a judgement rather than gaining agreement, but the former seems a mere formality that adds nothing to confirmation. For the problem that occurs with agreement also precludes our gaining certainty about communication. Ideally, if we knew we had communicated a judgement, then we could have some sense that ours was not a merely subjective pleasure because we did not depend only on our own fallible reflection. But here communication too still depends on fallible reflection, though now it rests on two (or more) of them. And it is not clear why additional fallible reflections will confirm a judgement when they are all still corrigible. In other words, we do not escape the fallibility of reflection by relying on a number of fallible reflections.

Here, communication does not seem to have any criteria. The suggestion is that other subjects gain pleasure when they make the same judgement. So we succeed in communicating judgements when others gain pleasure by making the same judgement as we do. But there do not seem to be any criteria for communication other than this experience of pleasure. Where we might test communication by observing the behaviour of the subjects we communicate to, in this case only the occurrence of pleasure can count as a proof. Yet, as it was precisely because an experience of pleasure did not suffice as a proof (in our own cases) that we sought confirmation, we seem to have no reason to accept someone else's experience of pleasure as a criterion for confirmation.[52]

Finally, the reference to confirmation through communication to other subjects also changes our focus: we are no longer simply concerned with the object that has aesthetic value. Instead the relation to an object becomes peripheral to the relation between subjects in a community who supposedly confirm our individual actual pleasurable judgements. In effect, then, we consider the object an aesthetic one only because the relation between subjects warrants it. Consequently, the object seems to lose its independent status.

We need not concede to these objections. For example, the claim that the object becomes peripheral is not really an objection to Kant's theory because that, in fact, is what he claims. He is clear that references to beautiful objects really denote the subject whose experience of a universalizable pleasure constitutes the judgement that an object is beautiful.[53] In an important sense, the object is peripheral to the validity of aesthetic judgements;[54] the subject's experience of universalizable pleasure is central; and if confirmation from the community warrants that experience, then the relation between subjects will naturally gain prominence.

Nor is the relation between subjects a problem. Certainly the occurrence of pleasure will not by itself guarantee communication. But in judgements of taste, when pleasure occurs, we can point to various features of the object to indicate why we gain a pleasurable but rule-governed use of mind. And although these rules are not determinate ones, their presence makes it possible for subjects to clarify how they arrive at the harmony of faculties which yields a universalizable pleasure. Through this clarification subjects can divine whether an occurrence of pleasure is a result of communication or is merely an accidental agreement.

Similarly, Kant finds a positive use for the corrigibility of judgements. Even if judgements are fallible, and no strict confirmation is possible, so that we can never know ultimately that our judgements are correct, nevertheless aesthetic judgements explore the nature of a community of subjects, whom they must understand and relate to as subjects in order to validate claims about the beauty of objects, and therefore, through that mutual understanding, will construct and sustain a community of subjects. Here, since judgements are fallible, our confirmation may be mistaken. But it does not follow that every claim is useless because mistaken in some part. If there is an error in confirmation, a critic must analyse the particular agreement to diagnose where the error lies. That again requires a deepening understanding of the ways of rational and feeling creatures like ourselves, in their relation to each other.

However, if judgements of taste are corrigible by nature, then arguably the need for other subjects will be of a particular kind. These others may be the only ones who can have the subjective experiences we do; but the corrigible nature of these particular judgements makes otiose the claim that we need other subjects to confirm our own judgements. If the particular judgements we make are by nature fallible, no confirmation is really possible or necessary.

This objection misunderstands the need to confirm particular actual judgements. The corrigibility of particular judgements of taste does not preclude confirmation so much as require it. If our reflection on the pleasure in a judgement of taste is fallible, then we cannot know that we have made an actual judgement of taste. But then we are in the absurd position that we know generally, from the deduction, that judgements of taste are 'possible', yet cannot ever know that we have made them. To overcome this absurdity, we may suggest, we acknowledge their universality. This implies that all subjects can accede to the particular judgement of taste we make; so to confirm whether we have actually made a judgement of taste we need other subjects to make the same judgement. If they cannot do so for the right reasons, then ours is not a judgement of taste. The last claim does not simply repeat the position earlier described as absurd because, unlike the latter, our position takes seriously the need for and possibility of confirmation from other subjects. Further, rather than ask whether and how many corrigible agreements make for the universality of, and so confirm a judgement of taste, our claim recognizes that the fallibility of judgements also promotes an interrelation of subjects. An objection such as the one just set out depends on a notion of community that can be defined in terms of a mathematical quantity – an approach that surely needs defence. By contrast, by Kant's account, aesthetic judgements construct and develop a community that treats subjects as rational and feeling beings who confirm judgements by making pleasurable yet universalizable judgements. For him beauty is not just an attribute of an object[55] nor can claim an objective nature independent of the judging subjects, but rather denotes a relation between reasoning and feeling subjects understood as subjects.

That relation deepens and enlarges the community of subjects. The subjectivity of aesthetic judgements prevents their experience of pleasure from being imposed on subjects because of some objectivity or acceptance by an impersonal community. Aesthetic judgements must address individuals as rational and feeling ends who will for themselves give assent to a judgement by making one in confirmation. Individuals' agreement cannot be required by any promulgated law; instead, subjects in effect construct the community through their agreement based on capacities they share with other subjects. They generate a social form through mutual agreement, thereby claiming for their participation the power to establish, and the freedom to produce more and progressively freer forms of social order: they constantly explore and construct the relation of individual to community, where an individual's autonomous judgement seeks a warrant from the community, which itself constantly develops by gaining agreement from its members.

Success and Confirming Judgements of Taste

The third issue we may raise concerns the success of actual judgements of taste. Through communication, it seems, we can confirm our judgements and thereby demand agreement because we know we have rightly assumed the common sense and satisfied the idea of the *sensus communis*. Without such confirmation, if our fallible self-reflection or 'communicability' were all we had, we would not be sure that the *sensus communis* was satisfied and could not exercise any demand.

Yet surely pointing to the ideal of the *sensus communis* does not clearly advance Kant's argument. We know that we satisfy the idea of the *sensus communis* only by successfully communicating a judgement; and only satisfaction of the idea of the *sensus communis* allows us to demand that others agree with our judgements. But then the demand made in actual judgements seems useless, for it seems we know that we can exercise that demand only in the situations where the *sensus communis* is satisfied, but these are precisely those situations in which the judgement is successfully communicated and so just where the demand is unnecessary. Thus, if this were the only kind of demand deployed in a judgement of taste, it would be entirely redundant. We could not demand agreement because that depends on confirmation; and we would not gain confirmation because we could not demand agreement.

One way to avoid this circularity while also gaining confirmation, we suggested above, is to find some external reason for seeking a universally communicable judgement. Kant hints at this reason at the end of Section 40. He writes that 'if we could assume the mere communicability as such of our feeling must already carry with it an interest for us . . . then we could explain how it is that we require from everyone else as a duty, as it were, the feeling [contained] in a judgement of taste'.[56] If it were a duty to communicate, and judgements of taste were instances of the ideal of subjective communicability, then other subjects are duty bound to 'accept' judgements of taste. They are obliged to make the judgement of taste for themselves because these are instances of a communication that involves a duty. By making those judgements other subjects would confirm the subject's claim that his is a judgement of taste.

But Kant also adds in parentheses that judgements of taste do not, as judgements of taste, involve this interest. We seek confirmation and therefore communicate the judgement; we do not communicate the judgement because we are trying to satisfy an interest. Confirming the judgement is a matter of establishing that the actual judgement is a judgement of taste rather than something else, and the need for such confirmation leads us to communicate the judgement. If we want communication, that is, it is not for the duty that it satisfies but because we need to confirm our own reflection. In other words, in the judgement of taste, communication does not serve any purpose beyond the judgement. Further, the fact that we gain communication and thereby confirm the judgement may result in a feeling of life because to have communicated the judgement is to have enabled another subject to make a judgement and to gain that feeling of life. But the occurrence of such a feeling of life does not satisfy some interest, not even an interest in communication.[57]

It is important to consider the last claims in relation to their context, for Kant goes on immediately after to consider what sort of interest we can combine with disinterested reflective judgements. He does so by considering the objects of taste: natural beauty and fine art; and what we may glean from the opening paragraphs of the following Section 41 is that he is seeking an interest that may be attached to judgements of taste without determining them. If we are to avoid the circularity identified above, it was suggested, we may find some other reason for seeking judgements of taste. Now, Kant says also:

> That a judgement of taste by which we declare something to be beautiful must not have an interest *as its determining basis* has been established sufficiently above. But it does not follow from this that, after the judgement has been made as a pure aesthetic one, an interest cannot be connected with it. This connection, however, must always be only indirect. In other words, we must think of taste as first of all connected with something else, so that with the liking of mere reflection on an object there can then be connected, in addition, a pleasure in the existence of the object (and all interest consists in pleasure in the existence of the object). . . . This something else may be . . . something intellectual, *viz.*, the will's property of being determinable apriori by reason. [It] involve[s] a liking for the existence of an object and hence can lay the foundation for an interest in something that we have already come to like on its own account and without regard to any interest whatever.[58]

We may discover such an interest in the judgement of taste, the suggestion is, by looking to the object of beauty rather than to features such as the communicability of judgements.

In other words, the sequence of argument moves from considering the deduction and the possibility of judgements of taste to issues of how we are to deal with the actual judgements of taste we make. In the footnote to Section 38, and in the second half of the following Comment, Kant raises this issue of the mistakes we might make. From there he turns to talk of taste as the *sensus communis* in terms of universal communicability (Section 40), and then considers the objects of beauty (Sections 41 and 42 on Natural Beauty, Section 43 onward for Fine Art). We may suggest that this sequence follows the problems raised by seeking confirmation through communication. For if judgements need confirmation, we could gain communication without making a circular demand if the successful judgement of taste could be given an external value. Kant's talk of seeking an indirect interest[59] seems to answer the issue, and he turns now to look at the objects of beauty and the interest we might attach to judgements through them. The suggestion is that if objects of taste – natural beauty or fine art – satisfy an interest, then we have reason for seeking these out. That means we have reason for making the judgements of taste which identify for us the objects of nature or art which are beautiful. But by making communicable judgements of taste, enabling other subjects to make the judgement, we also confirm each others' judgement.

In summary, if Kant is seeking to confirm actual judgements of taste, he needs to afford them communication, but if he must communicate them in order to confirm them, he has to generate confirmation by getting other subjects to make the same judgements. If they do not make the same judgements, then our judgements are not confirmed. So he has to find some interest in judgements of taste which is indirect and does not determine the judgement that an object is beautiful yet is an interest that leads people to make judgements that confirm others'. To find this indirect interest, Kant turns to the objects of beauty – fine art and natural beauty – to see if our interest in them will warrant a compulsion on subjects to make judgements of taste and thereby confirm through communication each other's judgements. Accordingly, from Section 42 onwards, he considers what sort of interest we may ascribe to objects for being beautiful – for satisfying judgements of taste. In Section 42, he considers our 'intellectual interest' in natural beauty to argue why we should seek out natural beauty. Given the assumption that there are only two kinds of objects of beauty – natural beauty and fine art – he next turns to fine art, to show why it too satisfies an interest.[60]

It seems then that if we can explain why natural beauty and fine art are of interest, we can explain why we should seek them out and so explain why we communicate and confirm aesthetic judgements. The claims Kant has made about the nature of judgements of taste lead him to consider the objects of beauty. And we shall consider these claims in the next chapter. For the present, now that the structure of the deduction is clearer, we may pause to consider how this account differs from those presented by other commentators.

OTHER WRITERS ON THE DEDUCTION

The intention behind such a comparison is not to decide that ours is the right version while the others are all wrong. Rather, by comparison we see how different approaches to the *Critique of Aesthetic Judgement* stress particular issues and lead to diverse results – even if they agree over some features of their approach. A robust concern with the rightness of Kant's arguments is of interest only if we can sympathize with his general approach, for if we do not think his way of setting up issues is fruitful, there is little point in considering the arguments he deploys in defending his position. Hence, some important part of our interest in *Kant's* aesthetic theory must concern itself with what is Kantian about it, and this will lead us to consider its wholeness, comprehensiveness, and so on. In this context, a comparison with other approaches to Kant's aesthetic theory clarifies what constitutes the wholeness of and our interest in that theory.

One of the more interesting recent studies of Kant's deduction of judgements of taste occurs in Donald Crawford's book on *Kant's Aesthetic Theory*. Crawford argues that Kant's justification of the validity of aesthetic judgements is not restricted to the Sections entitled the Deduction of Taste but extends throughout much of the text. The argument may be divided into five stages, he maintains, and, in the text, follows an 'empirical' deduction and precedes an 'antinomy'. The empirical deduction clarifies 'how we come to believe that judgements of taste have universal validity or what the empirical basis is for the claim to universal validity, namely a consciousness of the disinterestedness of our judgement'.[61] And the antinomy considers 'two seemingly incompatible propositions concerning the "logic" of judgements of taste . . .: How can a non-conceptual judgement, admittedly based on individually felt pleasure, implicitly claim to hold for all men and to demand their agreement? The answer to this question is the "deduction" of judgements of taste – their legitimation as a class of judgement'.[62]

Having so contextualized the deduction, Crawford proceeds to argue for five stages of the deduction. He treats issues from the Second, Third, and Fourth Moments as the first stages of the deduction, and his succinct statement of the whole is worth quoting.

> Kant has argued, first, that the universal communicability of a sensation or feeling is postulated or presupposed by the judgement of taste because in no other way, given the analysis of judgements of taste as nonconceptual and aesthetic, could the universal validity claimed by the judgement of taste be justified (Stage I). Such universal communicability, Kant argued in Stage II, can be grounded only in the conditions which make possible cognition in general – the harmony of the faculties used for cognition (the imagination and the understanding). In Stage III, Kant argued that this harmony of the objective faculties must rest on the formal subjective purposiveness of the object being considered. In Stage IV, Kant argues that the universal communicability of the mental state or feeling of pleasure based upon the experience of this formal purposiveness presupposes a common sense. This condition we must assume to be present in all men, for otherwise there would be no basis, and hence no justification, for the communication and knowledge we do actually possess.[63]

The last stage consists in 'justify[ing] our right to demand the agreement of others and find[ing] fault with them if they show no taste'.[64] And to provide that justification, Crawford turns to the symbolic relation between beauty and morality which Kant sets out in the final Sections of the *Critique of Aesthetic Judgement*.[65]

We shall return to the last stages of Crawford's deduction later, when we consider the issue ourselves. For the present we may note that although both his approach and ours are similar in trying to see the whole of the *Critique of Aesthetic Judgement* as leading us to recognize the moral connections of beauty, nevertheless, there remain some obvious differences between the two accounts of the four Moments and of the Deduction. What he sees as one continuous argument, we have presented as two different considerations. The first was intended to provide a coherent conception of our usual practice of making claims about the beauty of objects – Crawford's empirical deduction. Although it construed Kant's examination as a phenomenological analysis of judgements of taste, in that it set out the implications of having a subjectively valid judgement, it did not see this analysis as an integral part of the justification of the validity of such claims. In part, the distinction between the Analytic and the Deduction was put forward as one between description and justification. And in comparison with Crawford, the suggestion was that the characterization of judgements of taste would remain incomplete unless all the four Moments were used to set out the full implications of the claim to subjective validity. By contrast, it seems, Crawford takes the disinterestedness of judgements of taste as the descriptive element while the rest of the Analytic is a part of the deduction. Yet, by our account, disinterestedness seems inadequate to a full description of judgements of taste, while the rest of the Analytic seems inadequate as a Deduction.

To explain the last point further, we may remember that Kant characterized judgements of taste by reference to the four headings of the categories. There is an important sense in which disinterestedness, so far as it goes to explain the quality of judgements of taste, is not the basic characterization of these judgements. For, as we saw, Kant's interest is in the power of the activity of judging, which he construes as a subjectively valid procedure, and which he associates with aesthetic responses of pleasure. The Analytic proceeds by examining what must hold true of judgements claiming validity if these are entirely subjective. In this process, the disinterestedness of judgements of taste is only one element of the whole characterization of these judgements. The more Kant clarifies those other aspects of judgement of taste, the more he shows that there is a coherent conception of valid aesthetic responses. Consequently, when the Analytic sets out this description of judgements of taste, it shows that we are not merely and systematically confusing valid aesthetic responses with agreeable, charming, pleasant, etc., responses, none of which can claim validity. Instead, his description of judgements of taste makes clear what our expectations are of subjective validity, and so prepares the ground for their deduction. In this process, then, disinterestedness plays only a partial role. It is secondary to the basic claim for the subjective validity of judging, being only one among other qualifications a judgement must satisfy to be subjectively valid.

Moreover, as a part of the description of subjectively valid judgements, qualifications such as disinterestedness, aesthetic universality and logical singularity, form of purposiveness, and necessity are not part of the deduction of judgements of taste. For Kant goes on to the deduction by abstracting two peculiarities of judgement of taste from the description and showing why judgements with these peculiarities are justifiable. These peculiarities involve judgements being universal and, because they are subjective and autonomous, being incapable of proof. And he is able to abstract these because he has depicted aesthetic judgements in the Analytic. That is, having provided a satisfactory description of judgements of taste, Kant can clarify what logical characteristics are basic to that description, and can then proceed to deduce or justify the validity of judgements of taste by showing that such peculiarities are possible: that the description is not only internally coherent but also one which we may expect all rational and feeling beings like ourselves can make. In other words, judgements of taste of the kind described in the Analytic, claiming necessity and validity, are possible and so a legitimate expectation on our part from other subjects. Now, clearly this concern with the legitimacy of having such expectations is separable from the interest in describing coherently and fully how we construe the nature of judgements of taste. The latter seeks to distinguish taste from other judgements; Kant also hints that taste is related to various faculties and capacities, but he does not make clear the precise nature of such dependence. Thus, his talk of the *sensus communis* raises a number of issues, which are not clearly resolved until the Deduction. Only there does he argue that judgements of taste are transcendentally possible or that our claims for a universalizable pleasure, which the Analytic has shown was part of any coherent description of judgements of taste, are justified and legitimate.

Once we recognize that the Analytic and the Deduction make separable claims, we can also point to another difference between Crawford's account and our own. Crawford maintains that the Deduction is not completed by showing the possibility of judgements of taste but needs developing to explain a duty-like demand which Kant associates with them. By contrast, by our account the Deduction argues that judgements of taste are possible, and suggests that the Deduction succeeds in its purpose. There *is* another issue raised here, about the success of the particular judgements we make; but, again, this matter is separable from the general argument that judgements of taste generally are possible. And while a concern with actual particular judgements is implicit in Crawford's claim, that concern remains undeveloped. As a result, he sees the duty-like necessity which attaches to aesthetic judgements as what needs to be justified by the Deduction. And, as a consequence of this strategy, it may be suggested, he emphasizes the scope and power of a symbolic relation that beauty bears to morality.

We shall turn to that issue in the next chapter; the comparison of our account with others can be developed further here. Our claim that the Analytic and the Deduction exhibit distinguishable concerns is shared by some other commentators. Anthony Genova, Paul Guyer, and Jeremy Maitland make similar suggestions; Guyer also claims that Kant's Deduction remains unsuccessful. However, Guyer construes the Deduction as an attempt to prove that we can *a priori* know that a single best proportion of faculties can be gained. But given that the Deduction concerns the faculties generally necessary for making aesthetic judgements at all, Guyer's construal seems to conflate issues regarding the transcendental possibility of making aesthetic judgements generally with those attaching to the actual judgement. For the single best proportion goes to explain the criteria for success of the actual judgements we make, while the Deduction seeks to justify generally that judgements of taste are possible because they depend on faculties which we must all possess if we are to have the ordinary experience which we do seem to have. Kant makes claims for the single best proportion only in the Fourth Moment, where he considers actual judgements of taste and their necessity, rather than when dealing with universality or in the Deduction itself. To know that we can make judgements generally, it is enough to know that we all share certain faculties; the issue of whether we have all gained the best proportion of faculties seems to be a matter of whether our actual particular judgement is successful as a judgement of taste rather than something else and can be appreciated by all others who have a capacity for these faculties and their relation. We would, after all, make the same distinction in the transcendental argumentation of the First *Critique*. Knowing that our judgements must be about objects in causal relations tells us neither whether we have judged correctly in any single instance nor which causal relations or objects we will encounter in experience. If we think of determinate judgements about particular objects in terms of faculties, then every correct judgement about particular actual objects will require a precise relation between faculties which every other similarly correct judgement must also adopt. But such correct judgements are empirical matters, and Kant gives a transcendental Deduction only for the general possibility of making judgements.[66] He does not justify the particular judgements we make. Unfortunately, since Guyer conflates the two kinds of issues and necessity, he finds the Deduction of judgements of taste incomplete.

Second, Guyer construes the Analytic in terms of a distinction between the Moments. He argues that according to his interpretation the Analytic contains

> two strands of argument, analytic and explanatory, . . . on which its four 'moments' are divided into two groups of criteria, differing in function and status. Universality and necessity, Kant's second and fourth moments of the judgement of taste, define the status necessary for a feeling to ground this judgement, and are derived from an analysis of its form as a judgement. Disinterestedness and the form of finality, Kant's first and third moments, are criteria by which particular feelings of pleasure may be decided to have the requisite status for justifying a judgement of taste, and are derived primarily from the explanation of aesthetic response.[67]

This introduces a distinction into the description of aesthetic judgements whereby the Analytic provides an explanatory description, in which some features of our response are explained as the result of others. It is not clear that Kant himself proposes this construal of the Analytic, and Guyer is aware that his work differs from Kant's;[68] nevertheless, his approach seems to make possible an account of the coherence of the Analytic and to strengthen its argumentative relation to the Deduction. But, still, it is a way of construing Kant's claims that is not Kant's.

Third, Guyer sees the *sensus communis* as a regulative epistemic ideal rather than as a necessary condition constitutive of the validity of judgements of taste. While our account proposed that the *sensus communis* provides an ideal, it also argued that the *sensus communis* as common sense is a necessary condition for judgements, and that as an ideal it also has moral value. We have not yet made the latter argument, but we indicated the need for some such separate argument when discussing the need to confirm particular actual judgements. And by retaining the connection between common sense and *sensus communis*, our account also preserves the close connection Kant seems to maintain between our ability to make judgements of taste and the value we ascribe to such an ability in the larger context of his concerns with our humanity and the purpose of philosophy.

Finally, Guyer does not set out the issue in terms of seeking confirmation for actual judgements but considers principally the possibility of making judgements generally. In a later paper, he argues that the need for communication occurs in the *Critique of Judgement* only as a remnant of another theory which Kant once subscribed to but later abandoned.[69] However, if Kant rejected this theory, that fact is not clear from what he says in the Third *Critique*; and our examination of the text suggests, instead, that his theory needs or could use just that requirement of communication in order to confirm the particular actual judgements of taste we make. Indeed, that requirement of communication serves to bring moral and other demands to bear on judgements of taste.

In his book on *Kant's Aesthetics* Kenneth Rogerson proposes another way in which judgements of taste carry a demand. Arguing that Kant's deduction is intrinsically practical rather than simply epistemological, Rogerson asks us to rethink the relation of universal validity and necessity in judgements of taste. Others have distinguished the universal validity of taste from the demand that other subjects agree with the judgement of taste.[70] Rogerson denies that there is any real distinction here. Taking his lead from Victor Basch, he sees judgements of taste as 'aesthetic imperatives' and maintains that 'viewing judgements of taste as issuing a demand for all to agree is the only sense of universality Kant has at work'.[71]

This thesis is welcome so far as it reaffirms that aesthetic judgements embody subjects' activity and should be considered in relation to Kant's moral theory. Rogerson defends this thesis first by appealing to the German text to argue that 'demand' and 'universality' are not philosophically distinct and, second, arguing that only his position really makes sense of Kant's use of the common sense as a regulative principle. The German text, with its use of *muten* and *fordern* rather than *erwarten*, he suggests, 'indicates that Kant understands expecting (*muten*) as a demand (*fordern*) for agreement. After stating that judging something as beautiful amounts to expecting (*muten*) agreement, Kant seems to think that it follows without further argument ("hence") that we can demand (*fordern*) agreement from everyone, even criticize them for lack of taste if they fail to agree.'[72]

On the basis of this analysis Rogerson contends that the common sense can now be seen as regulative, which is how Kant often talks of it, and that 'common sense is a universal imperative ultimately justified by morality. As such common sense expresses a necessary but imperatival connection between form, harmony, and pleasure'.[73] To defend this claim, Rogerson emphasizes the two-step argument present in the first two *Critiques* – each Deduction only argues that the requirements for 'object-talk' or for reason to be practical have been met; a second step is necessary to show what kind of experiential and moral objects there can be for us human beings, living in space and time and prone to acting on the 'basis of needs, desires, and other sorts of incentives'. Similarly, the Third *Critique* first argues that 'free harmony is a mental state available to everyone'.[74] This free harmony is an expression of Ideas, and Rogerson argues that, second, the '[e]xpression of Ideas *satisfies a rational interest* in the sense that an object which expresses an Idea is one which is organised so that it conveys to us Ideas of Reason'.[75] Consequently, because we have an intellectual interest in judging objects as organized by Ideas, we can demand of others that they agree with our judgements of taste, for if they fail to make the judgement then they cannot appreciate that expression of Ideas and they will fail to satisfy that intellectual interest.

There are problems with Rogerson's account. For example, for all the distance he wants to put between his 'imperatival' universality and the alternative, the philosophical need for that distinction seems to me unclear. Surely we can ascribe a moral value to a judgement which uses cognitive faculties without having to argue that the judgement itself is a quasi-moral one. Here Kant's use of an imperative mode to characterize aesthetic universality itself stands in need of justification, and does not support any particular argument for justification. More disturbingly, I contend that Rogerson's claims for an intellectual interest in the expression of Ideas imply that fine art cannot have necessity. Although Rogerson maintains that fine art and natural beauty are both capable of form and expression, the intellectual interest he ascribes to the expression of ideas is one which Kant clearly and firmly associates with natural beauty only: because nature seems antithetical to reason, our discovery of beautiful objects *in nature* is of interest. Beauty is purposive for us, and natural beauty evinces that nature is suitable to our needs and possibilities in a way that 'objective' nature seemed to make impossible. Here fine art cannot claim the same interest because it is not antithetical to human possibilities in the first place. On the other hand, if an intellectual interest attaches to our organizing experience in accordance with an Idea of Reason, and so applies to both art and natural beauty because they both embody such organization, then the notion of 'aesthetic imperative' becomes rather loose. For that interest attaches to *any* organizing of experience according to Ideas, not just to an aesthetic organization of Ideas; and we need some further arguments, to specify what, if anything, is distinctive of aesthetic judgements, and why the latter remain only symbolic of morality. It also raises the possibility that natural science too, because it uses organizing Ideas, is subject to this interest; and this too would stand in need of explanation.

In *The Kantian Sublime, From Morality to Art* (1989), Paul Crowther presents another account of Kant's aesthetic theory. This one examines Kant's concept of the sublime, but it deals with the Deduction also. Moreover, as he suggests that the justification of aesthetic judgements will ultimately also suffice for the sublime, if these are properly understood, we may treat his book here.

Crowther's book is clear about its relation to Kant's work: he wants to abandon 'Kant's overall architectonics (including the doctrine of the faculties), his main "baroque" version of the mathematically sublime, and his *entire treatment of the dynamical mode, and the Deduction*' (135): clearly this Kant*ian* sublime will avoid many of the burdens of Kant's aesthetic theory.

Crowther's criticisms depend on ascribing to Kant a rather dry notion of disinterestedness (57–61) while reserving a more interesting version, which is rather similar to the one we have presented above, but which Crowther borrows from R. W. Hepburn, for a reconstructed notion of the sublime (143 ff, 149, 161). That richer version occurs, as we saw, in Section 49 of the *Critique of Judgement*, where Kant points out that the use of reason and imagination add 'an aesthetically unbounded expansion' to concepts. By this explanation, aesthetic judgements are disinterested because their use of concepts is much richer than that found in cognitive or moral claims (Baumgarten identifies this richness as *ubertas*), not because they are more abstract or have less content. The drier conception of disinterestedness may suit Crowther's argument and may, in many details, coincide with the formalist and New Critical understanding of Kant's aesthetic theory, but it is unjustified by Kant's discussions of the issue in the *Critique of Judgement*.

Similarly, like Guyer, Crowther maintains that Kant's Deduction of judgements of taste seeks to prove that '[T]here must be one . . . universally communicable proportion which is most conducive to stimulating the general accord of faculties' (62). But, he goes on, Kant's argumentation is inadequate because, even assuming our common possession of faculties, 'there still remains scope for considerable divergence of response according to difference in cultivation amongst the individuals concerned' (64). But *this is* Kant's argument. The one best proportion is not a transcendental condition for the possibility of judgements of taste but a characteristic of the particular claims we make about the beauty of objects. The Deduction seeks to establish only our common possession of the ability to make pleasurable aesthetic judgements; no transcendental argument determines which if any objects we will find beautiful and capable of generating a universal pleasure – the one best proportion.

Both these interpretations of Kant determine Crowther's conception of the sublime. The first allows us to explain the aesthetic as 'a domain of logically and phenomenologically cognate experiences at once definable and differentiable in terms of the contrasting senses of disinterestedness they involve, and in terms of their contrasting ways of embodying the felt compatibility of rational cognition with the sensible world' (145) – one such experience being the sublime. And so far as the deduction validates experiences of this kind, it will serve for the sublime. Indeed, Crowther intends his account to do better than Kant's justification. The latter, according to Crowther, occurs when Kant acknowledges that though 'judgements of sublimity do not require a Deduction along the lines of those required by beauty', they do require *some* justification. In this version Kant holds that 'judgements of sublimity presuppose[ ] a "susceptibility" to moral feeling; and since we can assume such a susceptibility in all men, such judgements can command assent' (126–7).

Now, third, Crowther contends of the 'deduction' of the sublime (126–7) that its reference to culture, society, and human nature – and so to our capacity for a ratiocinative freedom from nature and an attendant susceptibility to moral feeling – is not developed in the Third *Critique* (127). Therefore he turns to Kant's ethical writings. This surely ignores large sections of the text, including the Introduction (Section II, for example) and Sections 64–85, which we shall refer to in the next chapter.

In any case, in important respects arguably Crowther's 'reconstruction' is really a rediscovery of parts of Kant's aesthetic theory. These parts were neglected because people had previously tried to find the theory relevant for a highly formalist aesthetics which is now mostly redundant. Crowther's account of the Kantian sublime re-emphasizes the relation between aesthetics and morality. He argues that our pleasure in the sublime results from realizing that we can disinterestedly yet rationally conceptualize those large and overwhelming objects that we cannot grasp and link to the 'human frame' in 'imaginative or perceptual terms'. In 'such an experience, we feel ourselves as transcending the limits imposed by embodiment' (147). This leads in the last chapter to a multi-layered discussion of sublimity in art that is valuable in itself and also for reworking the relation between aesthetic judgements, a respect for persons, and the permanent value of things judged aesthetically. This relation was central to Kant's enterprise in the *Critique of Judgement*; by neglecting it in favour of exploring the cognitive features of aesthetic judgements, as some people have done, we do a disservice to ourselves and to Kant's deepest concerns.

A recent work takes careful account of those deepest concerns. Rudolph Makkreel's book *Imagination and Interpretation in Kant, The Hermeneutical Import of the* Critique of Judgement (1990), is a very welcome addition to the growing list of serious works on the Third *Critique*. In cool and clear writing it develops an original thesis about the role of imagination, reflective judgement, and the orientational role of the *sensus communis*. Its analyses provide a distinctive context for beauty, the sublime, and their part in culture, history, and the interpretation of our humanity.

The author breaks decisively with a tendency to explain aesthetic judgements by the agenda of the First *Critique*, and shows the systematic interrelation between, on the one hand, our experience of beauty and the sublime and, on the other, our orientation towards a 'subjective communal context' (p. 65) and sense of the subject (p. 85). He begins by arguing that the imagination's 'image-formative' function in the earlier writings gives way in the critical work to a synthesizing operation that makes possible the 'fundamental unities necessary for representation to constitute experience' (p. 25). This yields a conception in which we may talk of 'deciphering', 'reading', and 'interpreting' our experience of nature. To understand or have experience is to read nature whereas to organize our experience into a systematic order of nature is to interpret it. The former is constitutive of our experience;

the latter is merely regulative: we start with a sense of the whole and find an order for our experience and, by hypothesis, may have given our actual experience a different order. As Kant expresses it, 'nature is our task, the text of our interpretation' (*Reflexion zur Metaphysik*, 5637, cited by Makkreel, p. 35).

Any reading of nature must rely on an imaginative synthesis and its concomitant determinate temporal ordering. In the *Critique of Judgement* Kant develops his conception of the imagination beyond its part in constituting experience. Our experiences of beauty and the sublime can be interpretative because they depend on a distinctive operation of imagination. For example, the relation of imagination to understanding in a harmony of faculties involves a reciprocal relation between two distinct elements rather than, as in synthesis, a 'one-sided influence for the sake of a strict unity' (p. 47). In these reflective judgements the 'aesthetic form is a whole, whose parts are not discretely sensed but felt to be an indeterminate unity, [and] there is no need for special acts of empirical synthesis, whether of apprehension, reproduction, or recognition' (p. 51). Instead of the strict temporal determinations of cognitive experience, Makkreel argues, in our experience of beauty and the sublime we must look to a non-linear model of time, such as the notion of 'interior sense', distinct from the 'inner sense' we are familiar with from the First *Critique*, that Kant presents in *Anthropology from a Pragmatic Point of View*.

This understanding of the imagination in interpretation is part of a deeper theory in which Kant dignifies subjective aesthetic judgements by referring representations to a feeling of life – a sense of vitality and activity. The disinterested pleasure of aesthetic judgements has a life-enhancing character such that the 'play of the imagination in the judgement of beauty serves to intensify the activity of our mental life in general' (p. 92). The same feeling for life is present in genius and its works as spirit. 'The spirit of an art is a whole, a systematic method, which contains a comprehensive (*zusammenhängende*) idea' (*Reflexion zur Anthropologie*, 1509, cited by Makkreel, p. 97). Its products are inherently unified and need interpretation rather than the synthesis native to cognition. Another version of this idea of life occurs in the *Critique of Teleology*, being derived from the aesthetic sense. Both reveal a 'significant shift away from the essentially atomistic psychological assumptions of the first *Critique*' (p. 196). Makkreel argues that Kant affirms this shift also in the *Opus postumum* by contrasting the system of elements of the natural sciences, which presumably builds up from our experience of particular objects and their relations with each other, with 'the concept of the world system which must be represented as proceeding from the idea of the whole to its parts' (cited, p. 107).

This holistic perspective has implications for the role of imagination in interpretation. Ultimately the interpretative nature of reflective judgements allows us to construe beautiful objects in terms of their relation to our capacity for thinking generally – in terms of a common sense or *sensus communis* – that brings them 'into a subjective communal context more fundamental than an objective context' (p. 65). To interpret is to propose an order and meaning for some whole. Interpretation becomes possible when there is a sense of the whole though we lack objective principles by which to give its parts a precise order. In these cases we rely on subjective principles of reason to orient ourselves to the whole: the subjective principles serve as guidelines for the imagination when it proposes some ordering. Here, 'on the level of judgement', Makkreel proposes 'an aesthetic orientation that evaluates the world on the basis of the feeling of life and a teleological orientation that interprets culture on the basis of common sense or the *sensus communis*' (p. 156). Through the feeling of life they occasion we assess the value of things to our existence, while the *sensus communis*, in turn, orients the individual's judgement towards the larger perspective of the community. Such orientation deepens and enlarges our relation to other individuals, ultimately directing Kant's teleological interpretations of history and the development of freedom in politics and culture. It underlies too the notion of 'authentic interpretation' found in *Religion Within the Bounds of Reason Alone* and 'On the Failure of all Attempted Theodicies'.

For Makkreel, then, this relation of imagination to a holistic outlook in interpretation structures the *Critique of Judgement*, explaining how the text provides a distinctive perspective on Kant's critical project. His book's hermeneutical reading of the Third *Critique* provides us with a distinctive vocabulary for explaining Kant's aesthetic theory. Like only one or two other books in this field, it opens up a new area in this theory, giving us access to concerns that scholars had neglected because they lacked an appropriate language. We shall turn to these issues in the following chapters.

6

The Necessity of
Judgements of Taste

We suggested that Kant needs to discover some reason for making aesthetic judgements. Satisfaction of this need will provide confirmation *in judgements* for the particular actual judgements we make which, prior to confirmation, only have subjective necessity.

In the *Critique of Judgement* Kant goes on from the Deduction and his discussion of its implications to examine the objects of beauty. Aside from clarifying the nature of these objects, he argues for the interest we ascribe to them. Natural beauty signifies the possibility of realizing the moral law in our actions, and an interest in natural beauty exhibits possession of a good disposition among subjects, while fine art is of interest because it promotes *humaniora*.[1] However, these interests are additional to a symbolic relation that aesthetic *judgements* bear to moral good – regardless of the other interests fine art and natural beauty may satisfy by being the kind of objects they are.

The Necessity of Beauty

Kant sees beauty as a distinctively human experience. It involves reason and nature – the rational faculties and a felt pleasure – in a mix that is significant only for creatures like ourselves. This does not make the experience of beauty definitive of human beings, as Schiller maintained,[2] but for Kant the experience denotes a central feature of our humanity.

In Section 60, 'On Methodology Concerning Taste', Kant links the experience of beauty with *humaniora*, taking this classical notion of the humanities to mean 'both the universal *feeling of sympathy* and the ability to engage universally in very intimate *communication*'. These two qualities in combination 'constitute the sociability that befits [our] humanity and distinguishes it from the limitation [characteristic] of animals'.[3] Communication is a relation between two mutually responsive individuals, and our ability to

116

grasp the humanity of others, to treat them as subjects like ourselves, without subsuming them as objects that are means to our ends, is a disposition for treating others as ends and equals.

Kant links this human community with taste by pointing to the universality of aesthetic judgements.

> Taste is basically an ability to judge the [way in which] moral ideas are made sensible ([it judges this] by means of a *certain analogy in our reflection* about [these ideas and their very renderings in sensibility]); the pleasure that taste declares valid for all mankind as such and not just for each person's private feeling must indeed derive from this [link] and from the resulting increase in our receptivity for the feeling that arises from moral ideas (and is called moral feeling). Plainly then, the propaedeutic that will truly establish our taste consists in developing our moral ideas and in cultivating [*Kultur*] moral feeling; for only when sensibility is made to harmonize with this feeling can genuine taste take on a definite, unchangeable form.[4]

The universality of taste is a feature of judgements, meaning that we constitute aesthetic judgements as ones whose pleasure can be shared. This universality is an aspect of reflection – of the manner of judging.[5] Thus, the link to moral feeling that Kant presents here is not to a content – whether the object of beauty is *about* or represents moral subjects – but to the reflective form of judgements.[6] He is suggesting that the universality of aesthetic judgements cultivates moral feeling – the ability to treat other subjects as ends and to distinguish oneself as an agent having only 'private' feelings from oneself as an agent capable of a 'universal' perspective in which we accommodate ourselves to and share a sensibility with others.[7] The more we develop this sense of ourselves and others as subjects like ourselves, and do so by acknowledging that our exclusively private feelings are not the only model for subjectivity, the more we will develop moral feeling. The latter is a feeling of respect for moral ideas, which Kant defines by their universality.

Kant talks of this cultivation of moral feelings as culture. Aesthetic judgements are not the only vehicle for promoting culture; but our interest in them seems to arise, by this account, from the contribution they make to this cultivation. And the latter, in turn, serves the needs of morality. Kant sets out his notion of culture in a number of texts, especially the *Critique of Judgement*, but does not always refer to it in the same way. His use of the concept shows clearly that the cultivation of moral feeling is culture. On other occasions he considers 'natural perfection', but slips easily into talk of 'culture' and then gives natural perfection an association with morality that makes it significantly similar to the cultivation of moral feeling.[8] We saw also that he links communication, pleasurable aesthetic judgements, and their universality with enculturing moral feeling. We may also look back at his earlier claims in the *Critique of Judgement* and understand his concern for 'The Communicability of Sensation' (Section 39) and for 'Taste as a kind of *sensus communis*' (Section 40) in the context of enculturing ourselves to a subjectively universal moral feeling. The orientational role of the *sensus communis*, based on reflective judgements and their ability to examine the particular in relation to the whole, also sustains this aspect of Kant's thinking.[9] A number of other theses from *Anthropology from a Pragmatic Point of View* also contribute to this account of culture.

So far as morality is a matter of treating others as ends in themselves, culture develops our capacity for morality by promoting our ability to set and gain ends. First, Kant defines culture as the 'production' in man, a rational and animal being, of the 'aptitude and skill for [pursuing] various purposes for which he can use nature (outside or within him)'.[10] More than the ability to appreciate ends, it includes the power to set ends 'independently of nature'[11] and to establish the objective validity of ends. The latter is 'an essential part of our entire aptitude for purposes'.[12]

Second, Kant links this culture with our striving for morality. The 'power to set an end – any end whatsoever – is the characteristic of humanity (as distinguished from animality).[13] Unlike animals, who do not reflect on the end towards which they act, human beings set and consciously work towards particular ends. Kant explains this activity, in which we are guided by a reasonable principle towards some ends, as 'a choice that bases its acts on reason'.[14] Moral principles are the most rational form of behaviour because they promote a universal end – one which every rational creature will always strive for. As creatures capable of rational and animal bahaviour who, to develop their humanity, strive to follow the rational demands of universalizable moral rules, we try to overcome our animality for the sake of following rational and virtuous ends. Thus, so far as culture promotes our humanity as the ability to set ends, it promotes our capacity for morality. In Kant's words, 'the ideal of morality belongs to culture'.[15] Morality provides a direction for our activity of culture.

Two aspects are central to this process: culture as discipline and progressive culture. To explain culture, Kant contrasts human beings' natural and rational capacities. We may be motivated by reasoning about our ends, which leads us to act in one way, or by the satisfaction of certain bodily desires, for example, which leads us to act in another way. When we follow our natural desires alone, Kant suggests, we are subjugated to nature and inclination. In that case, not only may the strength of our natural desires prevent us from attaining our reasoned ends, but also when we try to satisfy sensual natural desires only, we seek ends whose satisfaction serves only the particular individual who has those desires. Consequently, the conflict between reason and nature in our actions becomes a conflict between individuals, all possessing similar desires but, because of a 'truculent egoism', rivalling each other for the satisfaction of their own inclinations. This isolates individuals from each other, as they treat others as means to the satisfaction of their own inclinations.[16]

When this state of affairs obtains, culture 'proceeds without a plan'.[17] Yet only 'in the state of perfect culture would perpetual peace be of benefit to us, and only then would it be possible.[18] To gain that state, we need culture as discipline. This strives for a community in which 'each member . . . should indeed be not merely a means, but also a purpose; and while each member contributes to making the whole possible, the idea of that whole should in turn determine the member's position and function'.[19] Here, while culture begins when human beings set themselves apart from other animals by thinking of themselves as ends, we need not think of ourselves only in terms of physical purposes or aims.[20] We are also capable of reasoning. In the latter case, when we consider ends we must subjugate nature to reason in the sense that we give priority to motivation determined by reason and accept only those natural inclinations which are compatible with treating human beings as reasoning creatures. Consequently an important part of culture, as the ability to set and gain ends, is the negative role of disciplining natural impulses in order that we are motivated by reason to ends other than exclusively individual ones. If virtue is the power to 'master one's inclinations when they rebel against the moral law',[21] then in its negative role culture promotes the power of choice over natural impulses. And where virtue is 'the possession of a moral strength of will' to follow reason, culture tries to promote our exercise of the ability to determine the will by reason.

Kant identifies virtue as tne *ideal of humanity* in its moral perfection.[22] In this context culture as discipline is the *emergence of humanity* – of the individual liberated from subjugation to natural impulses and truculent egoism and now considered as a reasoning moral end. In this process culture also has a progressive role. Beginning with the relation of reason to nature, in the 'conflict between natural and moral species', progressive culture develops our capacity for reason. It does not, like disciplinary culture, simply control natural impulses; rather, through exercising and developing reason in relation to nature, progressive culture 'progressively interferes with [nature] by altering the conditions to which [culture] was suited'.[23] When we control our nature, we also change the relation between nature and reason which constitutes culture. Culture and reason now have to operate on a relation between reason and nature that differs progressively, as we become more encultured into using reason and setting rational ends. And the less exclusively individual desires determine our actions, the more we use reason and enter further into the public and positive relation with other individuals that reason subtends. For Kant, in this process progressive culture 'mak[es] man more than man', turning us more towards a conscious humanity and away from pursuing animal inclinations. Culture leads us to treat *'man as such (humanity* really)'[24] or human beings generally as morally capable beings.

Only when individuals act autonomously do they express and develop their moral personalities. But this autonomy still bears reference to a unified community. The autonomous individual must exhibit a consistency in his or her moral judgements. If they are to be an expression of their moral personality, their moral judgements must form a unity. They cannot simply be made piecemeal, without integrating considerations of past and present behaviour or of consistency with others' judgements. Kant clarifies this sense of a determinate universality, as compatibility with others, in the *Critique of Judgement*, when he discusses the requirement of consistent thought.[25] Our moral behaviour is autonomous but neither isolated from that of other subjects nor removed from cultural progress. The individual must be capable of legislating for himself as a member of the Kingdom of Ends. '*Humanity itself* is a dignity',[26] and a subject cannot develop his humanity while disregarding others'.

The development of a moral personality takes us beyond the single act, and our humanity integrates our actions into a cooperative effort. For Kant, 'man is destined by his reason to live in society with other men'.[27] Human beings have 'an inclination to associate with others' because 'in society [man] feels himself to be more than man, (i.e.) more than the developed form of his natural capacities'.[28] This development beyond natural capacities to reason is the task of culture, which Kant defines as 'the social worth of man'.[29] He also goes on to define the good in social terms: the 'species of rational being is objectively, in the idea of reason, destined for a social goal, namely the promotion of the highest as a social good'.[30]

Although we strive for this goal, we cannot expect to gain perfection ourselves or 'within [our] mortal span'. Perfection 'cannot be attained by a single individual by himself' but only in the human race in history. Even then, we must understand the human race not 'according to the generic notion (*singulorum*) but as a totality (*Ganzes*) of men united socially on earth'.[31] Culture as discipline and progress, in promoting reason, sustains a social not exclusively individual good, whose universality Kant explains as the consistency of individuals with others.

Although culture promotes moral behaviour, it does not engender morality. Its success consists in bringing people to pursue moral ends, but it does not determine the latter. When 'nature within man tries to lead him from culture to morality and not (as reason prescribes), from morality and its laws as a starting point, to a culture designed to conform with morality . . . this course inevitably perverts his tendency and turns it against its ends'.[32] Nevertheless, cultural activity, our enculturation of ourselves, because it promotes our capacity for setting and pursuing moral ends, is part of our natural perfection. It is a matter of developing the abilities we have by nature, including our ability to reason, in the pursuit of moral ends. In this context, culture is directed at making morality possible.

Kant argues also that we have a duty to promote culture. In the *Doctrine of Virtue*,[33] he outlines a moral demand that we make the cultural effort to promote moral behaviour and motivation by reason, arguing that it is part of the search for natural perfection.

The latter is an end in itself, derived from the supreme principle of morality.

Given Kant's account of culture and its subjection to the duty to natural perfection, the necessity of aesthetic judgements is easily suggested. Beauty, the pleasurable experience of judgements of taste, is a part of culture, and thus has the moral significance that culture has. But the details of beauty's participation in culture take longer to set out. It occurs in a number of related forms, of which we shall consider two immediately.

First, as we saw, in the Analytic of the Beautiful, Kant argued that judgements of taste are disinterested, subjective, but universally valid experiences of pleasure resulting from an harmonious relation of faculties.[34] Because they are pleasurable, the judgements are also autonomous: no one else can feel the subjects' pleasure and make the judgement for them; and, as judgements result from a harmony of faculties, they must depend on subjects ordering and making the material their own. The only confirmation we can get for these autonomous judgements is through other subjects making their own judgements and *giving* assent.

The explanation that subjectively valid judgements seek confirmation from others in the aesthetic community suggests other things about them. Because they are based on an experience of pleasure, aesthetic judgements are not subject to the usual ways of generating assent. The claim that an object is beautiful depends essentially on an experience of pleasure and cannot be inferred or deduced from any general property of the object.[35] As the subject's feeling is crucial, the frequency, facility, or conviction with which judgements are made by others cannot form any basis for a subject's assent because the ground for *giving* agreement is the subject's own experience of an appropriate pleasure. For similar reasons, we cannot dismiss a contrary judgement as false because we cannot have evidence in our feeling for dismissing another's claim.

By this account, the actual judgement of taste must satisfy two criteria – particular judgements must gain confirmation from the community[36] and the confirmed judgement must depend on the subject's autonomous activity in grasping and ordering some material in a pleasurable judgement. In effect Kant's theory points to a mutual dependence between the subject and the community. Neither gains serious employment without the other. The subject's particular claims remain questionable until the community validates them, and the force of the community remains ineffective until the subject deploys it in the act of judging some material. The individual's acts have a social character at the same time as the social formation must make room for the individual's autonomous activity.

This account of the activity of judging subtends a conception of the subject. If judgements are subjective and autonomous but need confirmation, then the individuals who make such judgements will find their behaviour constrained by these expectations. Through the activity of judging they will enter into a particular relation with the aesthetic community. Given the autonomy and subjectivity of judgements of taste, individuals must treat each other as rational and feeling beings who are ends in themselves for these judgements and are equally capable of engaging in the activity of making judgements of taste. Autonomy implies treating judgements as recommendations because subjects must make the judgements for themselves and can neither have judgements imposed upon them nor simply have them rejected out of hand. But such autonomy does not imply a complete independence for the subject because while we presuppose subjects' freedom in making judgements, their sovereignty needs the community's warrant. A lack of agreement will make the judgement *merely* subjective and idiosyncratic, and will prevent subjects making that judgement from entering into dialogue or claiming validity for their judgement at all. The judgement would become something 'merely true for me'.[37]

In this sense the 'subject' involves at least two components, one that is entirely subjective and idiosyncratic and another that can enter into agreement with others. The first may be entirely sovereign – but this is because it is entirely subjective – while the second must be capable of a rational and feeling relation with other subjects. Even if individuals retain a power to accede to or reject the dialogue (because they must feel a pleasure for themselves), nevertheless the judgement's constitution of the subject must satisfy the requirements of intersubjectivity, in which the subject's autonomous decisions gain validity from the community. In this respect, individuals are not sovereign subjects, but are always 'suitor[s] for agreement' from others.[38] Their autonomy is warranted only in being confirmed by others.

This explanation of the act of judging shows that 'making experience our own' is in part a matter of accepting social constraints in order both to be an individual subject and to enter into a dialogue as an agent rather than as a 'subjective object' on whom natural desires, causal influences, and social forces merely impinge. The individual becomes an autonomous subject by setting aside the complete sovereignty of merely subjective responses and accepting the conditions necessary for an intersubjective validity that succeeds by gaining confirmation from the aesthetic community.[39] Here, in terms of arbitrating between individual autonomy and the social confirmation of a claim, Kant puts the onus on the social formation, to which the subject must *give* its agreement. The social formation must gain compliance when the subject makes the social character its own in an act of judging. Yet, at the same time, the social formation is necessary for warranting the subject's act of judging, for a lack of confirmation would reduce pleasure to a merely subjective response rather than an act of judging aesthetically.

Further, as the rules of judgements of taste are indeterminate, they will be fallible or corrigible. The latter allows Kant to propose that the community and judgements of taste militate towards a continuing and developing relation between subjects. Rather than make individuals into the replaceable ciphers of cognitive judgements – where any individual who fails to make the same assertion about a particular state of affairs also excludes himself from the rational community – judgements of taste, by their subjectivity and commensurate corrigibility, generate an interrelation between subjects as subjects. As their experience is corrigible, they cannot impose rules on others on the grounds of their objectivity. And because their experience is subjective, only other subjects can grasp it in its subjectivity.

Thus, judgements of taste sustain an exploration of the nature and form of the community of subjects. In seeking confirmation, we must address subjects as subjects capable of such universalizable judgements. As we saw, Kant neither makes beauty an attribute of the object[40] nor gives it an 'essence' independent of subjects. More than anything else, our particular claims that objects are beautiful denote a relation between subjects.

That relation develops through deepening and enlarging the community. It depends on treating subjects as rational and feeling ends who must for themselves give assent to a judgement by making one in confirmation. Their agreement cannot be legislated over by the community, though in effect subjects construct the community of taste by their agreement and because they share the capacities that allow them unity with other subjects.

Kant's recognition that a mutual relation between subjects is necessary for particular judgements to succeed thus affirms that the source of social forms lies in the individual's participation. Because it gives the latter the power to confirm the social order, it also gives us the possibility of generating new and liberating ones from that source by changing social life as our participation in the community develops. Judgements of taste celebrate the relation of individual to community, which is ever in process, for the individual's autonomous judgement is always in search of a warrant from the community, which is itself always in a process of development that depends on assent from its members. And, as the reader may have foreseen, to deepen our sense of the communal features of individuals and their subjectivity is to participate in enculturing ourselves. The sensitivity towards universality which Kant presents as part of the confirmation of judgements of taste is also the universal feeling of sympathy and communication which generates a moral feeling.

A second aspect of beauty's participation in culture turns on the *sensus communis*, which we saw was crucial to aesthetic judgements, and which articulates features of the communal role of beauty that we considered above. The *sensus communis* justifies the moral and cultural significance of aesthetic judgements and the experience of beauty because it functions as a form of progressive culture. Kant says that we must understand the *sensus communis* as

the idea of a *public* sense, i.e., a critical faculty which in its reflective act takes account (apriori) of the mode of representation of everyone else, in order, *as it were*, to weigh its judgements with the collective reason of mankind, and thereby avoid the illusion arising from subjective and personal conditions which could easily be taken for objective, an illusion that would exert a prejudicial influence upon its judgement. This is accomplished by weighing the judgement, not so much with actual, as rather with the *merely possible* judgements of others.[41]

By this account, the *sensus communis* is concerned with possible consciousness: with others making and being able to make the judgements we make and which express our humanity. It requires that we impute the capacity for states of mind and feeling to other

individuals, promoting a persuasive and intersubjective unity between reasoning and feeling individuals who participate in a
dialogue. Here, by 'weigh[ing] our judgements with those of
others', we also consider what others are or could be. For example,
subjects reflect upon a judgement on a beautiful object, considering its adequacy to the general harmony of faculties. In this,
subjects judge not only the object but also themselves. Considering the appropriateness of an object also implies reflection on their
own adequacy to the object and to dialogue with its audience. This
self-reflectiveness of aesthetic judgements allows us to participate
in culture, to 'progressively interfere' with nature, and to 'alter the
very conditions to which it is suited'.[42] It changes the very relation
between nature and reason in the individual on which it depends
for its appreciation. It cultivates our individual judgement through
a dialogue based on the capacities for reason and feeling which
we possess in common with others. Such reflection uncovers
'that which forms the point of reference for the harmonious
accord of all our [i.e. everyone's] faculties of cognition – the
production of which accord is the ultimate end set by the intelligible basis of our nature'.[43] It produces the unity and community
for which we are destined by our rational capacities, and so
participates in culture.[44]

The discussion above proposes that beauty and aesthetic judgements are a part of culture because they promote our humanity
through an activity in which we treat each other as subjects who
are ends in themselves, capable of reasoning and persuasion. We
have also suggested that we have a duty to develop our humanity
by rescinding the animal and exclusively individual part of
ourselves and furthering our capacity for acting and thinking of the
self in relation to other equally valuable selves.[45] Our experiences
of beauty provide instances which are universally subjective in the
required way, and in which all other subjects can participate
because they possess the faculties necessary to the *sensus communis*. If we have an obligation to promote culture, if our experience of beauty promotes culture, and all other subjects *can* also
make aesthetic judgements, then other subjects are obliged to seek
to assent to our claims about particular experiences of beauty. In
other words, all beings capable of reason and feeling have an
obligation to promote their humanity by developing their capacity
for reason and for setting ends. Beautiful objects provide occasions
in which subjects make pleasurable judgements, based on an

accord between reason and nature in themselves and others, that can develop every individual's capacity for reason in relation to a universalizable feeling. All human beings can make these aesthetic judgements because they all possess the necessary rational faculties. Therefore, a subject making a judgement is justified in thinking this warrants his claim that every other rational and feeling being *should* assent to his judgement about the beauty of an object.

All this goes to explain what the exemplary necessity of aesthetic judgements consists in. First, it involves our humanity, possessed of both an animal and a rational character, and the promotion of our capacity for reason and ends. Second, objects of beauty are significant only to humanity, and our judgement of beauty promotes our capacity for reason and for the determination of the will to rational universal ends by developing our sensitivity to other subjects as human ends in themselves. Moreover, judgements of taste have a universal validity because they are based on a relation of rational faculties and feelings that are also possessed by all those who are capable of ordinary experience. Consequently, we are concerned with promoting a capacity whose possession is not restricted to only some subjects. Third, the judgement of taste is exemplary. It is an example or instance of an accord between reason and nature that requires the relation of subjects to each other as subjects. The accord between our reason and feeling which the judgement subtends shows that the animal character of human beings is no longer conflictive. Instead, while remaining subjective, our animal character, our capacity for feeling, participates in a harmonious community with other subjects. These instances may count as proof that we can have a persuasive and universal experience that promotes our humanity generally. For this, the particular judgements are 'exemplary', serving as 'a standard or rule of estimating'.[46] Thereby, they invite comparison with something like 'the idea of humanity (what man ought to be)', which the obligation to culture requires us to attain. Thus, the obligation to culture warrants our particular claims that others should assent to our autonomous, persuasive, and intersubjective judgements.

The necessity of beauty here, then, is the significance it has for our moral and practical lives. This importance warrants us in demanding that we should seek out beauty. Our aesthetic judgements are instances that we claim are universally valid experiences of pleasure and which carry that warrant. This obliges others to try to make the same judgement – to assent to our putative aesthetic claims, in which we are suitors for their agreement, by making the aesthetic judgements for themselves. By acceding to that demand, by trying to make those aesthetic judgements, others will *confirm in judgements* the judgements we make.

Kant's account of necessity can stand more detailing in the following sense. He gives the necessity of beauty – the significance of instances of its occurrence – at least the following refinement. In considering fine art – beautiful art – he produces a hierarchy of these arts. His suggestion is that the different arts make distinctive contributions to cultural development because they embody particular relations between individuals. In other words, he seems to be proposing that we must deepen our understanding of the significance of beauty by considering the character of beautiful objects and the relation between subjects they sustain because these warrant the general demand to seek beauty in particular ways. The main division Kant has here is between fine art and natural beauty, and we may further our understanding of the necessity of beauty by considering the character of beautiful objects and our reasons for giving them significance.

The Interest in Natural Beauty

The significance we give to natural beauty turns on the fact that it is natural. The 'mind cannot reflect on the beauty of *nature* without . . . finding its interest engaged'.[47] Nature satisfies our interest because of the very fact that natural beauty exists. Its every occurrence gives us reason to suppose that nature can be in accord with rationality: that nature 'contains in itself some ground or other for assuming a uniform accordance of its products with our wholly disinterested delight'.[48]

Kant's interest in finding an accord between nature and the free use of reason has to do with the background to the *Critique of Judgement*. He is looking for ways of bridging the gap between a theoretical knowledge of nature and the practical exercise of man's reason in moral behaviour. Although theory and practice have been consigned to different domains, 'still the latter is *meant* to influence the former – that is to say, the concept of freedom is meant to actualize in the sensible world the end proposed by its laws; and nature must consequently also be capable of being regarded in such a way that in the conformity to law of its form it at least harmonizes with the possibility of the ends to be effectuated in it according to the laws of freedom'.[49]

The theoretical understanding of nature seems to leave no room for, and to be incompatible with the need for moral behaviour. According to the conception Kant favours, nature is a mechanism with rules and an order based exclusively on natural causes. The use of categories, which he argued is necessary for us to have experience at all, requires and legitimates explanations according to strict causal determinations. Events in nature are all causally determined, so that explanations of their occurrence need only refer to the causal connections which precede and determine them.

At the same time, the comprehensiveness of Kant's larger theory requires also that we must be free actors and that our moral ends can be realized, or else 'the moral law, which commands that it must be furthered, must be fantastic, directed to empty, imaginary ends, and consequently inherently false'.[50] The moral man must be able to believe that the order of the natural, causally determined world still allows moral ends to be actualized.

For Kant the study of aesthetic judgements is part of this underlying concern. The experience of natural beauty evinces an unsought but real accord of nature with human rational faculties where the free harmony of our faculties is taken to be an end for nature. What seemed to be two incompatible and even antagonistic elements provide evidence of compatibility and harmony. The presence of beauty then shows nature in a new light. In the pleasurable experience of beauty, we think of the object as having an order directed towards the free play of our faculties. We 'apply the term "final" to the object on account of its representations being immediately coupled with the feeling of pleasure. . . . [Aesthetic pleasure expresses] the conformity of the Object to the cognitive faculties brought into play, and hence a subjective formal finality of the Object.'[51] Where the beautiful object is an object of nature, it seems as if nature is directed towards this state of mind: 'susceptibility to pleasure arising from reflection upon the form of things . . . betokens . . . a finality on the part of the objects in their relation to the reflective judgement *in the Subject, in accordance with the concept of nature*'.[52] It indicates a conception of nature that has a regard for subjective ends and involves something other than objective determination according to causal laws alone.

Kant makes the same point about the possibility of a non-causal nature by reference to the faculty of understanding. This faculty, governed by categories, always operates on the basis of causal explanations. By contrast, Kant says, 'self-subsisting natural beauty reveals to us a technic of nature which shows it in the light of a system ordered in accordance with laws the principle of which is not to be found within the range of our entire faculty of understanding'.[53] In supposing nature capable of finality or purposiveness, we find another conception of nature. The principle by which we now order nature 'is that of a finality relative to the employment of judgement in respect of phenomena which have thus to be assigned, not merely to nature regarded as aimless mechanism, but also to nature regarded after the analogy of art. Hence it gives a veritable extension . . . to our conception of nature itself – nature as mere mechanism being enlarged to the conception of nature as art'.[54]

Kant is not claiming that nature is constructed by a deliberate act but that we can conceive of nature not only as a mechanism but also as bearing some design. For methodological reasons we think of nature *as if* it were created by an understanding *like ours for our understanding*.[55] We think of this heuristic device of the idea of God as 'divine wisdom' or as 'nature as the source of purposiveness in the world'.[56] Similarly, in aesthetic judgements, we think of the beautiful natural object as something created. And this creativity – this basis in freedom – lies behind the contrast between nature as mechanism and the nature capable of beauty. The pleasurable judgement of a free and harmonious relation of faculties, which is our experience of beauty, allows us to think of nature as if it had a 'finality apart from any end', as if it were something capable of design and making which is directed towards our aesthetic appreciation, not just a mechanism operating according to causal, determining laws.

The interest in this accord between a nature conceived of as designed and the pleasurable experience of a judgement of taste, and the satisfaction we gain from its occurrence, are not a moral interest or satisfaction. Only action motivated by duty, regardless of any inherent pleasure, can be moral. While the existence of beauty indicates that we may well be able to attain our goals and so is an added incentive to our efforts, it does not ground a moral imperative. Nor are interest and pleasure here merely psychological. Rather the interest in discovering a congruence between nature and rational faculties is 'akin to the moral' and refers to something of existential importance.

> [I]t is a great stimulus to moral effort and a strong support to the human spirit if man can believe that the moral life is something more than a mortal enterprise in which he can join with his fellow men against a blind and indifferent universe until he and the human race are blotted out for ever. Man cannot be indifferent to the possibility that his puny efforts towards moral perfection may, in spite of appearances, be in accord with the purposes of the universe.[57]

The accord of nature and reason in the free harmony of rational faculties is a support to the human spirit, letting man hope that his efforts toward moral perfection will not simply be overthrown by nature. Without justifying the exercise of our will in particular cases, the existence of beauty shows that nature and reason can be coterminal: we may yet act in the hope of achieving moral ends in a world not wholly indifferent to our aspirations.

In making a judgement of taste about an object of nature – in successfully gaining the pleasurable experience of a free and harmonious relation of rational faculties where the harmony is taken to be an end for nature – we gain some indication that the laws of freedom, morality, and the laws of the natural world can cooperate. The natural world appears conducive to the attainment of our ends, and this militates against scepticism about the possibility of morality ever being realized. Our moral disposition thus gains in strength and 'gain[s] a new object for its exercise'.[58] Not only do we gain the pleasure attendant upon the experience of beauty, but because natural beauty evinces the cooperation of nature and human ends, it becomes of existential importance. We are then 'not alone pleased with nature's product in respect of its form, but . . . also pleased at its existence . . .'.[59]

As the beauty of nature carries this significance, Kant can say 'we have reason for presuming the presence of at least the germ of a good moral disposition in the case of a man to whom the beauty of nature is a matter of immediate interest'.[60] 'Disposition' is a technical term Kant uses to describe the grounds for our action. In *Religion within the Bounds of Reason* he explains disposition as 'the ultimate subjective ground of the adoption of maxims'.[61] It is a tendency for choice *underlying* the particular principles of action or maxims we actually adopt, and so is in addition, but closely related to the particular moral rules we follow in any instance. It signifies a tendency we possess individually to adopt one kind of imperative or another. A good disposition is thus the tendency to adopt principles of action or maxims that lead to good, while a bad disposition is the tendency to adopt principles leading to evil. If an interest in natural beauty signifies a good disposition, then, we may expect that is because it supports our moral hopes by showing an interest in actualizing our moral ends in the empirical world. An individual with a bad disposition or an amoral person will be indifferent to the possibility that the existence of natural beauty reveals of actualizing our moral ends.

All this explains why natural beauty is of interest. We have reason to seek out its examples. When we do, we also contribute to the success of particular aesthetic judgements, for we may *confirm in judgement* other subjects' aesthetic claims – providing them more than subjective necessity. However, we must also make clear that a reason for seeking beauty does not determine what if anything we will find beautiful. An interest in natural beauty gives us reason for valuing its instances but does not mean that we will find something beautiful on moral grounds. The interest attaches to beauty; it does not determine what is beautiful.

This means that we ascribe this significance to objects of nature once we find them beautiful. Kant distinguishes the 'disinterested delight' of beauty from the 'interest akin to the moral' associated with the discovery of and concern for beautiful objects of nature. We have an interest akin to the moral in discovering that nature 'contain[s] in itself some ground for assuming a uniform accordance of its products with our disinterested delight'; and although we associate that interest with beautiful objects, it does not determine the pleasure which is our experience of beauty. 'It is not the object that is of immediate interest, but rather the inherent character of the beauty . . . a character . . . that belongs to the very essence of beauty.'[62] The object is not found more beautiful for satisfying an interest. This allows Kant to say that there are two sorts of objects, natural beauty and fine art, each of which generates its own interest, but that 'in the judgement of mere taste [they] could scarcely contend with one another for superiority'.[63] And that raises another issue: we are not to prefer either kind of object over the other for its beauty, so 'what then, is the distinction that makes us hold them in different esteem?'[64]

Certainly, for Kant, fine art cannot have the interest that accrues to natural beauty. He even talks as if the latter has an abiding and absolute superiority. 'The superiority which natural beauty has over that of art . . . [lies in] being alone able to awaken an immediate interest'.[65] Leaving aside issues of the relative superiority of the two kinds of object, Kant argues that fine art cannot have the same interest as natural beauty.

> The fact that the delight in beautiful art does not . . . involve an immediate interest . . . may be readily explained . . . [Art] is either such an imitation of [natural beauty] as goes the length of deceiving us, in which case it acts upon us in the character of a natural beauty, which we take it to be; or else it is an intentional art obviously directed to our delight. In the latter case, however, the delight in the product would, it is true, be brought about immediately by taste, but there would be nothing but a mediate interest in the cause that lay beneath – an interest, namely, in an art only capable of interesting by its end, and never in itself.[66]

This needs further explanation. Like natural beauty, fine art also depends on nature, albeit human nature. This signifies the cooperation between mind and nature, but, for Kant, their interaction in art does not have the cachet that attaches to natural beauty. In both, the relation of mind and nature is contingent: as not any object or product is beautiful, the unity of mind and nature remains serendipitous. But the contingencies of art and nature differ. The contingency of art has to do with whether a particular person produces a beautiful object, not with whether human beings can produce objects at all. We already suppose it possible for people to behave in a purposive manner and to construct objects, because the concept of human nature already incorporates this ability to construct things. By contrast, the contingency of natural beauty turns on the possibility of seeing objects as anything but determined according to causal necessities – whether any object can be seen as a construction at all, and as something directed towards an end which it satisfies. The uncertainty underlying this contingency of natural beauty is that the conception which attributes purposiveness to nature is not the conception used in scientific explanations and may not be possible at all. When we discover examples of purposiveness in natural beauty, when we discover a free cooperation between nature and our rational feelings, then an interest inspiring a feeling akin to the moral is concomitant with the experience of natural beauty and its revelation of a positive interrelation between reason and nature.

In art it is human nature that is active. As we suppose that human beings are capable of rationality and have natural inclinations, their production of a design and evidence of compatibility between nature and the mind do not show human nature in any new light. Sustaining no new reflective conception of the natural order or of the relation between the theoretical understanding of nature and practical reason, art is art. By contrast, the 'sole basis . . . of the interest in natural beauty is that the beauty in question is taken to be *nature's* handiwork'.[67] We construe the beautiful natural object as the *work* of a *nature* formerly thought mechanistic, whose objects were determined by their preceding causes. This is not a conception Kant attributes to *human* nature. 'To say that man [has certain qualities] by nature means but this, that [certain qualities] can be predicated of man as a species.'[68] But this does not set out how things *must* occur and it precludes any systematic account of human nature like that we give of empirical, non-human nature. Moreover, talk of human nature must also take cognizance of 'man as a totality united socially on earth',[69] which is some way beyond man as a biological or natural species.

This is not to say that no necessity of any kind can attach to our understanding of human nature. Given that we understand people to have certain qualities, dispositions, and capacities for action, we can require them to behave in particular ways necessitated by practical reason. Kant supposes human beings are rational and also subject to natural inclinations. The 'proper' relation between them is where the needs of practical reason and moral behaviour condition the satisfaction of natural ends. What we should do may be limited by what we can do by nature, but still we must understand what we can do in the context of moral behaviour and necessity. Natural inclinations appear to be part of moral thinking and are subject to moral necessity. We may discover that a 'moral' requirement is impracticable because of our natural limitations – the requirement never to kill any living creature in order to survive may prove practically untenable; but we cannot discover a natural limitation to cause a moral requirement in the way, say, one object causally affects another. In some cases we may suppress natural inclinations in accordance with moral requirements – we may suppress the desire to eat some fruit because of the way its harvesting puts migrant workers at risk; in other cases we can point to natural inclinations to mark the limits of moral compulsion. But these limitations and suppressions – this interrelation of reason and nature – occur within the context of moral behaviour and practical reason. Thus, the very relation of nature to reason in human nature, which underlies artistic beauty, differs from that underlying natural beauty. It is not surprising then that natural beauty has a significance for *its* relation between reason and nature that artistic beauty does not share on the basis of *its* relation of reason to nature.

Although we do not have the interest in fine art that we have in natural beauty, Kant thinks fine art has its own significance. To explain that, he must first clarify the nature of fine art. This leads Kant to present the notion of genius, which explains how fine art is produced. After that we can examine the importance of fine art itself.

The Case of Fine Art

Kant's conception of genius is comparable to the classical one. Aristotle explains it as the ability to strike upon the middle term of a syllogism.[70] This explanation proposes that we find the result of activity important, not the process. Were someone to strike upon a claim that made no sense it would not, despite its incoherence, become logically valid because it was uttered by a 'genius'. We are justified in describing a product as a matter of genius only when and because it fits an argument, and so satisfies criteria of reason. We will praise a person for his or her genius, then, by extension from assessing the value of their work.

This classical stress on judging the object that is produced rather than the producer is crucial to the account of genius Kant sets out in the *Critique of Judgement*. Genius (1) 'is a talent for producing something for which no determinate rule can be given,. . . . [H]ence the foremost property of genius must be originality. (2) Since nonsense too can be original, the products of genius must be models, i.e. they must be exemplary;. . . . (3) Genius cannot itself describe or indicate scientifically how it brings about its products . . .'.[71]

In saying that no determinate rule can be given for genius's production, I suggest, Kant is turning attention away from any concern with the process of producing works. In a sense, as his third point emphasizes, it does not matter how the work is produced, whether by accident or design, because we judge the product for what it does rather than for how it was produced. The most gifted poets can produce duds, which can be seen to be bad poems; and the relation between a work and its source – the domain of production – is only contingently related to the value of the product. In part, then, genius cannot 'indicate scientifically how it brings about its products' because there is no necessary link between the value of the work and its source. And the absence of that necessary link also explains why there cannot be a rule for producing works of genius. As we lack a necessary link, as the relation of value to source is contingent, there can be an infinitely large array of ways for producing a valuable object. No single determinate rule can be appropriate.

In this context, a rule for producing works of genius could have no function. Kant's emphasis on originality suggests that genius is a matter of producing new rules – ones that are publically assessable and can be followed by the genius as well as by others. But if the nature of genius is to produce a rule, then to ask for a rule for producing a rule will lead to an infinite regress. Moreover, as we assess the value of the product separately from issues about its production, the work is ruptured from its producer in the sense that the author does not have any greater authority in determining the meaning and value of the product than anyone else does. The work constitutes a rule, and the nature of rules is that they are, so to speak, part of the public domain.

In talking of our producing rules Kant is taking a step beyond the strictly classical account of genius. The latter supposes that the rules by which we assess a work are given and have authority. We try to attain them in our works because those standards are valuable. The form of a sonnet, for example, is given once and for all, and serves as a standard which we try to attain in the particular works we create. But by pointing to our production of rules, Kant denies the simple authority of given models, and allows for us to generate new values in producing new objects. By producing new rules we develop new standards and forms of poetry or art, and do not merely seek to fulfil the given standards in newly interesting ways. Nonetheless, Kant does not accede to a romantic rejection of all past forms and standards either. His emphasis on our universalizable experience of pleasure constrains an untramelled production of novel poems, images, and other works by reminding us that we must still warrant them and their value. This warrant is public and universal, just as classicism proposed, and claims a legitimating authority.

In any case, an assumption underlying the claim for genius's production is that we produce a rule rather than something arbitrary or nonsensical. The need to add this qualification emphasises again that the relation between the source and the value of the work is arbitrary. Our concern must be with the latter, which must satisfy rational standards. In the aesthetic case, this means the work must yield an harmonious relation of faculties and its resulting universalizable pleasure. Moreover, as genius is a matter of producing new rules, the work is only a particular example because it will not be followed by others, who produce their own rules, and at best treat the original product as an example of what can be done in devising rules. Of course, because it is aesthetic, our judgement is singular, and the beautiful object serves only as an instance or example of the product of genius for that reason too.[72]

Given this understanding of genius, Kant describes fine art generally as the art of genius. '[E]very art presupposes rules, which serve as the foundation on which a product, if it is to be called artistic, is thought of as possible in the first place.'[73] That production by human nature which we referred to earlier is production by genius.

Earlier we gave a value to natural beauty because it betokens an unexpected interrelation of nature and reason. We might now make a similar argument for the production of fine art. Genius is the element of human nature responsible for fine art, but its occurrence is contingent and serendipitous because not everyone can produce works of genius, and when they do, they produce a harmony between reason and nature. Unfortunately, this will not do. The contingency of genius concerns whether or not a particular product turns out to be a work of genius rather than simply nonsense or merely mediocre. It is not an issue of whether there can be any actors producing works at all. The contingency of natural beauty results from the doubt about whether we can at all conceive of nature and reason as coterminal in the way they are in natural beauty.

If the comparison with natural beauty fails, then we must look elsewhere for the significance of fine art. At the end of the *Critique of Aesthetic Judgement* Kant returns to his systematic concerns. He argues in Section 59 that beauty is a symbol of morality:

> I maintain that the beautiful is the symbol of the morally good; and only because we refer [*Rucksicht*] the beautiful to the morally good (we all do so [*Beziehung*] naturally and require all others to do so as a duty) does our liking for it include a claim to everyone else's assent, while the mind is also conscious of being ennobled, by this [reference], above a mere receptivity for pleasure derived from sense impressions, and it assesses the value of other people too on the basis of [their having] a similar maxim in their power of judgement.[74]

This comparison may be the basis for giving significance to fine art.

The last part of Kant's assertion parallels his claim that an interest in natural beauty shows the possession of a good moral disposition. In the present case too, we assess the value of others in terms of whether and how they respond to beauty: on their having 'a similar maxim in their power of judgement'. Further, 'only when we refer the beautiful to the morally good does our liking, [the universalizable pleasure we feel], . . . include a claim to everyone else's assent', and we gain that reference through beauty symbolizing the morally good.

Kant explains that a symbolic relation between two elements depends on identifying analogies between them.[75] Here the symbolic relation itself cannot yield the necessity of beauty: the morally good bear necessity, but we cannot argue successfully that *because* beauty is analogous to moral good, *therefore* it too will bear that necessity. Instead, for beauty to symbolize moral good, it would already have to bear the significant analogy of being necessary in a relevant way. And Kant affirms that their analogy consists in their having a comparable necessity, holding not only that both moral good and beauty strike us '*directly*' and '*without an interest*', but also that we base both on our capacity for freedom *and* think their principles necessary because universally valid. In other words, their symbolic relation depends on both being necessary; the relation then cannot justify the necessity of beauty.

Instead, I suggest, through the symbolic relation Kant points to the features of beauty which come to the fore when we think of beauty in terms of supporting 'a claim to everyone else's assent' and assessing 'the value of other people too on the basis of [their having] a similar maxim in their power of judgement'. Their interest in beauty, based on given features, shows the quality of people's moral sensibilities. In other words, beauty is significant because those features of it that we emphasize by pointing to its symbolic relation to moral good are the ones which promote culture and moral feeling, thereby helping bring about a moral order in our lives. If fine art exhibits these features, it is significant for these reasons, and we may use that significance to urge other subjects to make the aesthetic judgements which confirm our own claims.

The four points of similarity Kant sets out are: '(1) The Beautiful we like *directly*. . . . (2) We like it *without any interest*. . . . (3) In judging the beautiful, we present the freedom of the imagination (and hence [of] our power [of] sensibility) as harmonizing with the lawfulness of the understanding. . . . (4) We present the subjective principle for judging the beautiful as universal.'[76] The first two points we have dealt with already when considering the defining moments of aesthetic judgements.

We have seen also that Kant denied to fine art the significance we could give to natural beauty because the latter signalled an *unexpected* appearance of freedom in nature. Now Kant stresses the fact of freedom, which he earlier denied to nature, and thereby brings fine art to the fore. First, this freedom occurs through our use of imagination in constructing art. For Kant, 'beauty . . . may in general be termed the *expression* of aesthetic ideas'.[77] In expressing aesthetic ideas 'through the free employment of the imagination . . . a multiplicity of partial representations [is] bound up'. Imagination 'quickens the mind by opening up for it a view into an immense realm of kindred representations'. It 'prompts . . . so much thought as can never be comprehended within a determinate concept, and thereby the presentation aesthetically expands the concept in an unlimited way'. The 'imagination is creative in [all of] this and sets the power of intellectual ideas (i.e. reason) in motion: it makes reason think more . . . than what can be apprehended and made distinct in the presentation'.[78] The 'imagination ([in its role] as a productive cognitive power) is very mighty when it creates, as it were, another nature out of the material that actual nature gives it. . . . We may even restructure experience; . . . [and] in this feel our freedom from the law of association (which attaches to the empirical use of imagination)'. We process 'that material into something quite different, namely, into something that surpasses nature'.[79] Borrowing elements from nature, the imagination relates ideas according to expressive intentions rather than the determinate rules of cognized experience, and so permits a freedom from the restraints of determinate reality.

Expression and imaginative freedom are essential to our construction and reception of beauty. They constitute art objects by 'a production through freedom, i.e. through a power of choice that bases its actions on reason'.[80] This exercise of our free choice in imagination to construct a fine art that suits us is a crucial element in the symbolic relation between moral good and judgements of taste.

Kant repeats this emphasis on freedom in beauty when he says first that poetry is the most valuable of the fine arts because it 'fortifies the mind: for it lets the mind feel its ability – free, spontaneous, and independent of natural determination – to contemplate and judge phenomenal nature as having aspects that nature does not on its own offer in experience either to sense or to the understanding'.[81] This freedom, an essential component of the analogy between beauty and moral good, has as its corollary an independence from nature.

Second, Kant says that 'the mental powers whose combination . . . constitutes *genius* are imagination and understanding'.[82] Given that genius produces fine art, the quotation suggests that freedom is not just a freedom in imagination but also a constructive and real freedom to produce new rules and change the order of things. Fine art as the art of genius presupposes the ability to act on and effect the world. It involves the free exercise of imaginative freedom, which indicates how we would reconstruct nature. Fine art, then, embodies an analogy with the free but rule-governed activity characteristic of moral good. And so far as it cultivates this commerce with our freedom within the constraints of a free play of mind, both by producing objects and through our appreciating of objects in the consciousness that they were produced by human beings, fine art is significant because it promotes moral feeling.[83]

Further, if fine art is significant because of its commerce with a free production, another reason for giving it importance may be found in its capacity for universality. A concept of a cognized object may have a place within a structure of scientific knowledge, natural laws, and causal connections. By contrast, the objects of aesthetic judgements cannot be completely conceptualized because they have associations and meanings beyond their ordinary compass within the system of science. Kant talks of this as the imagination leading the understanding and of language never getting on level terms with the object. His other locutions include his emphasis on indeterminate concepts and giving the object more scope than concepts can grasp. But despite lacking the determinate order of cognitive conceptualization, clearly some measure of conceptualization is essential to our aesthetic judgement and to the universality of the latter. Beauty 'refers the imagination to the understanding *as a faculty of concepts*',[84] presenting associations between concepts that are richer than those of our cognitive judgements. This richness results from our imaginative freedom, but without rendering beauty devoid of concepts altogether. Nor does their indefiniteness make these judgements incapable of universality. Rather, instead of cognitive criteria, we use standards of appropriateness, and measure the meaningfulness of concepts by reference to a structure of subjects' feelings. As we proposed earlier, aesthetic judgements are comprehensive over subjects rather than objects, and their universality consists in treating subjects as rational and feeling subjects like ourselves, all equally capable of making judgements.

Both their freedom and their universality serve the analogy between fine art and moral good that allows a symbolic relation between them. The latter identifies the significance of fine art. As the aesthetic judgement is sufficiently like morality, then our attainment of fine art also supports morality. It gives us an experience in which we consciously construct an order that is sensitive to others as rational and feeling beings like ourselves. Our aesthetic judgements enable us 'to make the transition from sensible charm to a habitual moral interest' because they 'present the imagination as admitting, even in its freedom, of determination that is purposive for the understanding, and it teaches us to like objects of sense freely, even apart from sensible charm'.[85] In doing so, it cultivates moral sensibility, and so allows us to demand an interest in it from other subjects. Their attempt to satisfy such a demand will lead other subjects to make the aesthetic judgements which will give *confirmation in judging* to our own claims.

There are some more important details we must add to this account of the necessities of fine art and natural beauty. When Kant says that beauty is the expression of ideas, he clearly includes both fine art and natural beauty. The text I used from Section 51, has the following parenthesis where I have introduced an ellipsis: '(whether it be of nature or of art)'. This clearly indicates that Kant is writing of beauty generally, not just of fine art, although I used it to defend the parallels between moral good and fine art. Kant's argument must be that both fine art and natural beauty are symbolic of moral good, and so are significant for similar reasons. This does not detract from finding fine art of interest in the way I have just argued, but it suggests that natural beauty must also be significant in a parallel way – in addition to showing the possession of a good moral disposition. However, we may also note that the parallels with moral good which make beauty significant suit fine art better than natural beauty. While objects of fine art are the result of our actions, and so embody our freedom, naturally beautiful objects are only derivatively an expression of our freedom and are 'constructed' only in a sense borrowed from art. While we may talk of it as expressive,[86] in 'the case of beautiful nature, mere reflection on a given intuition, without a concept of what the object is [meant] to be, is sufficient for arousing and communicating the idea *of which* that object *is regarded* as the *expression*'.[87] By themselves empirical natural objects are neither expressive nor free. The natural object is only an occasion for our reflection and communicating an idea. We have to incorporate it into a structure of feelings and meanings that it does not have in nature. Its universality too will be commensurately restricted in comparison with fine art. And in this context, given that fine art is better suited than natural beauty is to the symbolic relation to moral good, any significance we give to beautiful objects because of their symbolic relation to the moral good will make fine art more important than natural beauty. The latter does not lose any of the significance it has from revealing the possession of a good disposition, by this move. Rather it shows that an interest in fine art similarly reveals something about subjects.[88]

Kant develops this relation between fine art and natural beauty without ascribing more or less value to either. Natural beauty has its own importance despite the apparently junior position he gives it in one respect in relation to fine art. In the *Critique of Judgement* Kant wants to explain the compatibility between reason and nature, and searches for a particular balance between them. He proposes that a self-conscious 'social communication' and 'social spirit' are proper to or 'befit' mankind. And while he contrasts this social spirit with our natural animal being, it is not at the expense of extirpating the latter entirely. The balance we gain through this self-conscious social thought cannot 'dispense' with nature, and even if cultural development makes us 'ever more remote' from it, we will never reach a point where its importance disappears. The forms of sociality that grow out of our nature can, in the course of social and cultural development, become more expressly social and less natural, as we replace natural determinations with rational ones. But if this process suppresses our nature completely, we will be left with 'no enduring examples of nature, [and] will hardly be able to form a concept of the happy combination . . . of the law-governed constraint coming from the highest culture with the force and rightness of a free nature that feels its own value'.[89] This will cause us to lose that part of our human nature which is an important source of our activity and creativity. To circumvent this forgetting and retain our creative nature, we look to morality and its relation of nature to reason to remind ourselves of a proper balance between the elements. In aesthetic considerations, by this analogy, we look for the 'mean between higher culture and an undemanding nature constituting the right standard, unstatable in any universal rules, even for taste, which is the universal human sense'.[90]

In this relation, because fine art is concerned with *humaniora* and with 'the ability to engage universally in very intimate *communication'*, it addresses the 'sociability that befits [our] humanity', which distinguishes the latter from the limitation [characteristic] of animals'. The significance of morality here is that it cannot structurally forget its relation to sensibility and nature. But this double determination of an indispensable and insuperable natural basis and the continuing transformation of this by mankind does make the production and development of human social existence into a central concern. It is in mankind and its objects, in its nature and the relationships between subjects, that this dual determination works itself out. In this context, aesthetic activity promotes this exploration because taste is the 'proper' relation of genius to communication, of a purposive nature to rational faculties, of nature to the sociality of mankind.

This dual determination is present in both fine art and natural beauty. In fine art, the aspect of nature is human nature, of which genius is a function. It implies freedom and creativity in expression, universality, and in the production of works. In natural beauty the balance is between reason and a nature to which we ascribe purposiveness and construction through analogy with art. The mean between nature and reason here shows nature is cooperative with reason and conducive to the universalizable pleasure which serves as an end. While we value natural objects for their part in this balance, it is a value that depends on our looking at nature in a particular way. Nature's purposiveness – its appearance of a regard for human ends – is *only the result of our thinking of the object in this way*.[91] The actual order of nature is according to causal connections.

Through the analogy with morality and its relation between nature and reason we can understand the relation between fine art and natural beauty. In moral goodness, reason serves as the 'unconditioned and unqualified' value. It determines the relation between itself and nature as the senior partner. If we take this to apply to natural and artistic beauty, then the seniority of reason leads us to accept that the two kinds of beauty are not identical or capable of being homogenized. They are both part of our aesthetic activity. However, we may also say that natural beauty exhibits the purposiveness of nature, showing that it is compatible with reason and can invite an immediate interest capable of supporting moral feeling. Natural beauty participates from the side of nature, so to speak, exploring how far nature can enter into relation with reason. In this sense, fine art participates from the side of reason, exhibiting the extent to which it is compatible with nature and our capacity for feeling. The social spirit of mankind arises out of a natural being in the course of developing social practice. This growth is a process that begins with creative projects and purposes, for which there must be scope in nature. There is no analogy for creativity in mechanistic nature, though we may discover one through a teleological conception of nature. This in turn depends on an analogy with art and on ascribing to nature properties it does not have.

Arguably, their relation to reason and nature conditions the relation between fine art and natural beauty: our experience of fine art conditions our regard for natural beauty. The interest in natural beauty arises from nature presenting itself as having a regard for mankind and its rational ends. Nature is valued here only because it is like art: 'the direct interest we take in [natural] beauty is based on [this] thought *alone*': that the beauty *'was produced by nature'*.[92] Fine art, by contrast, has a basis in nature but is also part of the development of reason which we examined in culture. Like the relation between reason and nature in moral good, taste provides in culture a constant and moderate discipline of our inclinations and our relation to nature. By a continuous cultural labour and growth, the firm resolve to do one's duty becomes a habit as we progressively free ourselves from the arbitrariness of nature. We promote the 'predisposition to good in human nature', especially those characteristics which are the 'aesthetic receptiveness to the concept of beauty'.[93] And our cultural experience and responses to art circumscribe our approach to natural beauty and its exploration of nature's capacity for reason. While we find both valuable, and would not mix them together,[94] one is valued without conditions and the other insofar as it is consistent with pursuit of the first. Our response to nature is conditioned by the demands of reason and the exercise of creativity. Artistic beauty is the unconditioned and unqualified development that is truly the result of a free autonomous and creative will. The limitations it accepts are those necessary to communication and rationality. Natural beauty is the conditioned and qualified development, determined by the demands of fine art, whose criteria of creativity and expression it satisfies only by being ascribed them externally. At the basis of fine art there lies a rational and active will that natural beauty only acquires by analogy.

In an important sense, neither fine art nor natural beauty has precedence over the other because they have distinctive values which Kant does not wish to mix. Both have significance for supporting moral aspirations and endeavours, though they do so in distinctive ways. But in another sense, fine art has precedence because of its better constitution of our freedom and its positive exploration of our rational and communal character. Natural beauty examines at best the relation between nature and reason to see how far nature makes space for reason. That is important but less so than the exploration of our capacity for morality and humanity. And in any case, its exploration is conditioned by art and fine art.

Natural Beauty and Fine Art, New Criticism, and Formalism

Part of the difficulty in clarifying the necessity of and interest in beauty is the way critics have conflated Kant's distinction between fine art and natural beauty with one between pure and dependent beauty.[95] They then use this conflation to condemn the fine art, saying that it must be inferior to natural beauty.[96]

Kant's theory has implications for the relation between fine art and natural beauty, as we have just seen, but he does not use it systematically in relation to the distinction between pure and impure judgements. The critics' conflation is not obviously present in his writing. To begin with we may clarify that Kant uses 'nature' in a number of ways: one is as a technical term to signify any object of our experience.[97] This use includes fine art as well as natural beauty, so far as these are objects of judgement, and appears in his examination of aesthetic judgements generally. A second use of nature is as the object of determinate judgements, that we place in a causal nexus within the system of scientific knowledge, to explain the character and behaviour of objects. This second sense excludes fine art so far as the latter concerns a meaningful object that results from human action rather than simply from the operation of objective natural forces.

Now, some critics have argued that because fine art cannot be produced naively, it can never be 'pure'. Art always involves an intention,[98] for to identify an object as art, we must see it as the product of some human agency; but to see it as the result of some agency is to identify it as the attainment of some intention. Therefore, we cannot identify an object as art unless we describe it in terms of the intention that determined its construction: unless we identify it under some description. But such a description clearly intrudes concepts and objective considerations, so that to see an object as art – or by extension, when we see it as fine art – we judge the object under some description, and so the aesthetic judgement on the object cannot be purely aesthetic if we see it as a work of art. Fine art, then, must always be dependent, it seems. By contrast, it is maintained, we can judge objects of natural beauty without recourse to explanations of their genesis or to descriptions of their nature. Therefore they are capable of being objects of pure judgements of taste. They also have a kind of priority over fine art because they sustain or are appropriate to pure aesthetic judgements.

Natural beauty is assigned priority for other reasons also, but we may begin to assess the above developments of Kant's theory by considering the proposed acclamation of natural beauty and its commensurate derogation of fine art. It is not clear that such evaluations can succeed. If we must depend on some description in order to identify an object as art, and if we thereby vitiate claims to purity for fine art, then surely that also precludes us from affirming objects as cases of natural beauty. For just as we must identify an object as fine art by applying *some* concept, similarly we must identify an object as a case of *natural* beauty by applying some concept, and must thereby bring in considerations of the object, its nature, and causal determinations. A judgement of natural beauty too must identify its natural object, and if this needs concepts, then natural beauty too is interested. What distinguishes nature from art is the genesis of the object, and to identify either we must refer to these ways of bringing the object into existence. Consequently, if we cannot identify an object as beautiful *and* a work of art, similarly we cannot identify an object as beautiful *and* an object of nature.

Moreover, it is clear from the examples Kant cites that purity is not restricted to either fine art or natural beauty. Thus, not only are fine art and natural beauty not given priority over each other on the grounds of the dependence of the first and the purity of the latter, but it seems also that fine art is not simply a matter of being dependent beauty only. Kant writes that 'many birds . . . and a lot of crustaceans in the sea are [free] beauties themselves [and] belong to no object determined by concepts as to its purpose, but we like them freely and on their own account. Thus, designs *à la grecque*, the foliage or borders on wallpaper, etc., are free beauties. What we call fantasias in music (namely music without a topic [*Thema*]), indeed all music not set to words, may also be included in the same class'.[99] But these latter are all fine art, constructed by us rather than born of nature alone.

Kant suggests that these objects are pure because they do not have any intrinsic meaning; 'they represent nothing, no object under a determinate concept'.[100] For beauty to be pure and free, the objects involved should mean nothing on their own, and so should not possess a meaning which they import into the judgement by their very presence. To examine an object for itself, we look at the relation between its parts, their balances, the tones, textures, and tactile qualities it has, the particular usages of words, colours, and sounds it contains, the coherence and unity of its elements. All these are capable of being grasped and appreciated without construing these elements in terms of any extraneous purpose they might serve. We may argue from there that the meanings of objects come from their place in a work or from the judgement upon them. Thus, even an imported intrinsic meaning

– say a stereotype of weakness and fragility brought in by giving a woman a particular role in a play – must be legitimated by the order and events in the work if that work is to possess a pure beauty.

We can multiply such examples and explanations without damaging Kant's notion of pure beauty or restricting purity to natural beauty. The distinction between free or pure beauty and dependent beauty, then, does not coincide with that between natural beauty and fine art, for free beauty includes both kinds of objects. Instead, as Kant makes clear in the title of Section 16 and in his positive explanation, dependent judgements use determinate concepts. Pure judgements of taste include both fine art and natural beauty, and so do not exclude our identifying the intent or nature of the object. What they exclude is perfection, purpose or extrinsic meaning. Pure judgements 'are based on no perfection of any kind, no intrinsic purposiveness to which the combination of the manifold might refer'. Or, the judgement must be on objects that 'mean nothing on their own; they represent [*vorstellen*] nothing, no object under a *determinate* concept'.[101] We cannot consider a beautiful object in terms of its perfection or its appropriateness to some conception we have of objects of its kind, but that does not exclude identifying it as a work of art or nature.

By this account, we might even see objects as churches, horses, or buildings, or as representations of these, and then find them beautiful so long as we do not suppose that the object is beautiful or ugly *because* it is a church, horse, or building. If our conception of churches is that they must have large crosses raised on high steeples, and we fail to find a building beautiful because it is a church yet fails to have a large high cross, then we should be determining our pure aesthetic judging by an extrinsic concept or meaning. Similarly, if we find a portrait of a soldier less than aesthetically valuable because her uniform is considered incomplete or improper or because the portrait shows her dishevelled in some unmilitary fashion, then again our judgement would be impure because beauty and our liking would be determined by extraneous factors. By bringing in 'intrinsic purposiveness' we introduce into aesthetic judgements considerations native to objects and events in their prosaic life and context – we insist on applying determinate concepts to the object regardless of the meaning or significance it gains from being the object of an aesthetic judgement. But none of these matters exclude fine art from being pure, for the judgement on a church, building, or portrait can be made without bringing in determinate concepts in the way set out earlier.

Kant exhibits other complexities in this account of pure judgement, showing that the indeterminate concepts which enter into aesthetic judgements on works of art do not prevent us from finding the latter beautiful. One such occasion is his explanation why aesthetic judgements are not capable of proof. He argues that a subject may 'mold his taste, familiarising himself with a sufficient number of objects of a certain kind', even though 'the fact that others have liked something can never serve him as a basis for an aesthetic judgement'.[102] The subject may 'clarify by examples'[103] what is significant in any work, comparing it with others to exhibit its particular qualities and meanings. A tradition may be formed here, without generating sufficient and necessary rules, and so without determining aesthetic judgements by concepts. Indeed, 'if each subject always had to start from nothing but the crude predispositions given him by nature, [many] of his attempts would fail, if other people before him had not failed in their's'.[104] But following such a tradition, with all it implies about the social and cultural background of both the subject and the work, the relation of the work to others, and so on, does not make our judgements any less free and pure.

As Kant makes clear, our expectation of subjects is that '[f]ollowing by reference to a precedent, rather than imitating, is the right term for any influence that products of an exemplary author may have on others'.[105] Following is a matter of the subject making his *own* judgements on the basis of sensitivity to various factors, whereas imitation does not carry any connotations of any independent judgement by the subject. In following, subjects use other examples as models, but make their own judgements, presumably using the models as guidelines in their own absorption and ordering of the tradition in making an independent judgement. The subject draws 'on the same sources from which the predecessor himself drew, and learn[s] from him only how to go about doing so'. And just because he uses others as models but still makes an autonomous judgement, his judgement remains aesthetic and free. For as a model, and by using examples, and itself being exemplary, the aesthetic judgement can bring in all the factors of social and political background, the place of the work in the history of arts, the intentions of the artist, and so on, without deriving conclusions about the validity of his judgement from any of these factors. At best he follows these factors in understanding how they serve to structure the work in question, but still he makes his own judgement on the basis of what is present in the work. Thus, this work continues to be the focus of his attention, and his judgement on the work will be about the meaning, order and significance of the parts of the work, and so will consider the work for itself, clarifying it by reference to the background yet without thereby making the judgement a dependent one.

A consequence of these reflections is that we cannot see Kant as a New Critic.[106] For as we see he does not intend to exclude such factors as meaning, history, background, and so on from the judgement of taste. We might suggest that if New Criticism takes its inspiration from Kant, it does so by over-emphasizing a particular conception of Kant's notion of disinterestedness. By that account, only foliages, designs *à la grecque*, etc. would satisfy the requirement of disinterestedness, and even that could only be because we did not consider them as meaningful, neither as fine art nor as natural beauty.

Another consequence aestheticians have found in Kant's purported preference for pure beauty is that it implies 'formalism'. Kant writes that the 'form of objects of the senses . . . is either *shape* or *play*', so that *design* or *composition* 'constitute the proper objects of a pure judgement of taste',[107] and later claims that where we 'judge free beauty (according to mere form) then our judgement is pure'.[108] These passages may suggest that Kant thinks of form in austere sensate terms and that free beauty excludes all concepts, whether these are determinate or indeterminate. Pure judgements of free beauty depend on only the composition and design of what we perceive through the senses.

However, Kant's analyses provide a very meagre basis for a major theoretical claim like formalism. First, to construe form in sensate terms, the formalist must apply Kant's conclusions about design and composition outside their context. Kant's argument is against the proposal that 'pure' sensations are proper objects of aesthetic judgements. He emphasizes that sensate experience must be ordered in space and time, so that we may speak of the latter's spatial or temporal form. We develop this form in shape and play, which are capable of design and composition. Because the latter depends on an *a priori* order the mind must have, it claims universal communicability. But this contrasts with mere sensation which, no matter how pure it is, is not a part of that form. Thus, Kant's concern with the senses, and the vocabulary he develops here, deal with the validity claimed by 'pure' sensation; and he argues that the latter lacks *a priori* validity and so cannot be confused with a judgement of taste. The argument does not warrant a general formalist theory.

Second, in the discussion of pure judgements at Section 16 Kant again rejects the rationalist association of beauty with perfection, which proposes an ideal for objects. Kant maintains that 'no concept of any purpose . . . and hence no concept [as to] what the object is [meant] to represent' such as its ideal state, determines a pure judgement of taste.[109] We neither find objects beautiful or ugly for their perfection nor suppose there is some *ideal* or perfect beauty. Any such determination of beauty by concepts of an ideal type would make it interested. However, in no case in all these arguments does Kant exclude indeterminate concepts.

Third, Kant later sets out an acceptable notion of 'form', which turns out to include indeterminate concepts. He writes of the arts of speech, vision, and the play of sensation, where the first includes poetry and its *'play* with ideas'. Artists make this play communicable by giving a form, where the ideas are in play yet in harmony. Similarly in the visual arts, where artists construct figures in space to *express* ideas. In none of these cases are ideas merely a redundant content, for the figures and their harmony embody ideas. The shapes and order depend on and thereby express these ideas.[110] And as we saw, we gained these by adding to concepts a subjective resonance that they did not possess in their objective uses. In other words, Kant is not a formalist.

7

The Context of Kant's Aesthetic Theory

So far we have examined Kant's aesthetic theory. To make fuller sense of its thrust, we would do well to relate it to Kant's deeper concerns about reason, freedom, nature and humankind.

In the *Critique of Judgement* Kant wants to explain the possibility of nature's relation to reason and freedom. We saw some aspects of their interrelation in our discussion of interest in natural beauty, and shall consider it further in this chapter.

Aesthetics and Morality: Freedom and Nature

As we explained in the first chapter, in the *Critique of Pure Reason* Kant argues that our experience must be constituted of causal determinations. His arguments are intended to establish that every event in our experience will be causal. They legitimate the application of causality to our experience, and ensure that our search for causal relations is not pointless. But they do not tell us which particular causes we will discover in our actual experience of nature. As Kant reminds us, '[s]pecial laws, as concerning those experiences which are empirically determined, cannot in their specific character be derived from the categories, although they are one and all subject to them. To obtain any knowledge at all of these special laws, we must resort to experience'.[1] The argument of the Transcendental Deduction of the *Critique of Pure Reason* only shows that nature in general is grounded in causality. To discover actual instances of causes we must examine contingent experience.

Kant suggests this distinction between the categories, which establish that all experience must be causal, and actual contingent experience as early as the Introduction to the *Critique of Pure Reason*. He writes of our need to appeal to experience, and reminds us that this appeal presupposes the categories. In empirical 'judgements, I must have besides the concept of the subject something else (X), upon which the understanding may rely if it is to know that a predicate, not contained in this concept, nevertheless belongs to it'. This X is the 'complete experience of the object which I think through the concept', and it depends on the categorical system. The latter, which we must first 'mark out', he proposes, 'forms a genus by itself . . . in a system, with completeness according to its original sources'.[2] However, to 'advance into the limitless field of knowledge *yielded* by pure understanding',[3] we need something more than just the categories themselves. That knowledge and experience needs its own standards. He argues that we need to find a systematic unity for that actual experience too, to give it a lawlikeness and necessity that parallels the systematic necessity exhibited by the underlying system of categories. 'The law of reason which requires us to seek for this unity' of a system of our empirical knowledge and experience, 'is a necessary law, since without it we should have no reason at all, and without reason no coherent employment of the understanding, and in the absence of this no sufficient criterion of empirical truth'.[4]

From the above, we may understand that for Kant a full account of any experience must satisfy two considerations. The first requires us to use concepts of an objective world in order to have experience at all. The second holds that we are interested ultimately in providing a coherent body of empirical knowledge within which we place an event and thereby explain it. Kant writes that '[s]ystematic unity is what first raises ordinary knowledge to the role of science, i.e., makes a system out of a mere aggregate of knowledge'.[5] The task of science is to discover the causal nature of the world in systematic detail by carrying out an empirical investigation of the natural causal laws that structure our experience of objects and events. In other words, this yields a conception of nature as determined and ordered according to the causal relations between objects.

However, given that scientific knowledge establishes the determinate causal order of events governed by natural laws, there does not seem to be any room for freedom *in* this determinate system. As we usually contrast the external compulsion of causal relations with the capacity for choice possessed by the spontaneous and free will, if we argue that all our experience must be causally determined and ordered into a system of science, there does not seem to be any occasion which can exhibit the exercise of our free will. If every event is causally determined, then we cannot see any event as an exercise of free will.

Unfortunately, the absence of freedom within the systematic order given to our causally determinate experience raises problems for the coherence of Kant's philosophical claims. If determinate experience excludes freedom, then the claims of morality become vacuous because they presuppose our freedom. If we are determined, then we cannot be free; consequently, we cannot be held responsible for actions, and so can never be morally culpable.

Kant explains this point in the following terms. He understands the validity of causal and moral laws in terms of legislation. Where we accept the validity of causal explanations, we suppose that it is legitimate for us to order events and objects according to the causal compulsions operating on them. In other words, causal principles legislate over these events and objects. The latter, then, form the territory over which causal principles have authority. In a parallel way, when we accept moral imperatives, we accept their validity or power to compel us. We think that they are legitimate and so allow that they can legislate over us. The area or domain where their compulsion is valid, the events and objects – the actions and persons – they govern, is their territory.

Using these terms, Kant explains in the Introduction that

> our cognitive power as a whole has two domains, that of the concepts of nature and that of the concept of freedom, because it legislates a priori by means of both kinds of concept. Now philosophy too divides, according to these legislations, into theoretical and practical. And yet the territory on which its [philosophy's] domain is set up and on which it *exercises* its legislation is still always confined to the sum total of all possible experience, insofar as they are considered nothing more than mere appearances, since otherwise it would be inconceivable that the understanding could legislate with regard to them.[6]

The legislative power of practical reason is made up of the moral rules we establish through the supreme principle of morality. And Kant is suggesting that whatever the validity of these rules, they must have application in our ordinary experience. The latter is the territory over which both practical reason *and* our theoretical or scientific understanding claim validity. Yet the former presupposes we are free, whereas for the latter our knowledge is constituted by the causal determinations of natural objects and events, and so cannot suppose that as objects in nature we are free.

Previously Kant had tried to reconcile the competing demands of freedom and causality by saying, in effect, that we could think of ourselves from two different viewpoints, even if we cannot actually take up both viewpoints points simultaneously, when examining human behaviour.[7] We could grasp the same event by using two languages, one consistent with causal explanations and the other with assumptions about our freedom. The two vocabularies, he suggests, are incommensurable with each other, in that we do not know how to translate the terms of one into those of the other. Each has its own rules, which are internally consistent and coherent. Consequently, the use of one to make claims does not contradict claims made in the other. For such conflict to occur, we must use the same vocabulary to articulate the nature of the dissonance. For example, because we think that freedom and natural causality are mutually opposed concepts, we expect their use to describe an event can lead to contradictory accounts of that event. But Kant is advocating a position where freedom and natural causality are not mutually opposed: he is asking us to reassess our use of the concepts and to recognise that they actually belong to different languages and their use in those languages is governed by different sets of rules. We cannot then expect to translate from the one language, of freedom, into the other, of causal determination, and so cannot generate a contradiction. Instead, we may continue to use both because they are incommensurable, although in doing so we must consistently use the appropriate rules.

Unfortunately, this kind of distinction did little to solve the problem that both were supposedly exercised in the same arena of our experience, and so, we may expect, required translation into the appropriate vocabulary. In a later text, the *Critique of Practical Reason*, Kant made another proposal to try to overcome the difficulty. This was the more radical claim, that although we could not suppose that our free agency intervenes at the required moments into the series of natural events, we still have reason to believe that the latter is always subject to the freedom of our wills, even at the moments when nature seems least tractable to free will.[8] However, leaving aside the plausibility of this claim, this still will not account for the most important factor in the problematic relation between reason and nature: that we must have some way of identifying certain events in our experience as the results of human action, even if we may also see them as natural and causally determined. Unless Kant can explain how nature allows for this, we cannot make full sense of experience as the legislative territory of practical reason in which we ascribe blame and praise. All we will have is a general sense that any causal description will fit under one based on freedom and reason, but no clear sense of why this event is a particular action and is praiseworthy.

For example, we may describe a particular event as a culpable action even though we can also explain its occurrence by reference to causal determinations. We can do this because we suppose generally that whatever the causal determination and description of the event, it will always be possible to grasp it with the vocabulary of free will and moral responsibility. So *any* causal explanation of an event may be subject to some reinterpretation in moral terms. But this licence surely leads to arbitrariness unless we have some constraints on the kind of considerations that lead us to redescribe a causally determined event as one subject to moral terms. And if there are such constraints, then not any event may be redescribed in the relevant way, and we have some account of how we can translate from the language of freedom to the language of natural causes. But if we have that, then we can generate a contradiction between the two. The only reason why the position of the *Critique of Practical Reason* was an advance on the position of the First *Critique* was that it added to the thesis of incommensurability a claim about the priority of the language of freedom. But unless that priority is spelled out, it becomes arbitrary to descriptions using the language of natural causes, and so offers no rules for the use of the language of freedom to redescribe naturally caused events.

What we need, we may suggest, is some way of showing how the language of natural causes allows for talk of freedom. Until we gain that, as Kant says, 'an immense gulf is fixed between the domain of the concept of nature . . . and the domain of the concept of freedom . . . so that no transition' from the one to the other is possible, 'just as if they were two different worlds, the first of which cannot have any influence on the second'.[9] In other words, we would have to revert to the claim about their incommensurability. But where this 'immense gulf' occurs, practical reason, the laws of morality, also lose their power. For if we cannot say of any event that it was free, we cannot think of it in terms of agents and their responsibility. 'Yet', Kant says, 'the [concept of freedom] *is* to have an influence on the [domain of the concept of nature], i.e. the concept of freedom is to actualize in the world of sense the purpose enjoined by its laws'.[10] This must be true if we are to take morality seriously. 'For no law of reason can command [us to pursue] a final purpose unless reason also promises [*verprechen*], even if not with certainty, that this final purpose is achievable, and hence also justifies us in assenting to the conditions under which alone our reason can conceive of that achievability.'[11] Kant repeats this *caveat* in the main text. Having clarified that the problem occurs because of an incommensurability between our theoretical knowledge of nature and our practical, free and rational activity, he writes that 'reason cannot command us to pursue a purpose that we cognize as being nothing but a chimera'.[12] If we have no room for actions in the causal determinations of nature, then moral demands remain a chimera, even if we can argue at some etiolated level of abstraction that all theoretical nature must be subject to the freedom of the will. For unless we can specify the moral duty in terms of our experience and action, it lacks any real link with the possibility of our actions in the single experiential territory in which we live and, apparently, are caused.

Kant also clarifies that the general argument will not do by distinguishing between the ideas of practical reason. Those ideas of pure reason consisted of freedom, God and immortality of the soul. Strictly, the last two were practical postulates – propositions we had to accept in order to make our moral notions coherent. We could not prove theoretically that God existed or that the soul was immortal, he argued in the *Critique of Practical Reason*, but without these suppositions his moral theory would be compromised.[13] If we did not believe that God gave us the holiness towards which we strive, we would not fulfil our ethical duties. There would be no reason to suppose that fulfilling them would lead to a moral state, and consequently no plausibility in their compulsion. The coherence and, ultimately, plausibility of the moral enterprise depended on these practical postulates, which we could not prove but which were practically necessary.

Freedom differs somewhat from the other ideas in that it is not so much a practical postulate as a presupposition of morality: if we are culpable, it is because we have the ability to choose our actions and so are responsible for them. Despite this difference between freedom and the other moral ideas, however, all three ideas of pure reason have their basis in practical reason and not in the realm of our theoretical knowledge of nature. But towards the end of the *Critique of Judgement* Kant adds another distinction between the three ideas, and contends that freedom is the only concept of the three 'which (by means of the causality that we think in it) proves in nature that it has objective reality, by the effects in can produce in it. It is this that makes it possible to connect the other two ideas with nature . . . .'.[14] And as this claim comes at the end of the *Critique of Judgement*, it suggests that Kant thinks he has shown in the book that determinate nature must allow for the possibility of our free actions – of events in nature which are caused by the operation of our will.

We may set out briefly, as the occasion allows, how Kant thinks he has replied to the general difficulty of finding room in our actual experience for freedom and its exercise. He does this through his analysis of teleological judgements. These allow us to see objects not as determined by the causes and events preceding them but as having an order arising from the object as an end. It is as if the concept of the object brings together its parts. The behaviour and order of parts then depends not on the causes which precede it but on the end – the object – that they go to construct. It is as if nature works to achieve particular ends rather than being determined by preceding causes.

In his consideration of teleological judgements, Kant also proposes the need for and irreducibility of events understood as purposes rather than the result of causes. He sets out the ground of this claim in earlier sections and can say, at the end of Section 78, that 'we are to explain all products and events of nature, even the most purposive ones, in mechanical terms as far as we possibly can (we cannot tell what are the limits of our ability for this way of investigating)'.[15] The most fundamental explanations are in terms of causes, which constitute our experience. However, he adds a significant *caveat*: in providing such explanations 'we are never to lose sight of the fact that, as regards those natural products that we cannot even begin to investigate except under the concept of a purpose of reason, the essential character of our reason will still force us to subordinate such products ultimately, regardless of those mechanical causes, to the causality in terms of purposes'.[16] In some cases our explanations cannot even begin to get off the ground unless we identify the object we want to explain as the result of a rational act. Explanations in causal terms cannot be substituted for our explanation of the event in terms of reason or the 'causality of purposes', then, because the event makes sense as an event or object of explanation only when we think of it as the result of purposes – when we think of it as an action. If we failed to identify it in terms of a 'purpose of reason', then causal explanations could not begin to be attached to the event because there will not be an event there in the first place. Only thinking in terms of reason and purpose makes an object available; we may seek causal explanations for it, but the latter will never be able to substitute fully for the former because their very appropriateness and possibility depend on thinking of it as the result of reason.

Kant also suggests, first, that a mark of rational ends is their contingency 'in terms of all empirical laws'.[17] The 'very contingency of the thing's form is the basis for regarding the product as if it had come about through a causality that only reason can have. Such a causality would be the ability to act according to purposes (i.e. a will), and in presenting an object as possible only through such an ability we would be presenting it as possible only as a purpose'.[18] The object would have a unity which 'is possible only in reason' and not by any non-rational cause. For example, seeing a hexagon in the sand, it would seem to the subject that 'although this effect [the figure] can be considered a purpose, it cannot be considered a natural purpose, but can be considered only a product of art (*vestigium hominis video*)'.[19]

Second, he distinguishes events that result from human actions from organisms by saying that the latter are both cause and effect of themselves. Trees generate other trees like themselves, and human beings too, like other biological creatures, produce their own like, as much as they were produced by their own like.[20] By contrast, actions and events that result from human actions are not 'physical ends': the latter is an object that is '*both cause and effect of itself*'.[21] Instead, in the case of actions and human products, the object can only be understood as the result of some external force: reason. The object is contingent according to natural laws.

Both natural beauty and fine art are made possible by teleological judgement. The latter allows us to see objects as art – as the product of a ratiocinative human willing rather than as the effect of determinate causes – and thence as fine art when these products satisfy our judgements of taste. Similarly, '[b]eauty in nature may rightly be called an analogue of art, since we attribute it to objects only in relation to our reflection on our external intuition of them, and hence only on account of the form of their surface'.[22] Without the validity of judgements that allow us to see objects as ends, we would not be able to see natural objects as organized to suit a harmonious relation of faculties – which is our judgement of taste – and so could not gain natural beauty.

By this account, then, teleological judgements and our ability to see objects and events as the result of rational human activity allows us to bridge the gulf between freedom and nature.[23] Fine art and natural beauty are made possible because that gap is overcome. In the case of fine art, we can now describe objects in nature as the result of human actions, and therefore can see some beautiful objects as produced by humankind. In the case of natural beauty, first, teleology allows us to see our knowledge of nature as a system of science. This means that we can identify the object, as a particular or kind in nature, because we can give it a determinate place within the causal nexus of the system of scientific explanation, and thereby identify its character as a natural object. Second, teleology allows us to conceive of natural objects as directed towards our disinterested and universalizable delight. When we feel the pleasure of judgements of taste on these natural objects, we take this to be an experience of natural beauty. For these reasons, fine art and natural beauty embody that bridging of the gulf between reason and nature.[24]

However, these aesthetic objects embody that bridging in ways distinctive from, say, morality. The most important distinction is that fine art and natural beauty are a part of our cultural development, which includes cultivation of our moral sensibility. The 'fine art[s] and the sciences, which involve a universally communicable pleasure as well as elegance and refinement, . . . through these . . . make man, not indeed morally [*sittlich*] better for [life in society], but still civilized [*gesittet*] for it'.[25] This cultural development promotes our capacity for behaving rationally rather than following our natural inclinations. Without saying that we should extirpate the latter, Kant insists that we should encourage those features of our natural being that are universalizable because this prepares us to act morally.[26]

We have already considered the details of the contribution fine art and beauty make to culture. As they are particular objects of beauty, the contribution they make *as* fine art and as natural beauty are part of the contribution that beauty makes to culture. The analysis we presented in earlier chapters suggested that Kant has a complex account of the contribution of aesthetics to culture and the conditions for morality. And we may complicate this conception further by developing some more details of beauty in culture.

The last chapters have shown that Kant puts forward an open-ended, active and participatory conception of beauty. This appears in many guises. The aspect of subjects' participation appears in Kant's explanations of universality. The latter is one of the defining characteristics of judgements of taste, and demands a Moment for itself. But Kant makes clear, as the text develops, that this is not a homogeneous and undifferentiated kind of wholeness. That it is a comprehensiveness over subjects rather than implying character-istic of objects, already announces part of its distinctiveness. Kant's theory suggests that the nature of the universality of aesthetic judgements emerges as they deepen the relation between subjects, exploring the details of their complex and changing community.

In the *Critique of Judgement* Kant signifies this substantive univer-sality through the maxims of the *sensus communis*. These are '(1) to think for oneself; (2) to think from the viewpoint of everyone else; and (3) to always think consistently'.[27] The first requires us to set aside our prejudices and habits, which we gain from external influences, and to judge things for ourselves, using our own capacity for reason. Given our orientation in reason, we shall not simply follow what others have said, nor give authority to anyone else. We retain our ability to legitimate aesthetic judgements through giving our 'agreement [as] free citizens, of whom each one must be permitted to express, without let or hindrance, his objec-tion or even his veto'.[28]

The second maxim balances this stress on the individual's power with the need to 'override[] the private subjective conditions of his judgement, . . . and reflect[] on his own judgement from a *univer-sal standpoint* (which he can determine only by transferring himself to the standpoint of others)'.[29] This maxim seems to allow that 'ability to engage universally in very intimate *communication*' which Kant explains as a part of 'the universal feeling of sympathy'[30] and associates with beauty. The need for a universal standpoint and for transferring ourselves to the standpoint of others suggests a *caveat* against any attempt to read Kant as condoning the feeling of sympathy that empiricists like Hume identified as the basis for society. While Kant's notion of sympathy is subjective, it is not an identification of ourselves with others, as a feeling of empathy. The latter, arguably, is a matter of projecting our own feelings on to another, and is therefore not an escape from our subjectivity.

We do not here transfer ourselves to the standpoint of others so much as extend our own standpoint to include others, seeing them as like ourselves in their subjectivity. Our assumption is that we have the same physiology, and therefore our feelings must have the same character. Consequently, we are just to others when we extend our understanding of ourselves and our natural judgement and feeling on to them. Kant's talk of sympathy and transferring ourselves to the viewpoint of others seems to ask for a step beyond extending our subjectivity to others, and so merely thinking of them as ourselves, to thinking of others as subjects capable of having their own understanding and structure of feelings. Only this sense of sympathy both allows for others as other subjectivities, with their own concerns, desires, and orders of preference, and also suits the first maxim of the *sensus communis*, that we must *all* think for ourselves, even those other subjects.

In this context, Kant's talk of 'intimate *communication*' affirms a reference to independent subjects and their particular subjectivities. Successful communication takes place between two or more participating individuals, by Kant's account, and is not simply a matter of one active agent talking to a passive one. It depends on a mutual recognition of the other as a separate, autonomous, and thinking agent with something to say, and requires agents to 'override[] the subjective conditions of their judgement'. The universality involved here, then, is a substantive one – an exercise in discovering actual present subjectivities with whom we communicate.

These two maxims are necessary for the third and most important one, which enjoins us to 'a *consistent* way of thinking'.[31] Kant says that it is 'the hardest to attain and in fact can be attained only after repeated compliance when a combination of the first two has become a skill'.[32] Although he talks of it as if it were a psychological practice, like all other thought experiments, this one too has a more stringent role to play, suggesting that the need for consistency governs our pursuit of the other two maxims. This is a double-edged claim: for consistency must provide rules for these activities as they are. By this account, then, Kant's requirement of consistency is not merely a striving for logical consistency, nor simply a demand for the coherence of each individual's own behaviour, nor simply a striving for comprehensiveness over subjects. It is all of these but in the particular conditions of our actual existence, where people think particular thoughts for themselves in relation to others as they are at any historical and social point. We relate our judgement to others' in our present community in the consciousness that this activity is not monolithic but a creative grasping capable of change. We seek consistency because it provides us with a mechanism for moving towards the inclusive order of the ideal of universality from our present community, with its determinate forms, arbitrary associations, and conflicts. The search for consistency becomes an examination of our responses to diagnose, in those instances where universality fails us, why that failure occurs. Through such continuous labour, the ability to think of others and of ourselves as members of a community presumably becomes more powerful.

Given the substantive notion of universality that seems to be at work in Kant's *sensus communis*, our search for community and universality does not lead to homogeneity. We recognize differences between ourselves as well as those features of our subjectivity which we share with and which are compatible with others' subjectivity. If our enculturation is a matter of promoting the social and rational parts of ourselves at the expense of the exclusively individual, then the forms of that enculturation will vary with the forms of our natural being. For Kant, there does not seem to be any natural limit to our tendency to exclusively individual pursuits. These are various and indeterminate; in that sense, they are infinite. Commensurately, our attempts to overcome it will be varied and complex.

Nor is the *sensus communis* a utopian dream. As we said, the search for consistency causes us to attend to our present situation, to analyze our particular involvement, and to diagnose the precise ways in which we fail our communal needs. Utopia functions here as a way of examining why our present situation fails the ideal and how it may be changed in the present circumstances. Nor have we any guarantee here that a progressive restructuring appropriate to a given moment will not need changing later, in the face of other changes.

From this activity our rational and animal character, our humanity, emerges as the forms of life which survive critical analysis and diagnosis. These forms allow us to be individuals in the communal setting of other subjects, without reducing the one to the other. Moreover, this is a continuing process. Ethical development is ever in progress, Kant maintains, because we are radically evil: the source of this evil lies in nature, and we can never escape our nature. Therefore we are always in danger of falling back from the culture and moral feeling we have developed, and there is never a situation when we grow completely out of the need for culture into some domain where we are beyond its interrelation between our rational freedom and our natural being. The point is not to overcome this distinction entirely by obliterating the lower partner, but to harmonize the two as best possible. By so doing, we overcome the gulf between nature and freedom which Kant set out in the Preface of the Third *Critique*.

The open-endedness of this progress suggests also that in setting out his theory Kant only identifies the parameters, the space, in which our humaneness appears. This is not a determinate set of characteristics but a structure of our relations with each other, compatible with certain activities – those which, because they are universalizable, are always acceptable. Through it Kant explores our humanity in an appropriate manner. In culture we are not objects to be dissected but agents involved in an activity that shows itself and grows in relation with the participation of other members of the community.

In this beauty is part of a larger endeavour. The model of the *sensus communis* derives from Kant's description of reason and method. He presents this also in the *Critique of Pure Reason*, in the Doctrine of Method. By this account, critique or philosophy is a method for displaying the structure of our reasoning.[33] As Onara O'Neil points out,

> The elements of human knowledge are not self-constructing; they must always be put together according to some plan or other. No master plan is inscribed in each one of us; rather we must devise a plan that assembles the various elements. . . . The most basic requirement for construction by any plurality of agents must then be negative. It can be no more than the requirement that any fundamental principles of thought and action we deploy be ones that it is not impossible for all to follow. There may be many differing detailed plans that fall within this constraint. . . . [A]ny principles of thinking and acting that can have authority cannot enjoin principles on which some members of a plurality cannot . . . act.[34]

The *sensus communis* shares this thrust towards a structure which sustains a plurality of sensible and rational free agents. And, in this context, where beauty contributes to culture through its interpenetration with the *sensus communis*, beauty is a part of this continuing task of philosophy to discover the structures of reason.

BEAUTY AND BIBLIOGRAPHY

In the past twenty or so years a number of books on Kant's aesthetic theory have appeared in English. These have given us some sense of the themes and purpose of the *Critique of Judgement*. For some years prior to that, anecdotal evidence suggests, people relied on H. W. Cassirer's *A Commentary on Kant's Critique of Judgement*, which was first published in 1938 and was reprinted by Macmillan in 1971. This commentary seemed to attend to issues of the epistemological status and nature of judgements of taste, understood by reference to issues drawn from the *Critique of Pure Reason*, rather more than to the relation between beauty and morality. The author omits from his commentary 'the section headed "Remark" which follows upon Section VII of the *First Introduction*, Sections 13–17 of the *Critique*, the section headed "General Remark upon the Exposition of the Aesthetic Reflective Judgements", Sections 40–2, 51–4, 58–60, 67–8, 72–3, and the whole of the Methodology. It would be tedious in each case to specify my reasons for omitting a passage', he writes, 'but I must explain why I have not dealt with Section 42 ("The Intellectual Interest in the beautiful"), Section 59 ("Beauty as a Symbol of Morality") . . . I have to confess that I have omitted them because I do not understand them properly. In them Kant puts forward the view that there is a necessary connection between morality and appreciation of beauty. I am unable either to follow Kant's argument here or to decide whether such a doctrine is or is not in keeping with the general principles of the Critique . . .'.[35]

Such honesty is laudable, but the result is a work that underplays the moral connection when Kant sees the *Critique of Judgement* as a bridge between theory and practice. A similar stress on epistemological issues determines Paul Guyer's book on *Kant and the Claims of Taste* (1979). He proposes that the then current 'insistence upon the moral aspect of Kant's deduction has actually deflected attention from the important and logically prior question of the strength of [Kant's] epistemological argument'.[36]

Certainly a concern with the relation between beauty and

morality was present in some published papers. As Guyer points out, R. K. Elliott, 'The Unity of Kant's "Critique of Aesthetic Judgement"', *British Journal of Aesthetics*, 8 (1968), 244–59 devotes more space to the moral connection than to the deduction. Similarly, A. Hofstader, 'Kant's Aesthetic Revolution', *Journal of Religious Ethics*, 3 (1975), 171–91; M. Johnson, 'Kant's Unified Theory of Beauty', *Journal of Aesthetics and Art Criticism*, 38 (1979), 167–78; R. Kuhns, 'That Kant did not complete his argument examining the relation of Art to Morality and how it might be completed', *Idealistic Studies*, 5 (1975), 190–206; K. F. Rogerson, 'The Meaning of Universal Validity in Kant's Aesthetics', *Journal of Aesthetics and Art Criticism*, 40, (1982); G. Weiler, 'Kant's "Indeterminate Concept" and the Concept of Man', *Revue Internationale de Philosophie*, 16 (1962); J. B. Wilbur, 'Kant's Critique of Art and the Good Will', *Kant Studien*, 61 (1970), and D. A. White, 'On Bridging the Gulf between Nature and Morality in the *Critique of Judgement*', *Journal of Aesthetics and Art Criticism*, 38 (1979), all examined aspects of the relation between beauty and morality.

In addition to the papers listed in the last paragraph, two books presented Kant's aesthetic theory as an argument for relating theory to practice and, by implication, epistemology to morality through the nature and scope of judgements of taste. Donald Crawford's *Kant's Aesthetic Theory* (1974) proposes that the whole of the *Critique of Aesthetic Judgement* is a single argument designed to link theory with moral practice, while F. X. Coleman's *The Harmony of Reason: A Study of Kant's Aesthetics* (1974) maintains, as the title suggests, that the experience of beauty resolves the apparent tension between theoretical knowledge and moral practice.

But if a concern with moral aspects was then current, it did not last long. Papers such as Karl Ameriks, 'Kant and the Objectivity of Taste', *British Journal of Aesthetics*, 23 (1983), 3–17; H. Blocker, 'Kant's Theory of the Relation of Imagination and Understanding', *British Journal of Aesthetics*, 5 (1965) 37–45; G. Buchdahl, 'The Relation between "Understanding" and "Reason" in the Architectonic of Kant's Philosophy', *Proceedings of the Aristotlian Society*, 1976; K. W. Cooley, 'Universality in Kant's Aesthetic Judgements', *Kinesis* 1 (1968), 43–50; J. Fisher and J. Maitland, 'The Subjectivist turn in Aesthetics: A Critical Analysis of Kant's Theory of Appreciation', *Review of Metaphysics*, 27 (1974), 726–51; M. J. Gregor, 'Kant's First Deduction of Taste', *Proceedings of the Fifth International Kant Congress*, 1981; and J. Maitland, 'Two senses of necessity in

Kant's Aesthetics', *British Journal of Aesthetics*, 16 (1976), 347–53, among others, all attended to epistemological issues in the *Critique of Judgement*.

Indeed, over the next six or seven years it began to seem that an epistemological concern determined most of the interesting examinations of Kant's aesthetic theory. This may have been the result of the mindset first established by Cassirer's commentary – for a long while it was the only book-length work on Kant easily available in English – and then given impetus by Guyer's detailed examination of the deduction. In any case, in *Kant and Fine Art: An Essay on Kant and the Philosophy of Fine Art and Culture* (1986), I thought that although an epistemological approach to the *Critique of Judgement* yields many significant insights, nevertheless it does not do justice to the relation between beauty and morality. Similarly, Rudolph Makkreel, in *Imagination and Interpretation in Kant, The Hermeneutical Import of the Critique of Judgement* (1990), as the title suggests, questions the usual stress on Kant's epistemology and explains the power of imagination in the interpretative task of constituting and understanding culture and history.

Moreover, the epistemological slant seems to have almost completely neglected other aspects of Kant's aesthetic theory, such as his conceptions of art, fine art, and cultural activity, all of which he discusses in detail at crucial points in the *Critique of Judgement*. To understand the latter we must turn to consider Kant's deeper purposes in writing the *Critique of Judgement*. In his book on *Kant on History and Religion* (1973), Michel Despland sets out some details of that deeper purpose; J. D. McFarland, in his paper on 'The Bogus Unity Between Physical and Moral Teleology' in P. Laberge, F. Duchesneau, and B. E. Morrissey (eds), *Proceedings of the Ottawa Congress on Kant in the Anglo-American and Continental Traditions* (1976), examines Kant's central claims for the relation as presented in the Third *Critique*; and *Kant and Fine Art* examines a number of issues about culture, morality, and beauty.

One consequence of this approach is that we must limit the scope of the Deduction to showing the transcendental possibility of judgements of taste – as I proposed in Chapter 5 above. Other more recent books have taken a different line. In *Kant's Aesthetics: The Role of Form and Expression* (1986), Kenneth Rogerson argues that aesthetic judgements and their deduction are best understood by using the vocabulary of morality to talk of 'aesthetic imperatives'. Mary M. McCloskey in *Kant's Aesthetic* (1987), in addition to ensuring that her book precedes Rogerson's in any alphabetical listing of titles of books on Kant's aesthetic theory, maintains that the 'ought' involved in judgements concerning the beautiful is 'a non-moral ought' that functions 'independently of the moral ought'.[37] Unfortunately, the coherence of this assertion and her authority for making it remain highly questionable.

Another aspect of Kant's aesthetic theory which a stress on epistemological aspects of the Deduction leads us to neglect is the nature and role of the sublime. This concept is considered in various ways in some of the books mentioned above, of course, but few books made it central to their concerns. The authors who have given importance to the sublime include Paul Crowther, whose title *The Kantian Sublime, From Morality to Art* (1989) indicates its contents, J.-F. Lyotard whose book on *The Differend, Phrases in Dispute* (1988) finds the Kantian sublime a rich source for answers to issues about reason, Jacques Derrida, whose *The Truth in Painting* emphasizes the allusive open-endedness of Kant's notion of the sublime, and Peter de Bolla, whose interesting book on *The Discourse of the Sublime, History, Aesthetics and the Subject* (1989) examines the English discussion of the sublime that influenced Kant's thinking on the subject.

In addition to the book-length studies of Kant's aesthetic theory which we have listed above, there are at least three collections of essays on the subject. Eva Schaper published her collection, *Studies in Kant's Aesthetics*, in 1979, while Ted Cohen and Paul Guyer edited and published a collection of *Essays on Kant's Aesthetics* in 1982. In a more recent essay in *Aesthetic Reconstructions* (1988), Anthony Savile treats Kant's theory in the context of essays on Lessing's *Laocoon* and Schiller's *On the Aesthetic Education of Man*.

Other collections of papers appear as special issues of journals. 1990 marks two hundred years since the *Critique of Judgement* was first published, and *Revue Internationale de Philosophie* and *Nous* published papers on the subject. Papers on this subject are also published in the *Proceedings of the Sixth International Kant Congress*, 1985 (1990) and the *Proceedings of the Seventh International Kant Congress*, 1990. Other recent papers on Kant's aesthetic theory include Casey Haskins, 'Kant and the Autonomy of Art', *Journal of Aesthetics and Art Criticism*, 1989, 43–54, which helps redress the neglect of Kant's theory of fine art, and T. A. Gracyk, 'Sublimity, Ugliness, and Formlessness in Kant's Aesthetic Theory', *Journal of Aesthetics and Art Criticism*, 1986, 49–56. More extensive bibliographies on

Kant's aesthetic theory appear in the Cohen and Guyer collection mentioned above and in Werner S. Pluhar's translation of the *Critique of Judgement* (1987).

Secondary readings should not replace the text they are about. Pluhar's new translation of the *Critique of Judgement*, with its introduction, glossary, index, and bibliography, makes the text and its arguments much more accessible than they were previously. And this introductory book that you have just read, which I hope is close in spirit and letter to Kant's writing, should now lead you to the *Critique of Judgement* itself.

Notes

1 The Background

1. Immanuel Kant, *Critique of Pure Reason*, A21/B35–6. I have followed the usual practice of referring to pages in the two editions of the *Critique of Pure Reason* by using A to denote the first edition and B to denote the second. In what follows, I shall refer to the *Critique of Pure Reason* by noting only the relevant pagination.
2. A50/B74.
3. Recent work on Kant's epistemology suggests that the faculty should be treated distinctly from the concepts it informs. Previously, Jonathan Bennett among others had argued that judgement plays an idle role in explanations of how we make assertions by applying concepts. See, for example, Hubert Schwyzer, *The Unity of Understanding. A Study in Kantian Problems* (1990), Chapters 1–3.
4. B131.
5. The use of 'I think' is not intended to lessen its certainty as if we were now falling short of asserting X and had to be satisfied with saying that 'I think that X' in the sense that 'It is my opinion (only) that X'. Rather, the claim is only that I can talk about what I am thinking of.
6. This and the above arguments are culled from Kant's *Critique of Pure Reason* and from *Kant's Transcendental Idealism*, by H. E. Allison. The latter seems to me to contain the most plausible recent account of Kant's central arguments.
7. Cf. Graham Bird, *Kant's Theory of Knowledge*, (1962) and Gerd Buchdahl, *Metaphysics and the Philosophy of Science* (1968), both of whom develop accounts of the difference between transcendental and empirical necessities.
8. Bxiii.
9. Ibid.
10. Sections 383, A. G . Baumgarten, *Metaphysica* (Hildesheim, 1963).
11. Ibid., Section 462.
12. G. W. Leibniz, *New Essays Concerning Human Understanding*, Section 11.
13. *Vernunftige Gedancken von Gott, der Welt, und der Seele des Menschen* (1720), (Abbreviated as VGG), Section 276.
14. Wolff also proposes a distinction between figurative and intuitive knowledge (VGG, Section 316) by which to refine Leibniz's account of perfect and imperfect knowledge. In spite of their differences, both provide degrees of knowledge.
15. Section 123, A. G. Baumgarten, *Aesthetica* (Hildesheim, 1970).
16. *Aesthetica*, Section 619.
17. *Aesthetica*, Section 22.
18. *Aesthetica*, Section 2.

19. *Reflections on Poetry*, Section 13.
20. Ibid., Section 13.
21. Sections 14 and 15.
22. Section 19.
23. Section 38.
24. Section 40.
25. *Aesthetica*, Section 177.
26. *Aesthetica*, Section 181.
27. Kant's *a priori* justifications of validity deny the power of inductive generalizations about our actual behaviour, such as Hume and Burke propose, to justify the validity of aesthetic response. I have not developed the contrast between Kant's theory and empiricist explanations of aesthetics because a great deal of work is already available in English on this subject. The relation between Kant and the rationalists is less studied, and I thought it would be more useful to develop some details of the theories here. Paul Crowther discusses some aspects of the relation between Kant, Burke, and Addison in Part I of *The Kantian Sublime. From Morality to Art* (1989).
28. Kant wrote this book under the influence of Burke's *Philosophical Enquiry into the Origins of our Ideas of the Sublime and the Beautiful*, and entertained pronouncements on how ideas of beauty varied between countries, cultures, and races.

2 The 'Analytic of the Beautiful'

1. Though they associated it with perfection.
2. They are also aesthetic in the first sense, of course, but that claim does not need argument because it only says that judgements of taste are judgements of taste. In the second sense it says that judgements of taste have to do with our feelings and sensations.
3. Immanuel Kant, *Critique of Judgement*, Section 1, 204. See also Section 25, 228, where Kant notes that the aesthetic judgement gives us no knowledge, not even confused knowledge, of an object. I have usually used the translation of the *Critique of Judgement* by Werner Pluhar, published by Hackett (1987). Page numbers refer to the Academy Edition of Kant's works, which Pluhar cites in the margins. In some instances I have used the translation of the *Critique of Judgement* by James Creed Meredith because of the felicity of its phrasing. In what follows, I have abbreviated the *Critique of Judgement* as KDU.
4. B171.
5. These ways, we know, depend on the twelve categories. Kant classifies those twelve categories under four major headings of Quantity, Quality, Relation, and Modality. Thus, causality, substance, and reciprocity belong under the rubric of Relation, while possibility, necessity, and existence belong with Modality. Any sentence, thought, or judgement must use at least one category from each of the four rubrics. We cannot assert at the same time that the same thing is possible *and* necessary or existent, but it must be one of those. Similarly, that item must constitute a causal relation or one of

substance and its accidents, and so on. Cf. B106, for the list of categories.

6. A133/B172.

7. Ibid.

8. A134/B173–4.

9. My attempt to separate out an act of judging from the particular application of a concept may seem problematic, especially given the criticisms familiar in analytic philosophy against such a distinction. Jonathan Bennett, for example, argues that Kant's distinction is fraught with difficulties and makes an unnecessary complication out of the schematism. More recently, this position has been questioned, I think effectively, by Stuart Bell, 'The Art of Judgement and the Judgement of Art', *Mind*, 1987, and *The Unity of Understanding, A Study in Kantian Problems* by Hubert Schwyzer (1990). My account of judgement owes considerably to these two publications.

10. Cf. the Introductions to the *Critique of Judgement*.

11. But also, because we gain this appreciation of order in judgement, it involves the faculty which is distinctively Kantian. If Kant can associate taste with the activity of this faculty, he will avoid many of the problems afflicting earlier aesthetic theories, which fell victim to a number of problems because they did not make good use of a concept of judgement and associated taste with mere sense, and sensate knowledge with perfection.

12. KDU, 169. It may be as well to emphasize here that for Kant judgement shows itself in the beauty of both art and nature. Such an emphasis should go to counter the tendency, prevalent for too long in secondary literature, on Kant's aesthetic theory, to claim that his concern is with natural beauty principally. Rather, given his interest in the spontaneous and creative activity of judgement, Kant is unlikely to be satisfied by its exhibition in natural beauty alone, for fine art best embodies the creative power of judgement, of the activity of discovering order, in which the creative power is at its most exemplary in making us conscious of the fact of grasping a richly novel and valuable material produced by our genius, where genius shares in the spontaneity native to judgement.

13. KDU, 169.

14. KDU, 194.

15. KDU, 215. Italics added.

16. KDU, 203 n1.

17. See KDU Section 59 for the claims about realism. The issues appear also in S. Kemal, *Kant and Fine Art*, 131–4.

18. KDU, Section 43.

19. We should make clear that most claims about the *Critique of Judgement* are controversial. Although the text has gained serious attention from Kantians only in recent years, in this short span it has generated debate over precisely what its issues are. For example, even if we are agreed that intersubjective validity is a crucial issue, the role it plays and its scope are still open to discussion. In this situation any thesis may be found controversial, and although it is not possible for us to enter into discussion with everyone about everything, in this intro-

ductory book we will usually indicate in the end-notes what disagree-
ments there are and what diverse positions authors have identified or
developed.

20. KDU, 211.
21. KDU, 219.
22. KDU, 236.
23. KDU, 240.
24. KDU, n 203.
25. KDU, 204. See the interesting papers by Rudolph Makkreel, in which
    he develops Kant's talk of a 'feeling of life' by reference to Dilthey's
    work, to show that aesthetic judgements have a wider role to play in
    our practical lives. The formal properties of aesthetic judgements,
    therefore, must be put in the context of Kant's more general philo-
    sophical concerns. Makkreel identifies a hermeneutical issue in the
    Analytic and later sections, where by displaying the role and nature of
    the 'productive imagination' Kant's work can be seen as a contribution
    to the debate between explanation and understanding. R. Makkreel,
    'The Feeling of Life: Some Kantian Sources of Life-Philosophy',
    Dilthey-Jahrbuch für Philosophie und Geschichte der Geisteswissenschaften,
    Band 3, 1985, 83–104; 'The Role of Synthesis in Kant's *Critique of
    Judgement*', *Proceedings of the Sixth International Kant Congress*, 1985,
    (1990). The results of these papers are presented in R. Makkreel,
    *Understanding and Imagination in Kant. The Hermeneutical Import of the
    Critique of Judgement* (1990).
26. KDU, 203.
27. Of course, it is also the case that thinkers at various times have
    accepted that some role is played by pleasure, but have denied it the
    centrality which Kant accords to it.
28. In any case, Kant does provide something of a more basic defence of
    his association of pleasure and beauty, for he sees pleasure as distinc-
    tively subjective, and so is able to use it to explain the nature of the
    activity of judging. We saw that this activity was subjective, and could
    serve as a propaedeutic to all philosophy. As pleasure is entirely
    subjective and incapable of describing or denoting the object, it can
    serve well as an instrument for grasping the scope and nature of the
    subjective side of judging.
29. When Kant distinguishes aesthetic responses from interests, interested
    pleasure includes what the rationalists and empiricists see as aesthetic
    judgements. The notion of a disinterested pleasure shows the subjec-
    tivity of aesthetic judgements is compatible with Kant's critical theory
    and also goes to explain why he rejects the empiricist or rationalist
    account. However, we can understand the First Moment in its own
    terms and not merely as a rejection of empiricist and rationalist
    theories.
30. Section 1, 203. The rejection of empiricist and rationalist epistemology
    thus seems to lead Kant to exclude *all* sensate material that could be
    cognitive. Kant is not just rejecting claims to validity based on sup-
    posing that sensate experience is imperfect knowledge but rejecting
    everything that could count as sensate knowledge, even in this sense,

by basing aesthetic responses on something that could not possibly count as sensate knowledge and so is something for which the question or issue of objectivity could not arise directly or indirectly through cognitive experience. He is setting himself the very difficult task of arguing that aesthetic response must be valid despite being *entirely* subjective.

31. Section 2, 204.
32. KDU, Section 5, 209.
33. Ibid.
34. This relation to a particular might be expressed as a disinterested aesthetic pleasure that has nothing to do with objects. The suggestion is that reference to an object possessing determinate properties invites considerations of interest because it must involve the use of determinate concepts in existential judgements to make such references. The latter are not subjective but denote something in the object, and they bring in all the confusions between sensate knowledge and aesthetic response that beguiled the rationalists and empiricists into providing either a quasi-cognitive account of validity or a sensualist conception of validity and universality. The only way to guarantee the distinctiveness of subjective aesthetic response, it seems, is by showing its independence of the determinate properties of objects. And at times Kant seems to propose that this end requires us to exclude the modes of language by which objective experience is grasped. Only in the domain of subjectivity, it seems, free of all such reference to objects, can we proceed to provide a validity for aesthetic responses. However, we may argue that it is unnecessary to so completely exclude concepts and objects for fear of introducing interests into what should be a purely aesthetic response. What is important is that aesthetic response be understood as being independent of the uses which an object may serve, for it considers the object for itself rather than for any other purpose. How that consideration of the object is pleasurable and what we consider of the object are issues Kant has yet to deal with in the Second Moment.
35. For a further development of this kind of openness in Kant's philosophical method and its consequences for aesthetic theory, see S. Kemal, *Kant and Fine Art* (1986), Chapters 5 and 6. More recently, O. O'Neil, in *Constructions of Reason, Explorations of Kant's Practical Philosophy* (1990), has given a very useful account of this feature of Kant's conception of reason. See Chapters 1, 2, 4 and 5.
36. KDU, Section 6, 211.

3 The Second Moment

1. See Anthony, Earl of Shaftesbury, *Characteristics of Men, Manners, Opinions, and Times*, Volumes I and II (edited by J. M. Robertson, with an Introduction by S. Green (Indianapolis, 1964)).
2. A70/B95; and *Logic*, 102–3.
3. If concepts apply to subjects, then they too must be considered as part of a causal nexus.

4. KDU, Section 2, n206.
5. Ibid.
6. KDU, Section 41.
7. KDU, Section 60, et al.
8. Another essential point is this: the criterion of disinterestedness does not allow us to distinguish between objects such that some are identified as fine art and other objects are ones of natural beauty. Either may be disinterested, for each may give rise to pleasure on being considered for itself.
9. KDU, Section 58, 346ff.
10. See Chapter 1 above.
11. KDU, Section 49, 316.
12. KDU, Section 49, 314.
13. KDU, Section 49, 315–16.
14. KDU, Section 49, 315, italics added.
15. Ibid.
16. KDU, Section 9, 217. See also 219.
17. In the early sections of the *Critique of Judgement* Kant seems to exclude concepts altogether. See for example Section 8, 219 and 285; Section 9, 217, 219; and Section 6, 211. See also Section 16, 230, where Kant suggests that by using concepts we limit the imagination. There is another strain in the *Critique*, though, that seeks to exclude only determinate concepts or the use of concepts in making cognitive claims. This strain is seen most clearly not only in Section 16, whose title specifies that 'A judgement of taste by which we declare an object beautiful under the condition of a *Determinate* judgement is not pure' (KDU, Section 16, 229/76; italics added) and in the account of expression in art, but also in the Remark following (e.g. Section 49, 313–19; R1, 343).
18. KDU, Section 49, 314: 'we may even restructure experience; . . . [and] in this process we feel our freedom from the law of association (which attaches to the empirical use of the imagination). . . . We process the material [which nature lends us under laws] into something quite different, namely into something that surpasses nature'.
19. Ibid. The 'imagination ([in its role] as a productive cognitive power) is very mighty when it creates, as it were, another nature out of the material that actual nature gives it'. Consequently, its concern is not with objects as given in nature but with the use we might make of these objects in making aesthetic judgements.
20. Our response depends on 'attributes that accompany the logical ones and that give the imagination a momentum which makes it think more in response to these objects [*dabei*], though in an undeveloped way, than can be comprehended within one concept and hence in one linguistic expression' (KDU, Section 49, 315). We 'conjoin [with a] presentation . . . [that] which arouses a multitude of sensations and supplementary presentations for which no expression can be found', ibid.
21. KDU, Section 49, 314.
22. See S. Kemal, 'Presentation and Expression in Kant's Aesthetic

'Theory', *British Journal of Aesthetics*, Volume 15 (1975), where I argue that nature expresses the idea of the Finality of Nature. See also K. Rogerson, *Kant's Aesthetics* (1986) for a detailed consideration of the role of form and expression in aesthetic judgements.

23. KDU, Section 51, 320. Italics added.
24. Charles Dickens, *Pickwick Papers*, Chapter 27.
25. Rupert Brooke, 'Lines Written in the Belief that the Ancient Roman Festival of the Dead was called Ambarvalia'.
26. Lewis Carroll, *Through the Looking Glass*, Chapter 4.
27. 'Song of Myself', *Leaves of Grass*, Walt Whitman.
28. William Shakespeare, *King John*, Act IV, Scene 1, 41. Clearly, *Othello* is not Shakespeare's only use of handkerchiefs.
29. I do not mean to introduce a distinction between form and content in talking of the internal order of events represented on the stage. The order is one of meaningful events, and so is not distinguishable from the latter.
30. KDU, Section 9, 217.
31. KDU, Section 9, 217.
32. It is Kant's version of an older thought, perhaps best exemplified in Aristotle's claim that in beauty we perfectly apprehend perfection, that the perfection of the object suits a perfection of the operation of our cognitive and affective capacities.
33. Such a freedom from arbitrariness legitimates one aspect of our talk of beauty. We usually refer to objects as beautiful; but if the account of pleasure and aesthetic response given above is any guide, then beauty denotes the subject's experience of a disinterested pleasure. Kant has also proposed that if pleasure is disinterested, then it may be expected to denote something in the subject which differs from the arbitrary and varied features which give rise to interests. Whereas interests are divisive, disinterestedness militates towards unity because a disinterested pleasure is available to all subjects so far as they can overcome those of their subjective and idiosyncratic points of view that generate interests. His assumption is that there is some locus for pleasure which is common, and this will have to be explained; but if pleasure can be subjective yet universally available, if it is disinterested, then asserting that it denotes subjects adds nothing to our knowledge and experience of pleasure. We do not qualify any particular experience of disinterested pleasure in any significantly meaningful way by saying that it denotes the subject. And this frees us to use the experience of pleasure in another way: it can be used to indicate the object to which we refer our experience by saying that 'This object is beautiful'. It will mean that the pleasure in the object is disinterested and, because it is universal, is being 'imputed to everyone' (KDU, Section 8, 214) in that the subject's pleasure is referred to the object but is available to all subjects.
34. KDU, Section 8, 215.
35. KDU, Section 8, 216.
36. KDU, Section 33, 286.
37. KDU, 212.

38. KDU, 214.
39. KDU, Section 8, 216.
40. Ibid.
41. KDU, Section 8, 216. Italics added.
42. Ibid.
43. The need to separate these two parts of judgement is suggested by Paul Guyer in *Kant and the Claims of Taste*, p. 110.
44. This is the mode of reference Pluhar indicates in his translation of the Third *Critique*.
45. KDU, Section 9, 217.
46. See Guyer, 'Pleasure and Society in Kant's Aesthetic Theory' in T. Cohen and P. Guyer (eds), *Essays on Kant's Aesthetics* (1982), in which he suggests other reasons.
47. KDU, 219. Such an account raises a number of issues. The judgement of taste is said to denote the subject and to refer to the object; but both the subject and the object are construed in a distinctive manner. It is necessary to understand how pleasure arises from such a construal of the object, for we may also learn more about the claim to universal validity made for the subjective pleasurable response generated in these cases, and thereby clarify what Kant intends to justify in the transcendental deduction of taste.
48. KDU, Section 9, 217.
49. Ibid.
50. KDU, Section 9, 218.
51. KDU, Section 8, 216.

4 The Third and Fourth Moments

1. In what follows, I shall use 'finality of form' and 'finality' in preference to 'form of purposiveness' and 'purposiveness'. The latter seems more cumbersome.
2. KDU, Section 10, 220.
3. Ibid.
4. KDU, Section 10, 220.
5. Which you call it depends on whether you use the Meredith translation ('finality') or the Barnard and Pluhar translations ('purposiveness').
6. KDU, Section 10, 220.
7. *Critique of Teleological Judgement*, Section 64, 370.
8. KDU, Section 10, 220.
9. KDU, 221.
10. KDU, Section, 11, 221.
11. KDU, Section 17, 236.
12. KDU, Section 21, 238.
13. KDU, Section 19, 237.
14. In her book on *Kant's Aesthetic* (1987), M. McCloskey entirely misses the significance of Kant's distinction between subjective and objective necessity when she says '[i]t is noticeable that in dealing with the peculiarities of a judgement concerning the beautiful involving

necessitation, Kant does not, as he does with the peculiarities of its being universal, begin to speak of "subjective" as opposed to "objective" necessitation' (57). The title of Section 22, 'The necessity of the universal assent that we think in a judgement of taste is a subjective necessity that we present as objective by presupposing a common sense' (239), rather contradicts McCloskey's claim. She may have missed this issue because she seems to identify the necessity and universality of aesthetic judgements. Her discussion of the two occurs in the same chapter, without any consideration of the difference between the issues. Karl Ameriks, in his paper 'Kant and the Objectivity of Taste', *British Journal of Aesthetics*, 23, (1983), 3–17, makes a similar conflation.

15. KDU, Section 21, 138.
16. Ibid.
17. Section 22, 239.
18. KDU, ibid.
19. One influential version of this claim is proposed by W. K. Wimsatt, Jr and Monroe C. Beardsley in their paper on 'The Intentional Fallacy': See W. K. Wimsatt, *The Verbal Icon* (1954).
20. KDU, Section 16, see Chapter 2 above.
21. KDU, Section 14, 226/72.
22. See *Truth in Painting*, p. 9. Derrida talks of this role of framing in terms of the outside being tied in to the inside and so on, but I take it that he means what I have said. His talk of 'frames' extrapolates from Kant's talk of 'ornamentation', but the point Derrida makes by using the concept of a 'frame' does not apply to Kant.
23. KDU, Section 50, 319. Kant writes that art becomes 'durable, fit for approval that is both lasting and universal, and [hence] fit for being followed by others and fit for an ever advancing culture'.
24. See Jacques Derrida, *The Margins of Philosophy*, 'Structure, Sign, and Play in the Human Sciences', and the 'Interview' with Derrida in *Literary Review*, No. 14, 1980.

5   Judgements of Taste and their Deduction

1. Section 33, 284.
2. KDU, Section 32, 282.
3. KDU, Section 33, 284.
4. Ibid.
5. KDU, Section 34, 286. Kant says there that critics 'should investigate . . . [and] clarify by examples' the pleasure we feel so that others may come to recognize what they might have missed in their own responses.
6. Cf. Richard Shiff, *Cézanne and the End of Impressionism*, for an interesting analysis of Cézanne's style and work.
7. KDU, Section 33, 285.
8. 'Hence a judgement of taste has the following two-fold peculiarity, which is moreover a logical one: *First*, it has apriori universal validity, which yet is not a logical universal validity governed by concepts, but

the universality of a singular judgement; *second*, it has a necessity (which must always rest on apriori bases), and yet a necessity that does not depend on any apriori bases of proof by the presentation of which we could compel [people to give] the assent that a judgement of taste requires of everyone' (KDU, Section 32, 281).

9. See John Fisher and Jeremy Maitland, 'The Subjectivist Turn in Aesthetics: A Critical Analysis of Kant's Theory of Appreciation', *Review of Metaphysics*, 27, (1974), 726–51.

10. KDU, Section 37, 289.

11. KDU, Section 36, 288.

12. The paragraph summarizes some of what he has said about this issue when discussing the nature of beauty in the Analytic, so it shares a theme with the Third and Fourth Moments. Commentators have argued that Kant's claims here add little to what he said in the earlier sections. There, in Sections 18 to 21, among other things, Kant had proposed that necessity was subjective or objective depending on whether we could presuppose a common sense. We are 'suitors' for agreement from everyone else 'because we are fortified with a ground common to all'. On the basis of our own experience of pleasure, and the supposition that we have a common sense, we are able to impute the judgement to others. Of course, our judgement may be mistaken, and we need also some way of confirming the judgement by bringing others to have it. And had we some way of confirming judgement, then we might also demand the judgement of others. In this context, Kant went some way towards explaining our ability to impute judgements by saying that we had good reason for supposing that we had a common sense and could expect to share pleasure in judgements. But the thrust of his claim there was a negative one, directed against scepticism about the possibility of a common subjective experience. That argument is also capable of a more positive use, however, and in the Deduction itself Kant relies on this positive thrust. Yet, because he is using more or less the same argument, commentators usually suppose that he is merely repeating himself.

13. See Kenneth Rogerson, *Kant's Aesthetics*, pp. 74–6. See the last section of this chapter for further consideration of this work. Rogerson argues that 'communicate' is an imprecise rendition of the sense of harmony, etc., that Kant wants to gain. For Rogerson, Kant was more interested in explaining universal validity in terms of subjects' ability to have feelings which tallied or harmonized with those of other subjects. However, it is not clear that such harmony or tallying can be gained to any purpose if it is merely an unstudied coincidence. Whether we seek to harmonize or tally with each other, we must still know that we have this harmony, and that surely depends on being able to communicate to each other the response we have in judging an object aesthetically.

14. KDU, Section 35, 287.

15. Section 38, Comment, 290.

16. Pages 88ff, fn 107.

17. B137.

18. Ibid.

19. A345–5; A398; B131; B423, note; B407–10.
20. A341/B399.
21. A155–6.
22. A155/B194–A157/B196.
23. KDU, Section 38, 290.
24. Ibid.
25. Whether they actually do so and whether we can know that they do is another matter.
26. KDU, Section 39, 292–3. Another objection to this might be that pleasure has not been accounted for: we have no guarantee that a harmony of faculties is pleasurable. For some it may be nauseous, for others pleasurable, for yet others it may be something entirely different. Different answers have been given to this claim. One was proposed at the beginning of Chapter 2, when Kant's association of pleasure with a harmony of faculties was said to be an insight he had, which is not open to further justification in terms of some more basic concepts. We cannot expect to justify the conclusion, that a harmony of faculties is pleasurable, by pointing to some other premises from which the connection between pleasure and harmony follows. What we can do, instead, is to justify the association by developing a theory on its basis that accounts for our many intuitions about beauty.

    Now it may be said that nausea at harmony is one of our intuitions about beauty – and there does not seem to be any reason for excluding this claim. In reply we might point out that, second, Kant sees a 'feeling for life' as fundamental to taste, not simple pleasure. Where pleasure is universalizable, it is one of the responses which goes to make up that feeling for life. It provides a central and important exemplification of our feeling for life and, so, exhibits what we take life to be. Perhaps, here, we might see that nausea at harmony can be included as an instantiation of a feeling for life. If so, then nausea will function formally in just the way pleasure does when it is understood as the feeling for life. It will have to be entirely subjective yet able to claim universality or comprehensiveness over subjects, and so on. In other words, nausea may be the feeling attendant on making a judgement of taste, so long as it functions in the same way as pleasure does – though any subject's willingness to adopt it as the central feeling for life will tell us something of his or her expectations of life. Harmony would be considered painful, nausea would become central, and aesthetic judgements would still claim validity because the harmony of faculties could be shared.

    Third, nor does this necessarily go against the universality of aesthetic judgements. There may be a failure of universality in pleasure in the sense that pleasure may not be universalizable here because other subjects may feel nausea at the harmony of faculties in their experience. But in a sense that does not show anything really significant about the *universal validity* of aesthetic judgements, for the universality of the 'feeling for life' is still preserved. Whether other subjects feel nausea or pleasure, in both cases, where such feeling occurs it will not be arbitrary but related to the harmony of faculties. The feeling for life involved here may continue to be negotiable in that subjects need to consider whether their feeling is a harmony of faculties, and may have to accept that pleasure is not the sole criterion for recognizing a harmony of faculties. Fourth, the issue of whether a feeling of pleasure or nausea signals the occurrence of a harmony of faculties is really an issue of the particular actual judgements we make – of whether this feeling in this instance is universalizable or not. But because it concerns the actual judgement, the issue is secondary to our present concern with the condition for judgements of taste being possible. And so far as the latter is concerned, it is enough to show that we can all share the harmony of faculties and the attendant feeling.

27. KDU, Section 18, 237, italics added.
28. KDU, Section 19, 237, italics added.
29. KDU, Section 22, 239.
30. Ibid.
31. KDU, Section 41, 296.
32. Cf. Karl Ameriks, 'Kant and the Objectivity of Taste', *British Journal of Aesthetics*, 23 (1983), 3–17.
33. KDU, Section 22.
34. KDU, Section 19.
35. KDU, Section 40, 296.
36. KDU, Section 8, 216.
37. KDU, Section 40, 293–4.
38. KDU, Section 38; see also the Comment following.
39. It is important to note that the *sensus communis* is not premised directly on the transcendental deduction of the First *Critique* but is premised on the possibility of communicating our knowledge claims.
40. Ibid.
41. KDU, Section 8, 216.
42. KDU, Section 8, 216.
43. KDU, Section 40, 293.
44. KDU, Section 40, 295.
45. KDU, Section 22, 239. The last quotation is taken from the Fourth Moment. It expresses the use of *sensus communis* that Kant puts forward in Section 40, though in the Fourth Moment itself Kant's claims are fairly tentative. He suggests only where we might look to understand the necessity of judgements, and leaves open the issue of whether the common sense is presupposed as a necessary condition – such as the subjective conditions involved – or is a guiding principle by which we organize our aesthetic response and so is an ideal we create by making aesthetic judgements. Because these questions are left unanswered at this point, it may be suggested, Kant does not make explicit or discuss his concern with actual particular judgements rather than with the necessary conditions for these judgements – though what he says does seem directed at dealing with our actual judgements. It is only in Section 40, after the deduction has clarified what the necessary conditions are and shown that they are satisfied, that Kant turns to the actual judgements again. He treats them initially as the actual felt effects and then as reflection on the source and

applicability of that feeling. In these dealings with actual judgements, he expands on the suggestions and question he has raised in the Fourth Moment, and now organizes his conclusions so that their concern with actual judgements is more prominent. Thus, in Section 38 his footnote raises the issue of the actual judgements and the mistakes we might make in actual judgement, and most of the following Comment points to the 'unavoidable difficulties' that afflict our concern with actual judgements. In both cases, his point is that the problems we face in dealing with actual judgements do not 'detract from the legitimacy of the power of the judgement's claim in counting on universal assent' (Section 36, Comment, 291). And in the following Sections he goes on to deal with actual judgements, proposing the *sensus communis* as the feeling we share and the ability to judge that the feeling is shared.

46. Section 22, 239.
47. KDU, Section 38, 290.
48. KDU, Comment, 290–1.
49. KDU, Section 49, 317.
50. Further, the mental state brings with it the effect of the free play of the harmony of faculties that we earlier described as a 'feeling for life'. In view of the complex process of articulating that feeling for life in indeterminate concepts, ideas, expression, subjective resonances, and other means, we may suggest now that the feeling is more than pleasure alone, and depends in part on the character of the particular harmony of faculties involved. Such pleasure as there may be in gaining coherence and unity for all these subjective resonances and expression, we may suggest further, must be complicated by considerations of the 'texture' of what is articulated. This may include material to which diverse subjects react with nausea or pleasure, yet one subject's nausea may be understood by others as the feeling for life appropriate for him but not for themselves. By articulating his feeling the subject shows that nausea is his feeling for life, while others may exhibit their own pleasure as the feeling for life, which they make clear by both example, illustration, indeterminate concepts, and subjective resonances.
51. KDU, Section 21, 238.
52. Elsewhere Kant talks of a pleasure in communication, and it may seem that such an occurrence will confirm communication. But when considering judgements of taste, pleasure in communication is not at issue, for the relation between pleasure and communication we are concerned with is the pleasure of making a judgement of taste that is communicated rather than a pleasure in communication that arises from communicating a pleasurable judgement.
53. The First Moment defines the beautiful object by reference to a particular kind of liking; for example, *Critique of Judgement*, 211.
54. See T. W. Adorno, *Aesthetic Theory* (1984) for an illuminating discussion of objects and objectivity in Kant's aesthetic theory.
55. Ibid.
56. KDU, Section 40, 296.

57. He asserts first that 'a concern for universal communication is something that everyone expects and demands from everyone else, on the basis, as it were, of an original contract dictated by [our] very humanity' (Section 41, 297). Given that the ideal of the *sensus communis* embodies the successful communication of judgements of taste, we may expect that any interest in universal communicability which attaches to judgements of taste will be addressed to them as instantiations of the idea of the *sensus communis*. Consequently, if we can account for this interest, then we justify the importance given to the *sensus communis*. If the latter is valuable, and can be satisfied by a judgement of taste, then we will have explained why subjects should make judgements of taste to gain that ideal. That is, the ideal exercises a demand which we seek to satisfy by making aesthetic judgements; where we make judgements of taste successfully, there we satisfy the ideal. But here, the ideal has a moral connotation or is a moral interest, and so the need to satisfy it does not stem from a judgement of taste but is attached to a judgement of taste that is successful. But Kant goes on to make clear that this must not be an empirical interest, for that would make the necessity and confirmation of aesthetic judgements contingent on the presence and satisfaction of an interest.
58. KDU, Section 41, 296.
59. Op. cit.
60. In fact his argument will not really be complete until Section 87 of the *Critique of Teleological Judgement*, but that is a separate matter.
61. Crawford, p. 61.
62. Ibid.
63. Ibid., 125.
64. Ibid., 145.
65. It is only fair to add here that Donald Crawford has since changed his position on the nature and function of this symbolic relation of beauty to morality.
66. In the *Critique of Pure Reason*, 'The Transcendental Employment of Ideas', Kant argues that we need a separate set of criteria for the empirical judgements we make. He proposes that without some systematization of our knowledge we would lack any criteria for empirical truth.
67. Guyer, 122–3.
68. See *Kant and the Claims of Taste*, Chapter 1.
69. See *Essays on Kant's Aesthetics*.
70. See Karl Ameriks, op. cit.
71. K. Rogerson, *Kant's Aesthetics*, 6, cf. also 80ff.
72. Ibid., 86 (sic).
73. Ibid., 90.
74. Ibid., 33.
75. Ibid., 138, italics added.

6   The Necessity of Judgements of Taste

1. See Section 60ff.
2. In the *Aesthetic Education of Mankind*, Schiller claims that 'We are completely human only when we play'.
3. KDU, Section 60, 355.
4. Ibid. Italics added.
5. The distinction between form and content cannot be made in the standard way for Kant. Content and form are not contingently related as if the same form could apply to other content or the same content could be paraphrased and presented in a different form. In aesthetic judgements, the expression of ideas is the formation of meanings, which are intransitive outside that particular use.
6. Guyer entirely misses the point about the comparison between aesthetic and moral judgements being in terms of a 'certain analogy in our reflection' when he says of fine art that it cultivates moral feeling by setting forward moral ideas in its content. (I have discussed this further in Chapter 5, note 17.) Not only is a distinction between form and content of the kind Guyer implies difficult to make for Kant, but Guyer's claim makes redundant the analogy Kant himself puts forward between the mode of reflection – the manner of judging – in art and morality. See Paul Guyer, 'Feeling and Freedom: Kant on Aesthetics and Morality', *Journal of Aesthetics and Art Criticism*, 48, 2, Spring 1990, 137–46.
7. To continue the thought from the last note, the ability to treat others as ends needs more than, say, in art, setting a moral content as an end. Instead of understanding the ability to set and gain ends as this concern for having a morally uplifting content, we should recognize that aesthetic judgements contribute to culture because they cultivate our ability to treat others as ends with whom we share our pleasurable judgement of taste. This pleasure does not and cannot, for Kant, come from the content. See for example, KDU, 292–3, beginning with 'On the other hand, the pleasure we take in the beautiful is a pleasure neither of enjoyment nor of law governed activity nor yet of a reasoning contemplation governed by ideas, but is the pleasure of mere reflection. . .' . If the pleasure came from the content, it would be an interested pleasure. The content is not universalized in aesthetic judgements, and does *not* warrant treating others as rational and feeling ends in themselves because it is alleged to have a moral role in aesthetic judgements. Our pleasure in judging is what allows us to treat other subjects as ends in themselves.
8. See *The Metaphysics of Morals*, pp. 64ff, where Kant argues for a duty to natural perfection that makes it seem like culture. I have developed this in more detail in *Kant and Fine Art* (1986), Chapter 6.
9. A very interesting discussion of the manner in which reflective judgements allow for the hermeneutical business of culture through their orientational and regulative role is presented by Rudolph A. Makkreel, in *Imagination and Interpretation in Kant. The Hermeneutical Significance of the Critique of Judgement* (1990).

10. KDU, Section 83, 430.
11. KDU, Section 83, 431; see also *Doctrine of Virtue*, 91.
12. KDU, Section 83, 432.
13. *Doctrine*, 91.
14. KDU, Section 43, 303.
15. Universal History, 26.
16. KDU, Section 43.
17. Conjectural Beginnings, n118.
18. Conjectural Beginnings, 121.
19. KDU, Section 65, n375.
20. *Critique of Practical Reason*, 62.
21. *Doctrine*, 383.
22. *Doctrine*, 404.
23. Conjectural Beginnings, 117.
24. *Doctrine*, 386, italics added.
25. KDU, Section 40, 295.
26. *Doctrine*, 462.
27. *Anthropology*, 324. Only in society does man feel himself to be 'not merely a human being, but one who is also refined in his own way' (KDU, Section 41, 297). To feel oneself to be more than just an animal in society is to be acknowledged as a human being by other people. Culture concerns the relation between people and not that between, say, animals. If a man can be a person after his own kind only in society, it is because only with other human beings can he expect treatment as a person. Dogs, rivers, and cabbages react very differently to him. Only as a person and in society with others can human beings expect to progress to living '*under* moral laws' (KDU, Section 87, 448). When commentators have ignored these consistent and systematic claims about culture, which Kant presents in the *Critique of Judgement* and other texts, they have produced rather pale accounts of Kant's concerns for the practical connotations of aesthetic activity.
28. Universal History, 21.
29. Universal History, 21.
30. *Religion within the Bounds of Reason Alone*, 89.
31. Human Race, 79.
32. *Anthropology*, 328.
33. 386–443.
34. *Critique of Judgement*, 203–44.
35. See KDU, 216.
36. As the latter included everyone who is capable of our ordinary experience, the aesthetic community potentially includes all rational and feeling subjects.
37. KDU, Section 7, 212.
38. KDU, Section 19, 237.
39. This claim is not an isolated instance in Kant's work. Variations of it occur throughout his moral writings, in which the moral subject makes himself or herself by following the dictates of reason rather than sense. In *Religion within the Bounds of Reason Alone*, the agent becomes a moral agent not by being 'free' in some unconstrained

sense, but by behaving according to a rational autonomy. See *Religion*, Introduction by John Silber, lxxxix ff.

40. See above; the discussion of Derrida makes this clear.
41. KDU, Section 40, 293.
42. Op. cit.
43. KDU, Section 57, 344.
44. A third aspect of beauty's participation in culture occurs in the hierarchy Kant proposes for the fine arts. But as we have not as yet broached the issue of the objects of beauty in the context of their necessity, I shall leave the third aspect for a later section.
45. Kant does not want to extirpate natural impulses: that would be destructive of humanity. He only wants to regulate their satisfaction by the demands of reason.
46. KDU, Section 46, 309.
47. KDU, Section 42, 300.
48. KDU, Section 42, 300.
49. KDU, II, 176.
50. *Critique of Practical Reason*, 114.
51. KDU, VII, 190.
52. KDU, VII, 192. italics added.
53. KDU, Section 23, 246.
54. KDU, Section 23, 246.
55. KDU, IV, 180.
56. B727.
57. H. J. Paton, *The Categorical Imperative*, p. 256.
58. KDU, Section 86, 446.
59. KDU, Section 42, 299.
60. KDU, Section 42, 301.
61. *Religion*, 20.
62. KDU, Section 42, 302.
63. KDU, Section 42, 300.
64. Ibid.
65. Section 42, 299.
66. KDU, Section 42, 301.
67. Op. cit.; italics added.
68. *Religion*, 27.
69. *Strife Between the Faculties*, 87.
70. *Posterior Analytics*, 89b 34.
71. KDU, Section 46, 307–8.
72. I have dealt with these issues in more detail in *Kant and Fine Art*, Chapter II, 43ff.
73. KDU, Section 46, 307.
74. KDU, Section 59, 353.
75. KDU, Section 59, 352.
76. KDU, Section 59, 353–4. Both natural beauty and fine art satisfy the first two criteria. We cannot distinguish between them on the grounds of their aesthetic value or beauty – 'in the judgement of mere taste [they] could scarcely contend with one another for superiority' (KDU, Section 42, 300) – and the judgement of taste is always

disinterested and the pleasure it yields is immediate. The second two criteria seem well-suited to fine art.

77. KDU, Section 51, 320. Kant's text has the following parenthesis where I have introduced an ellipsis: '(whether it be of nature or of art)'. This clearly indicates that Kant is writing of beauty generally, not just of fine art. However, my concern is with fine art, and what he says applies; it also applies to natural beauty, but I shall ignore that for the present for two reasons. One, I would argue that although Kant includes natural beauty, the claims he makes are more clearly and fully applicable to fine art rather than to nature. Second, to bring in a comparison between natural beauty and fine art at this stage is to confuse two issues: those of what the significance of natural beauty is and those of which of the two has priority. I shall return to consider the latter issue later in the chapter.

78. 314–15.

79. KDU, Section 49, 314.

80. KDU, Section 43, 303.

81. KDU, Section 53, 326.

82. KDU, Section 49, 317.

83. However, it does not simply reveal the possession of a good moral disposition, as an interest in natural beauty does.

84. KDU, Section 29, 265–6, italics added.

85. KDU, Section 59, 354.

86. Natural beauty expresses the Idea of the Finality of Nature. See 'Presentation and Expression in Kant's Aesthetics', by S. Kemal, *British Journal of Aesthetics*, 1975.

87. KDU, Section 51, 320, italics added.

88. The parallel can be extended because Kant says that in certain circumstances fine art too may show us the possession of a good disposition: when it appears to us like nature.

89. KDU, Section 60, 356.

90. In the paper cited above, Guyer maintains that 'this text' does not carry that 'lovely echo' of culture as bridging a gulf between nature and reason. His footnote does not make clear which text his comment relates to: the *Critique of Judgement*, the *Critique of Aesthetic Judgement*, Sections 59–60 of the *Critique of Judgement*, or his own paper. Only the last gives his claim some chance of being true in any significant sense. Although Kant does not talk of overcoming a gulf at Section 60, unless there were some important difference between mere nature and a free reason, there would be no need to set out the need for their interrelation through culture.

Guyer's reference is to a passage which Meredith translates as 'how to *bridge* the difference between the amplitude and refinement of the former and the natural simplicity and originality of the latter', thereby stressing the idea of a gulf or gap that needs overcoming (italics added). Pluhar translates this as: 'and by discovering how to make the improvement and refinement of the first harmonize with the natural simplicity and originality of the second', and so forbears from that stress on bridging a gulf. Perhaps Meredith's translation intentionally echoes the idea of overcoming the gulf between freedom and nature, which Kant puts forward in the Preface, suggesting that this overcoming occurs through culture. While it would be wrong to rely on Meredith's translation to make the argument for the role of culture, Kant says so often that his concern is with enculturation and the development of moral feeling that it is rather pointless to deny this association between culture and beauty simply because Meredith's translation echoes talk of overcoming a gulf more than the original does. Kant so often makes the point that we need to argue for this possible harmony between nature and our rational capacities, and does so even at the end of the paragraph that contains Meredith's 'bridge', that it is unnecessary to divert attention (from the connection Kant makes between culture and the exercise of freedom in nature) by pointing to Meredith's extrapolation. Beauty is a feature of our sociability, which is the 'goal' set for us by our rational nature. In the *Critique of Judgement* Kant is clear that culture develops our capacity for reason by contrast with nature. That does not so much echo talk of the gulf between nature and freedom that needs to be overcome as it *is* part of Kant's analysis of how the gulf is to be overcome. Kant presents the details of this account in the *Critique of Judgement*, though not in the aesthetic part. The systematic link between the two parts of the Third *Critique* shows well enough that anyone who concentrates on the first part to the exclusion of the second will seriously misunderstand Kant's theory and fail to recognize the determinate forms of our enlightenment and humanizing activity. To ignore all this is to have a distorted view of Kant's endeavour – to treat him as a formalist. See also Chapter 6 below.

91. See *First Introduction to the Critique of Judgement*, V, 213′–16′.
92. KDU, Section 42, 299.
93. Immanuel Kant, *Critique of Practical Reason* (1956) 109.
94. Immanuel Kant, *Anthropology from a Pragmatic Point of View*, translated by Mary J. Gregor (The Hague, 1974), Section 88, 277.
95. The conflation occurs in the commentaries by Crawford, Guyer, Scarffe, Lorand, Gotshalk, and others.
96. The distinction of pure from dependent beauty and of pure from impure judgements of taste has generated some debate. Much of that debate seems spurious in the face of the dual process involved in aesthetic judgements, for the appraisal of an object need involve no reference to its determinate properties while the communication of our judgements may use indeterminate judgements. Other issues connected with this debate include the claim considered below, that fine art is impure while natural beauty is pure. Others have argued that Kant is pointing to a notion of decorum that is intrinsic to beauty, while some have used the purity of beauty to exclude even indeterminate concepts. See Paul Crowther, *The Kantian Sublime* (1989).
97. See Gerd Buchdahl, *Metaphysics and the Philosophy of Science*, (1969), Chapter 8.
98. KDU, Section 43, 303.

99. KDU, Section 16, 229.
100. KDU, Section 16, 229.
101. KDU, Section 16, 229. Italics added to clarify that 'representation' is being understood here in terms of particular determinate mimesis.
102. KDU, Section 33, 284.
103. KDU, Section 34, 286.
104. KDU, Section 32, 283.
105. KDU, Section 32, 283.
106. This claim apparently remains a radical one, and has generated some controversy among those who prefer to stress Kant's conception of disinterestedness and to see Kant as a New Critic.
107. KDU, Section 14, 225.
108. KDU, Section 16, 229.
109. KDU, Section 16, 229.
110. KDU, Section 51, passim.

7 The Context of Kant's Aesthetic Theory

1. B165, *Critique of Pure Reason*.
2. A10, *Critique of Pure Reason*.
3. Ibid.
4. A652/B680. My concern here is with presenting Kant's claims, and the occasion does not permit examining them in any critical detail. Graham Bird and Gerd Buchdahl, in their respective books, discuss some of these issues further.
5. B860/A832.
6. Introduction, Section II, 174.
7. See the *Critique of Pure Reason*, A536/B564-A558/B586, etc. A useful statement of Kant's position will be found in Roger J. Sullivan, *Immanuel Kant's Moral Theory* (1989), 281ff.
8. See R. C. S. Walker, *Kant* (1985) for an account of this claim and criticisms of it.
9. KDU, Section II, 176.
10. Ibid.
11. KDU, Section 91, 472, note.
12. KDU, Section 91, 472.
13. See, for example, the *Critique of Practical Reason*, 122–32, and *Religion within the Bounds of Reason Alone*, 45, 52, 75–6, etc.
14. KDU, Section 91, 474. As Guyer ignores these factors, he misunderstands the 'gulf' between reason and nature. He argues that 'the gulf that needs to be bridged is not that between noumenal and phenomenal causality, but between feeling and freedom' (p. 139, Paul Guyer, 'Feeling and Freedom: Kant on Aesthetics and Morality', *Journal of Aesthetics and Art Criticism*, 48, 2, Spring 1990, 137–46). This contention is questionable on a number of grounds, not the least serious of which is that it does not tally with what Kant says. Indeed, as feeling is a part of our nature, the truth of Guyer's claim that the real resolution is between feeling and freedom will depend on supposing that the two legislations have some relation to each other. That, in turn, must

presuppose that the great gulf between freedom and nature, between theory and practice, can be resolved.

15. KDU, Section 78, 415.
16. Ibid.
17. KDU, Section 64, 370.
18. Ibid.
19. KDU, Section 64, 370.
20. See KDU, Section 64, 371 and later Section 65, 372–6. Kant's discussion contains more details than I shall deal with here. My concern is not to examine this claim in detail but to set out the order and concerns Kant brings to teleology.
21. KDU, Section 64, 370.
22. KDU, Section 65, 375.
23. The explanation is rather more complicated than I have suggested here. Basically, Kant dissolves the issue of determinism by pointing out in the *Critique of Pure Reason* that the necessity attaching to our knowledge of natural events – which include all our actions, so far as they occur in nature, and so are causally determined – derives from their place within the system of science. The latter is governed by regulative ideas which, by their nature, are not constitutive and are contingent in the sense that we may develop other systems of knowledge than the one we have: a recalcitrant experience may make us rethink the system rather than lead us to propose *ad hoc* hypotheses to allow for the event. The result is that the necessity of causality that is usually associated with determinism here becomes a necessity gained from membership of a regulative and contingent system. Kant then argues, in the *Critique of Judgement*, that such a principle of causality need be neither exhaustive nor exclusive of teleological explanations. Consequently, since human actions are understood through one kind of teleological explanation, by showing the compatibility of the regulative principles of mechanical and teleological explanations, Kant shows how free will and explanations of events as causally determined are compatible.
24. A number of other events and actions also contribute to this task. Fine art and natural beauty, though, are distinctive in the manner in which they bring together human beings in their exploration of sensibility in relation to reason.
25. KDU, Section 83, 433.
26. Guyer's account of 'Feeling and Freedom', cited above, makes a number of undefended assumptions in this regard. He distinguishes the role of fine art from natural beauty in the culture of moral sensibility, and proposes that the purity of natural beauty allows it to sustain that culture in a way that artistic beauty cannot. But he argues that fine art is never pure on the ground that only crustacea and foliage are disinterested and, by implication, pure. As Kant includes works of art – music of certain kinds, some designs constructed by us, and so on – among the pure judgements, Guyer's ground for distinguishing fine art from pure judgements of taste does not coincide with Kant's. Further, talk of fine art as the product of human inten-

tionality does not make these objects any less capable of sustaining pure judgements – or at least Kant must have thought so or he would not have included works of art among examples of pure judgements. Conversely, if we think that in the case of impure beauty we judge an object aesthetically by first identifying it, then we must accept that *natural* beauty, too, because it requires us to identify the *object as nature* (and to think of nature as art), will also be impure because we cannot judge the object without first identifying it as an object of nature. But if we accept that, then there is little left that can be the object of a pure judgement of taste. So Guyer must either allow fine arts the same purity as natural beauty, and the same power to cultivate the mind, or deny that there are any objects of natural beauty that promote such culture.

Kant himself goes with the first, but he does *seem* thereby to exclude fine art. He says that '[u]nless we connect the fine arts, closely or remotely, with moral ideas, which alone carry with them an independent liking, . . . [increasing dullness of sensibility] is their ultimate fate. They serve in that case only for our diversion, which we need all the more in proportion as we use it to dispel the mind's dissatisfaction with itself, with the result that we increase still further our uselessness and dissatisfaction with ourselves. For the . . . [culture and attunement of our minds] it is generally the beauties of nature that are most beneficial, if we are habituated early to observe, judge, and admire them' (Section 54, 326). This may seem to support the kind of claim Guyer makes.

But even here Guyer cannot defend his construal of Kant's point about the need for moral ideas in fine art (KDU, Section 52). The argument and context are more complicated than Guyer's discussion allows.

(1) Kant is arguing that we cannot consider only the matter of sensations when valuing works of fine art, because these do not sustain the validity of aesthetic judgements. The latter must be meaningful, and so simple sensation does not provide the proper occasion for reflection and reflective judging. This claim follows from what he has said earlier about sensations, colours, etc. in Section 51, which I discussed at the end of the previous chapter.

By contrast with Guyer, Kant says that 'the pleasure we take in purposive form is also culture, and it attunes the spirit to ideas, and so makes it receptive to more such pleasure and entertainment' (Section 52, 326). Kant's concern here is with the mere play of sensations, where 'the aim is merely enjoyment, which leaves nothing behind as an idea and makes the spirit dull, the object gradually disgusting, and the mind dissatisfied with itself and moody because it is conscious that in reason's judgement its movement is contrapurposive' (ibid.). He is criticizing any attempt to claim a ratiocinative universality for a mere play of sensation, which has no meaning: the context of his complaint is that concern with mere plays of sensation, and so with a particular brand of formalism. Given this, any extrapolation of his arguments to more general concerns with fine art and natural beauty must be handled rather more carefully than Guyer's paper does.

(2) Kant then goes on to say that moral ideas are necessary for fine art to have any serious weight and longevity. Guyer rightly identifies these moral ideas with expression – what I have pointed to as meaningfulness – but goes on to claim that fine art cannot have the same relation to expression as nature does and so cannot have the same value. But, here too there are more complications.

(a) Guyer does not acknowledge that natural beauty too is expressive. Kant is clear that '[w]e may in general call beauty (*whether natural or artistic*) the *expression* of aesthetic ideas' (Section 51, 320, italics added). So the relation between expression and moral ideas must include natural beauty.

It may be as well to add here that expression does not imply or depend on a distinction between form and content. Expression *is* the formed content, so to speak, which sustains a judgement of taste, and we do not suppose that there is some content, capable of separate expression, which is given a contingent form. For Kant expression is intransitive. (I have discussed this issue above, when considering the conflation of the distinctions between fine art and natural beauty and pure and impure judgement of taste.)

(b) When Kant talks of moral ideas, he identifies 'the three pure ideas of reason [as] freedom, God and immortality', and maintains that 'freedom is the only concept of the supersensible which (by means of the causality we think in it) *proves in nature that it has objective reality, by the effects it can produce in it*' (KDU, Section 91, 474, italics added). If fine art must be brought into association with these moral ideas, then, because they differ in their scope, the association will also differ. As freedom differs from the other moral ideas because it is the only one that shows itself in our experience, and Kant governs freedom by reason, even if ideas were something like the 'content' of expression, freedom would not be a simple factor in the 'content' of expression. Instead, I suggest freedom shows itself in the universality of aesthetic judgements, which treat subjects as free, feeling, and rational beings capable of grasping and appreciating the work and behaving as the ends of these objects. God and immortality may provoke a series of imaginative products whose meaningful order we can appreciate, but even this is far from clear: other ideas can also gain expression; moral ideas are not the only ones available. In any case, Kant's reference to the need to associate fine arts with moral ideas, because it is not simply a matter of content, is best understood as the universality of ratiocinative judgements of taste and their deepening of the aesthetic community by commerce with the orders available through those pure ideas, including ones of God and immortality.

Expression does not simply rely on ideas as a content. If it were simply a matter of content, then it would be an illicit interest determining the judgement: we would be expected to find expressive objects beautiful (regardless of whether they are natural or artistic, since both are expressive) because of the ideas they express, and not for their universality etc. Indeed, Kant himself is clear that moral ideas are not simply a matter of content. Instead, he suggests that 'moral ideas' are rendered 'in terms of sense' or brought into our experience 'through the intervention of *a certain analogy in our reflection on both*'. (KDU, Section 60. I have used the Meredith translation here rather than Pluhar's because the latter extrapolates phrases that militate towards a particular understanding of the issue.) The moral ideas then, are not rendered into sensibility by being the content of the judgement; rather, Kant's talk indicates that the manner of our reflection – what Guyer would call 'form' – is what their analogy consists in.

(c) Further, our account of the role of moral ideas is also consistent with the occasion of Kant's argument, in which he wants to clarify that sensations cannot form the basis of any judgements claiming universal validity for sensations. If natural beauty is 'generally the most beneficial' to culture, it is because we cannot identify it as beautiful without having to think about what we are looking at. Some objects constructed by us, which may therefore claim to be fine art, by contrast, *can* be the mere play of sensation; and where they are, we must reject their claim to being fine art, for the mere play of sensation cannot be universalizable in the way required for aesthetic judgements – the way I pointed out at the end of the last chapter in discussing 'formalism'.

(d) That Kant sees natural beauty by analogy with art suggests also that what we say of judgements of taste and their *reflective analogy with moral ideas* will also apply to our judgements on natural objects.

In any case, a consequence of this understanding of moral ideas in fine art is that we cannot accept Guyer's claims because he fails to analyse Kant's account of the relation of aesthetic judgements and expression to moral ideas.

Further, (3) Guyer's use of a quotation from *Religion*, containing Kant's response to Schiller, is questionable. As Kant misunderstood the precise differences between himself and Schiller, we cannot without qualification use what Kant has to say of sensibility in this passage to support a reading of his intentions. For a discussion of the relation between Kant and Schiller, see Hans Reiner, *Duty and Inclination* (1983), Part I.

27. KDU, Section 40, 294.
28. *Critique of Pure Reason*, A738/B766.
29. Ibid., 295.
30. KDU, Section 60, 355.
31. Ibid., 295.
32. Ibid.
33. See *Kant and Fine Art*, Chapter 5, on the *sensus communis*. O. O'Neil develops an interesting account of this conception of reasoning in *Constructions of Reason, Explorations of Kant's Practical Philosophy* (1990), Part I.
34. Ibid., 20–1.
35. H. W. Cassirer, *A Commentary on Kant's Critique of Judgement*, 1938.
36. P. Guyer, *Kant and the Claims of Taste*, 261. See also footnote 19, 426.
37. Mary M. McCloskey, *Kant's Aesthetic* (1987), 90.

Index